T0302358

A GUIDE TO SUCCESS FOR TECHNICAL MANAGERS

A GUIDE TO SUCCESS FOR TECHNICAL MANAGERS

SUPERVISING IN RESEARCH, DEVELOPMENT, & ENGINEERING

ELIZABETH TREHER
DAVID PILTZ
STEVEN JACOBS

Illustrations by Timothy Carr

A JOHN WILEY & SONS, INC., PUBLICATION

Copyright © 2011 by John Wiley & Sons, Inc. All rights reserved

Published by John Wiley & Sons, Inc., Hoboken, New Jersey
Published simultaneously in Canada

No part of this publication may be reproduced, stored in a retrieval system, or
transmitted in any form or by any means, electronic, mechanical, photocopying,
recording, scanning, or otherwise, except as permitted under Section 107 or 108
of the 1976 United States Copyright Act, without either the prior written
permission of the Publisher, or authorization through payment of the appropriate
per-copy fee to the Copyright Clearance Center, Inc., 222 Rosewood Drive,
Danvers, MA 01923, (978) 750-8400, fax (978) 750-4470, or on the web at
www.copyright.com. Requests to the Publisher for permission should be
addressed to the Permissions Department, John Wiley & Sons, Inc., 111 River
Street, Hoboken, NJ 07030, (201) 748-6011, fax (201) 748-6008, or online at
http://www.wiley.com/go/permission.

Limit of Liability/Disclaimer of Warranty: While the publisher and author have
used their best efforts in preparing this book, they make no representations or
warranties with respect to the accuracy or completeness of the contents of this
book and specifically disclaim any implied warranties of merchantability or
fitness for a particular purpose. No warranty may be created or extended by
sales representatives or written sales materials. The advice and strategies
contained herein may not be suitable for your situation. You should consult with
a professional where appropriate. Neither the publisher nor author shall be liable
for any loss of profit or any other commercial damages, including but not
limited to special, incidental, consequential, or other damages.

For general information on our other products and services or for technical
support, please contact our Customer Care Department within the United States
at (800) 762-2974, outside the United States at (317) 572-3993 or fax
(317) 572-4002.

Wiley also publishes its books in a variety of electronic formats. Some content
that appears in print may not be available in electronic formats. For more
information about Wiley products, visit our web site at www.wiley.com.

Library of Congress Cataloging-in-Publication Data:

Treher, Elizabeth N.
   A guide to success for technical managers : supervising in research,
development, & engineering / Elizabeth Treher, David Piltz, Steven Jacobs.
        p. cm.
   Includes index.
   ISBN 978-0-470-43776-6 (cloth)
   1. Industrial management–Vocational guidance.   I. Piltz, David.
II. Jacobs, Steven.   III. Title.
   HD38.2.T74 2010
   658.4′09–dc22

                                                                    2010010326

Printed in the United States of America

10 9 8 7 6 5 4 3 2 1

For Gus Walker,
one of the few original thinkers about R&D
management and special friend

CONTENTS

CHAPTER 10   *POINTERS ON MANAGING PROJECTS AND DECISIONS*   171

CHAPTER 11   *SUGGESTIONS FOR MANAGING UP*   191

CHAPTER 12   *LET'S USE IT RIGHT: A SUMMARY OF SUGGESTED APPROACHES*   205

PREFACE

Technical managers and supervisors, both new and experienced, face a variety of challenges in managing professionals whose personal styles, education, values, and attitudes lead them to prefer self-direction and independent work. Over the last 20 years, in answer to the question we ask in our workshops—*How many of you have worked for at least one outstanding manager?*—generally only 20 to 30% say yes. Perhaps 5 to 10% say they have worked with or known more than one such individual. This in large part contributes to the issues we see in those responsible for managing technical professionals—individuals are not learning managerial, leadership, and communication skills in school, and there are few excellent role models to coach, mentor, and lead by example.

The good news is that the number of individuals who now say they have worked for at least one excellent manager (20 to 30%) has doubled over the last 20 years, perhaps because more organizations offer effective training and coaching. Yet, there is still a long way to go.

This book is based on decades of experience in both managing technical professionals and teams and providing training and coaching to individuals from industry, national laboratories, government, and academia. Much of the content and ideas for the book originated with our programs *Supervisory Skills in R&D, Managing in R&D*, and others. Our thanks go to the thousands of technical professionals we have trained, coached, or managed over the last 25 years. Their insights, ideas, and stories are incorporated throughout the book.

If there is a single theme in most of the chapters, it is communication. We have included ways to use the Myers–Briggs Type Indicator® (MBTI®) in many of the chapters since it is a powerful addition to any communication arsenal. We have experienced the impact of the MBTI first hand both personally and professionally. Using only the MBTI, even dysfunctional, unproductive groups and departments have become positive and effective. Providing a framework to understand yourself and your colleagues better, the MBTI helps us recognize our impact on others. It gives us a language to discuss differences and to realize another's approach may be different but that it is not wrong. The result can be humor, respect, and friendship so that our different ways become our strengths and are no longer an issue.

Rather than use strictly a management text format, the approach we have taken is to:

- Introduce a topic with a short case example(s) for analysis.
- Offer suggestions for handling the cases and real-world outcomes, when available, at the end of each chapter.
- Incorporate quizzes and assessments for self-diagnosis and development planning.
- Include content to review and consider.
- Have chapters stand alone as much as possible, considering the relationship between the topics.
- Provide checklists and tools for future use.

Examples include typical issues technology managers face. They serve as a tool for readers to "experience" a situation, to recognize and analyze the issues, and to think through how they might handle them. We provide approaches known to be successful for comparison. Also included is the Manager–Scientist Inventory, originally published by The Learning Key® in *The 2000 Annual: Vol. 1 Training* by Josey-Bass Pfeiffer. *Manager or Scientist: An Attribute Inventory*, was developed by one of us (E. Treher) with Augustus (Gus) C. Walker, a creative thinker who contributed to the development of many engineers and scientists. Gus made a transition similar to that of Elizabeth Treher—from leading technical professionals in research and development to a second career providing coaching and training and otherwise supporting the development of professionals in the research, development, and engineering (R&D&E) community.

We hope in this way to help readers build diagnostic and judgment skills, as well as to contrast and compare their own managerial approaches with those we have found to be successful.

We welcome input, suggestions, and learning about your alternative approaches. Please contact us at techprofessionals@thelearningkey.com.

Many of the concepts we present are not new. They can seem simple, especially in contrast with the technical knowledge and skills necessary for career success and promotions to supervisory and managerial roles for scientists, programmers, engineers, and other technical professionals. The concepts are simple, their implementation is not. As our good friend Gus Walker points out: *It's not the power of the tool that makes it useful. It's the use that makes it powerful.*

We trust this book will lead to improved managerial skills and behaviors for you and many other professionals in technology-based organizations. Increasing the number of good supervisory role models in R&D&E will enhance the work environment for all non-supervisory professionals.

Elizabeth N. Treher
The Learning Key, Inc.

CHAPTER 1

TIPS ON TRANSITIONS FOR TECHNICAL MANAGERS

TRANSITION SITUATIONS

Harry

Harry took a job at a prestigious laboratory eager to use his skills for new research projects and get to work. After only a few months, his abilities in the lab were clearly recognized. Leaders of this department of 100 decided to assign him 2 technicians, so he could be even more productive. Thus, for the first time for someone just out of school and new to the organization, they offered Harry the chance to become a supervisor.

Harry was astonished. He had never considered managing anyone, although he had been in supervisory roles in other jobs as he worked to pay for school. He felt he had gone to school and studied so he could do research himself, not to watch someone else do it for him. He loved his work and was anxious to prove himself. He felt he had no time, and little interest, to supervise anyone. Harry was afraid to say no, and so said nothing. He went home upset that night, looking forward to getting some advice from his family.

How would you feel in his place?

How would you coach Harry, if you wanted him to take a supervisory role?

See the end of this chapter for how the situation was resolved.

A Guide to Success for Technical Managers: Supervising in Research, Development, & Engineering, by Elizabeth Treher, David Piltz and Steven Jacobs
Copyright © 2011 John Wiley & Sons, Inc.

Anna

Anna, a highly respected geologist, had been working successfully for 7 years. She published frequently and was often an invited speaker. Anna was pleased to be offered the role of group leader to oversee a group of 35 geologists. She appreciated the recognition, salary increase, and renewed respect among her colleagues. She was well liked and she expected to have no difficulties as a group leader.

Five months after accepting the position, Anna admitted to herself that she was unhappy. She also had no difficulty in assessing the reasons why. She lived to be in the field, working. In her prior role, she did field work for days at a time. In her current role, she spent most of her time in meetings and on administrative tasks. Her geology was mostly limited to talking with and reviewing her colleagues' work. Her reputation as a respected geologist was going to be jeopardized over time, but her biggest concern was being away from the work she loved. She missed her work and being outdoors.

If you were Anna, what would you do?

If you coached Anna, what would you say?

See the end of this chapter for how the situation was resolved.

Perhaps the most important, and certainly the least addressed, of the issues faced by technical managers are those experienced in transitioning to managing other professionals. Notice we didn't narrow this just to "new" technical managers or supervisors. Transitions occur in stages over an entire career. These transitions are not often recognized nor are their importance planned for or considered.

The most obvious transition occurs when a technical professional begins to manage one or more technicians or other specialists in his/her own field. One of the most challenging transitions cited by many workshop participants is that of supervising former peers—not knowing how to balance friend versus boss and being uncomfortable giving feedback. Certainly supervising a former colleague and friend presents challenges, but two even bigger issues for most are the shifts that need to occur in our motivations and work values. The ways we derive satisfaction from work and are comfortable being recognized need to change. This doesn't happen easily, as is seen in the answers to the questions:

1. How many of you have worked for at least one outstanding manager?
2. How many of you have worked for two or more outstanding managers?

The answers vary somewhat by industry and profession but in the groups we have worked with, on average, only 25% say yes to the first question. Perhaps 5 to 10% say they have worked with or known more than one such individual.

As one of our colleagues, Gus Walker, is fond of saying— every organization says it hires the best, gives them the best facilities, and demands the best. So what happens to these "best" professionals when it comes to managing others? There seem to be four keys to making a successful managerial transition:

1. Motivation to help others succeed
2. Willingness to give credit to others
3. Openness to other's ideas
4. Interest in taking new roles

Success in technical work depends on both skills and knowledge. Early in a career as a manager, you are assumed to have both. As your career progresses, however, you are no longer the person most able to perform a specific technical task. In other words, managers (U) pass through transitions that reflect their ability relative to their employees (E). These managerial transitions are important factors in our career growth.

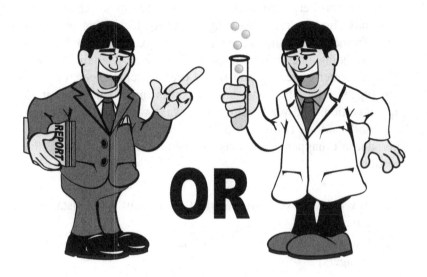

There are three broad ranges for U/E. The typical situation, when a technical professional receives a first supervisory assignment, is U >> E. Usually, there are few direct reports, and they act as assistants or simple extensions of the professional. Since this relationship is similar to many found in universities, it is relatively familiar and comfortable, at least for the supervisor. However, greater skill, training, or experience in one area can convince U of superiority over E in other skills as well. This halo effect often leads to overdirection and micromanagement. It can also lead U to miss an E's special abilities. Generally, routine problem solving is more efficient in a U >> E situation with close direction. However, over time, groups are usually more effective when skills are distributed.

$U \approx E$ is the next stage and requires a transition. In this role, you and some of your employees have equivalent technical or other capabilities. The ability to handle these interactions is a critical test of managerial aptitude, and delegation is important to success.

This is a difficult transition for several reasons. We often continue to rely on the close direction that was successful when $U \gg E$, even when it is inappropriate. Our training and experience often create strong feelings about the right approach to a problem, so we promote that approach. However, the same is true for employees who may resent having little influence on direction.

While problem-solving efficiency in $U \gg E$ depends strongly on supervisory control, success in $U \approx E$ depends more on collaboration and interactions with subordinates. This becomes increasingly important for generating creative solutions.

$U \ll E$ occurs when a manager has a large organization, is in a new position, or is dealing with interdisciplinary teams. It does not suggest incompetence. Rather, it reflects the reality that organizational goals require the efficient use of expertise and other resources. This requires that tasks are integrated and prioritized— both needed additional skills. Managers should have a broad understanding of goals and the experience and ability to achieve them. Compared with $U \approx E$, the manager has less need for personal technical competence. Authority and respect flow from general knowledge and the ability to manage resources.

These three transition stages are faced multiple times in technical careers and are most easily handled when they are recognized and thoughtfully considered.

Often we do not see ourselves as others do, and we make assumptions about our abilities to make such transitions. For this reason, one of us co-published the Manager–Scientist Inventory. We include it here as a way to gain insight into your managerial versus "scientist" preferences. Having a strong preference for managing or science does not ensure you will excel at either. Conversely, a low score does not mean you cannot become successful. The scores typically indicate a preference for one over the other and should give insight to those who have or will transition to the role of manager. The indicator has helped others better understand some of the issues they have experienced as managers or consider those they might face on moving to such a role.

MANAGER OR SCIENTIST?
AN ATTRIBUTE INVENTORY

This section is adapted from the inventory by The Learning Key®
published in Treher and Walker (2000), *Manager or Scientist: An
Attribute Inventory.*

Extensive research into differences between managers and
scientists/engineers has yielded consistent, distinct behavior patterns and preferences of these two groups. Data from the literature
and from the authors' experience in managing technical managers
and groups was distilled to provide the self-report inventory to
highlight individual preferences toward managing others and doing
technical work.

It is important to note that a strong profile in either direction
does not preclude success. It does, however, indicate that you may
face difficult transition issues.

Directions

Read each of the pairs of statements on the inventory and mark the
index below. If you strongly agree with the statement on the left,
circle 1. If you strongly favor the one on the right, circle 6. If you

are uncertain, circle the number that best represents your feelings. There are no right or wrong answers. Use your own views, not those you think others might have or prefer.

1	In solving non-routine problems, the leader should provide support.			In solving non-routine problems the leader should give directions and ideas.		
	1	2	3	4	5	6
2	I prefer to have all the facts before making a decision.			I am comfortable making decisions based on partial information.		
	1	2	3	4	5	6
3	The organization I work for is my primary source of satisfaction and professional recognition.			I get satisfaction and recognition from outside professional contacts and associations.		
	1	2	3	4	5	6
4	I prefer to do many varied things and not get into any one activity too deeply.			I prefer to focus my attention on one important thing and get to the bottom of it.		
	1	2	3	4	5	6
5	I prefer to work in my own area of expertise and not get involved in projects crossing several technical disciplines.			I enjoy working as a generalist or on interdisciplinary problems.		
	1	2	3	4	5	6
6	I like to generate new information and results on problems.			I like to see that available information is found and used effectively.		
	1	2	3	4	5	6
7	Decisions should be made analytically on the basis of the facts.			Political and human considerations should influence all decisions.		
	1	2	3	4	5	6
8	I like to run things and be highly visible.			I prefer to influence decisions quietly through my own expertise and reputation.		
	1	2	3	4	5	6

9	I prefer to consider my ideas carefully and put them in writing.			I prefer discussing my ideas with others and giving presentations.		
	1	2	3	4	5	6
10	When something goes wrong, the individual responsible should take the blame.			When something goes wrong, the manager should take the blame.		
	1	2	3	4	5	6
11	I enjoy working with people from other departments and functions.			I prefer working with people with similar backgrounds and interests.		
	1	2	3	4	5	6
12	It is usually better to figure out what the real problem is than to take quick action.			I have a strong sense of urgency and like to react quickly when something goes wrong.		
	1	2	3	4	5	6
13	When my colleagues have arguments, I like to help resolve them.			When my colleagues have arguments, I prefer not to get involved.		
	1	2	3	4	5	6
14	People and decisions interest me more than things and ideas.			Things and ideas interest me more than people and decisions.		
	1	2	3	4	5	6
15	The most important thing is to understand and solve the problem.			The most important thing is to meet goals and objectives.		
	1	2	3	4	5	6
16	I work well under stress and with urgent schedules. Things drift without deadlines.			I work best when the pressure comes from my own interests and schedules are realistic.		
	1	2	3	4	5	6
17	I enjoy interpreting the business goals of the organization and deciding how technology can help achieve them.			I enjoy theoretical and experimental work. In the long run it is the principal basis for growth and profit.		
	1	2	3	4	5	6

18	I like to identify a problem and solve it myself.			I like to see that problems are identified and solved as efficiently as possible.		
	1	2	3	4	5	6
19	I like to get to work early and leave late. A sense of urgency is important to the organization.			I like flexibility to come and go as my work demands. Creative insights cannot always be produced by schedules and pressure.		
	1	2	3	4	5	6
20	Generally, I study something only long enough to satisfy an immediate need.			Generally, I study something thoroughly so that I can understand and use it well.		
	1	2	3	4	5	6
21	I prefer shared accountability and interdependence.			I prefer individual accountability and independent work.		
	1	2	3	4	5	6
22	I believe that independent groups of specialists pursuing their own projects get the most done.			I believe that integrating technical groups is essential to getting the most done.		
	1	2	3	4	5	6
23	Organizational politics play a necessary role in setting goals and getting work done.			Organizational politics waste time and energy and get in the way of quality, creative work.		
	1	2	3	4	5	6
24	I sometimes ignore others' views in defending my position when I believe I am right.			I am flexible and willing to compromise my ideas for the organization's good.		
	1	2	3	4	5	6
25	A technical manager is a manager of people with technical training.			A technical manager is a technically trained person with additional management responsibilities.		
	1	2	3	4	5	6

26	I like to solve problems in clever and unusual ways.			I like to solve problems in familiar and established ways.		
	1	2	3	4	5	6
27	Understanding how things work is a major source of stimulation for me.			Getting things done and seeing practical results is what motivates me.		
	1	2	3	4	5	6
28	I enjoy helping others find their own answers and solve their own problems.			I prefer to answer questions and solve problems on my own.		
	1	2	3	4	5	6
29	To be respected, a technical manager should always know more than his or her subordinates.			To be respected, a technical manager must be able to recognize, use and acknowledge subordinate strengths.		
	1	2	3	4	5	6
30	I like to speculate and approach problems from a theoretical and abstract point of view.			I like to identify the goal and work toward it in a practical and realistic way.		
	1	2	3	4	5	6

MANAGER–SCIENTIST INVENTORY SCORE SHEET

To score the inventory, check your answer to each question and circle this answer on the scoring key (Table 1.1), where M = manager and S = scientist.

Then add the numbers circled in each column and enter that total at the bottom of the column. Calculate $M = 2M1 + 1.5M2 + M3$ and $S = 2S1 + 1.5S2 + S3$.

Subtract the smaller of M or S from the larger. The difference represents the preference for either the manager or scientist activity pattern.

Sum the numbers in each column on the manager side of the scoring sheet. Say you get $M1 = 19$, $M2 = 29$, and $M3 = 7$. Then $M = [2(19) + 1.5(29) + 7] = 89$.

TABLE 1.1   Inventory Scoring Key

Question Number	Manager's Activity Profile			Scientist's Activity Profile		
1	1	2	3	4	5	6
2	6	5	4	3	2	1
3	1	2	3	4	5	6
4	1	2	3	4	5	6
5	6	5	4	3	2	1
6	6	5	4	3	2	1
7	6	5	4	3	2	1
8	1	2	3	4	5	6
9	6	5	4	3	2	1
10	6	5	4	3	2	1
11	1	2	3	4	5	6
12	6	5	4	3	2	1
13	1	2	3	4	5	6
14	1	2	3	4	5	6
15	6	5	4	3	2	1
16	1	2	3	4	5	6
17	1	2	3	4	5	6
18	6	5	4	3	2	1
19	1	2	3	4	5	6
20	1	2	3	4	5	6
21	1	2	3	4	5	6
22	6	5	4	3	2	1
23	1	2	3	4	5	6
24	6	5	4	3	2	1
25	1	2	3	4	5	6
26	6	5	4	3	2	1
27	6	5	4	3	2	1
28	1	2	3	4	5	6
29	6	5	4	3	2	1
30	6	5	4	3	2	1
Add and enter the total of each column	$M_1=$	$M_2=$	$M_3=$	$S_3=$	$S_2=$	$S_1=$

Sum the numbers in each column on the scientist side of the scoring sheet. Say you get $S1 = 6$, $S2 = 18$, and $S3 = 24$. Then $S = [2(6) + 1.5(18) + 24] = 63$.

Take the absolute difference between S and M.

The difference represents your preference for either the manager or scientist activity pattern. In the example you get an excess $M = 26$. If the scores had been $M = 70$ and $S = 90$, you would find an excess $S = 20$, which is borderline.

INTERPRETATION

If you have a total score of $M - S$ equal to or greater than 25, it suggests you are somewhat more comfortable with the activities and work patterns of a manager than those of a scientist. If $S - M$ is equal to or greater than 25, the reverse is true. The higher the excess, the greater the discomfort level is likely to be for someone working in the other domain. Excess values less than 25 cannot be interpreted.

Please note that even a large excess value does not imply that you cannot perform well in the opposite domain. It does suggest that you may find your opposite pattern uncomfortable. At the first line of technical supervision there usually remains a large amount of hands-on technical work. However, with continued advancement to higher levels, the activities of scientists and managers become much more distinct, and the pressures resulting from high S or M scores can feel greater.

QUESTIONS TO ASK YOURSELF

For those who score high S and are S:

> Do these results fit me?
>
> What issues might I face if I become a manager?
>
> What are likely to be my biggest challenges on becoming a manager?
>
> Do I really want to go the management route?

For those who score high M and are M:

> Do these results fit me?
>
> What has helped me develop management skills?
>
> Where might I have differing views from those of my staff?
>
> How can I help others develop the attributes of a good manager?

For those who score high S and are M:

> Do these results fit me?
>
> What are some of my frustrations in managing technical work?
>
> What gives me the greatest satisfaction at work?
>
> How might I develop my management skills and interests?
>
> How might I gather feedback on how I am doing as a manager?

For those who score high M and are S:

> Do these results fit me?
>
> What gives me the greatest satisfaction at work?
>
> How might I develop my management skills?
>
> How can I demonstrate my management interests?
>
> Who might help me develop into a manager?
>
> How can I combine my technical responsibilities with my management interests?
>
> What are the roadblocks, if any, to my becoming a manager?

TRANSITIONS SITUATIONS—SOLUTIONS

Coaching Anna

This is a situation with little ambiguity. Anna has experienced the role, and short of delegating most of her responsibilities away, probably does not have the option to spend days working in the field. The group needs leadership, and her strong preference is one of an individual or team contributor. We would advise Anna to follow her heart and return to her previous role. She is motivated to be outdoors and do the research she loves, not help others do it for her.

Actual   Anna did return to her former job (one of the only professionals we have known to "go back"). She is still happily working in the field 12 years later.

Coaching Harry

At this point Harry sees no good reason to become a supervisor. He loves his work and wants to keep at it. His motivation seems to be around the work itself, like Anna the geologist. However, his work environment and new job expectations do not preclude him continuing his research. If you can help Harry see how supervising two techs will allow him to work on even more of his ideas at one time, he is likely to be excited at the prospect. He can continue to lead the work he wants and provide equally meaningful work to two others, testing some of his other ideas. This small team could actually help him generate new and perhaps even better approaches.

Actual Harry assumed this supervisory role. His own enthusiasm and love of the work was contagious, and his two direct reports became indispensible. His natural style of sharing information and seeking input from others created a strong team of three. Both technicians did well and grew in their roles. One began graduate school part time.

REFERENCES

Domhoff, G. W. *The Scientific Study of Dreams: Neural Networks, Cognitive Development, and Content Analysis.* American Psychological Association (APA), Washington, D.C., 2003.

Goleman, D. *Emotional Intelligence: Why It Can Matter More Than IQ.* Bantam Books, New York, 1995.

Hallowell, E. *CrazyBusy: Overstretched, Overbooked and About to Snap.* Ballantine Books, New York, 2006.

Klein, G. *Intuition At Work.* Doubleday, New York, 2003.

Locke, E. A., and Latham, G. *Goal Setting: A Motivational Technique That Works.* Prentice Hall, Englewood Cliffs, NJ, 1984.

Stone, L. "Living with Continuous Partial Attention." From the article "The Harvard Business Review List of Breakthrough Ideas for 2007." *Harvard Business Review*, Vol. 85, No. 2, February 2007, pp. 28–29.

Treher, E. N., and Walker, A. C. *Manager or Scientist: An Attribute Inventory. The 2000 Annual: Vol. 1, Training.* Josey-Bass/Pfeiffer, San Francisco, 2000, pp. 153–166.

Wiseman, R. *The Luck Factor: The Four Essential Principles.* Miramax Books/Hyperion, New York, 2003.

BIBLIOGRAPHY

Badawy, M. K. *Developing Managerial Skills in Engineers and Scientists.* Van Nostrand Reinhold, New York, 1982.

Badawy, M. K. "Managing Career Transitions." *Research Management*, Vol. 26, No. 4, July–August, 1983, pp. 28–31.

Badawy, M. K. "Why Managers Fail." *Research Management.* Vol. 26, No. 3, May–June, 1983, pp. 26–31.

Bailey, R. E., and Jensen, B. T. "The Troublesome Transition from Scientist to Manager." *Personnel*, Vol. 42, September/October, 1965, pp. 49–55.

Bayton, J. A., and Chapman, R. L. "Making Managers of Scientists and Engineers in the First-Level Manager" in *Selected Papers from Research Management.* Industrial Research Institute, New York, 1985.

Bayton, J. A., and Chapman, R. L. "Transformation of Scientists and Engineers into Managers." *NASA National Academy of Administration*, NASA S P-291, 1972.

Lea, D., and Brostrom, R. "Managing the High-Tech Professional." *Personnel*, Vol. 65, June, 1988, pp. 12–22.

Manners, G. E., and Steger, J. A. "Implications of Research on R&D Manager's Role to Selection and Training of Scientists and Engineers for Management." *R&D Management*, Vol. 9, No. 2, February, 1979, pp. 85–91.

McBean, E. A. "Analysis of Teaching and Course Questionnaires: A Case Study." *Engineering Education*, May–June, 1991, pp. 439–441.

Medcof, J. W. "Training Technologists to Become Managers." *Research Management*, Vol. 28, No. 1, 1985, pp. 18–21.

Oppenheim, A. N. *Questionnaire Design and Attitude Measurement.* Basic Books, New York, 1966.

Overton, L. M., Jr. "R&D Management: Turning Scientists into Managers." *Personnel*, Vol. 46, May–June, 1969, pp. 56–63.

Pearson, A. W. "Management Development for Scientists and Engineers." *Research Technology Management*, Vol. 36, No. 1, 1993, pp. 45–48.

Pickett, R. B. "The Four Stages of Management Part 1." *Lab Manager*, Vol. 3, No. 2, July 2008, pp. 16–19.

Treher, E. N., and Walker, A. C. "The R&D Environment: Roles and Issues." *Managing in R&D, A Program for Technical Managers.* The Learning Key, Inc., Washington Crossing, PA, 1992, 2006.

Walker, A. C. "Effective Technical Management." *American Chemical Society*, Washington D.C., 1990.

CHAPTER 2

ADVICE ON CREATING A MOTIVATING CLIMATE

MOTIVATION SITUATION

Jack moved across the country to lead a group that has been together for several years. The previous leader, Jessi, is still there, and he will report to her. Jack gets an earful during his first few lunches with the group members—all are hostile to Jessi and complaining is a way of life. One individual is excited about Jack's optimism but worried it won't last, given that he reports to Jessi. Another group member had been a candidate for Jack's position. Jessi says the employee who applied for his position is very disgruntled and likely to create problems.

> How would you handle this group and the individual who was passed over when Jack was hired?
>
> How should Jack handle this "disgruntled" employee?
>
> *See the end of this chapter for how the situation was resolved.*

A Guide to Success for Technical Managers: Supervising in Research, Development, & Engineering, by Elizabeth Treher, David Piltz and Steven Jacobs
Copyright © 2011 John Wiley & Sons, Inc.

Technical environments and work assignments often have characteristics that can demotivate technical professionals. Particularly at the technician or individual programmer level, problems are typically assigned and there is less of a feeling of choice. From entry-level staff to those with advanced degrees, expectations of creative assignments often turn into routine assignments. Past training may not fit assignments. In our project-focused technology world, assignments can be changed for nontechnical reasons. Business decisions override personal technical interests, and, for those industries with a high rate of failure, such as pharmaceuticals, project focus may shift frequently. These characteristics drive the need for technical managers to spend time thinking about ways to foster a motivating environment for their staff.

WHAT MOTIVATES YOU?

Exercise: Motivation Octagon

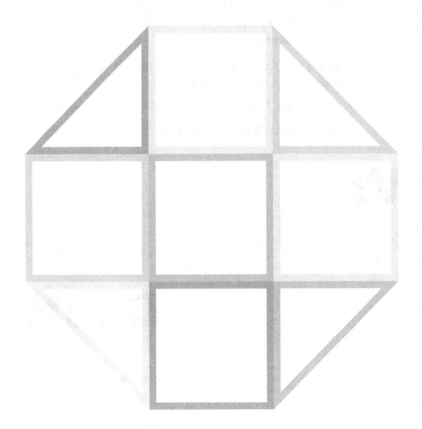

Using the Motivation Octagon:

1. Place a single motivator in each space. These can be things that motivate you or someone you know.

2. Next, circle those things you can influence as a supervisor.

3. Review your nine entries. How many can you influence?

If you listed salary, benefits, or state-of-the art facilities, those are probably outside your realm of influence. The key thing to notice is that many items on your list are actually within your control and provide opportunities for creating a motivating environment. If you do this activity with others, you are likely to see their lists and yours are not the same. Examples from our workshop participants include pizza or other food, challenge, friendly manager, clear goals, teamwork, positive feedback, encouragement, and many others over which they have direct impact.

Find out what is important to those you manage. Pay attention. Clues can come from the ways individuals spend their time on weekends or from their hobbies. Some of us like independence and the ability to figure things out on our own. Others prefer a structured environment with detailed information about what and how to do things. Giving someone who prefers structure and details the freedom to proceed as she/he chooses is likely to increase his/her stress and lower motivation.

Learning about what motivates your colleagues is one thing; using this information to foster a motivating climate is another. Technical managers often focus primarily on the work itself and overlook the enormous benefits (estimated at 20 to 50% in various studies) possible from better people management. Under the appropriate conditions, employees can greatly expand their contributions. Whenever you can, link your approach in managing others to what is important to them.

Understanding what motivation is and why it is important can help to create a motivating climate. Motivation refers to the internal and external needs, wants, opportunities, and influences that determine our courses of action. It is difficult to know how motivated someone is. Nor is it easy to identify and measure the many influences that contribute to selecting a particular course of action.

There are several key characteristics of motivation. For example, a motivated individual wants to achieve a goal or improve performance. This person has "purpose" and adapts his or her behavior and resources to achieve that purpose. The motivated state is learning and adaptive.

Motivation can be goal oriented, particularly for relatively simple activities. There are, however, many complicating factors. Individuals do not have a single goal; they have multiple goals that differ in importance and priority and may not even be compatible. For example, smoking or eating high-fat, high-calorie diets are in direct conflict with the longer-range desire to stay healthy.

To be useful in an organizational context, personal and organizational goals need to be compatible. This is particularly true in complex areas of science and technology that depend on long hours of study and concentrated effort for success. If we have strong interests in our field, we tend to focus on personal goals, even when they drift away from those of the organization. Motivated individuals resist and resent interruptions in the pursuit of goals that interest them. Managers who must terminate a project or shift its focus often face this problem.

A motivated state is one of high and focused energy. The emotional energy that occurs when we are motivated focuses our minds and creates periods of concentration essential for productive work. Even though many creative insights have been reported after periods of unfocused daydreaming, usually intense concentration and an incubation period comes first.

Different people express motivation differently. It is not always possible to tell when individuals are motivated. It is even more difficult to determine when their motivations are useful to the organization. Some individuals provide lots of feedback on their level of motivation; others provide little. In any case, different personality types influence and mask what is going on internally in different ways. Extraverts behave differently from introverts. Practical individuals, oriented around their senses and the present, behave differently from those who are more intuitive. Those who prefer to base judgments on thinking differ from those who rely on their feelings. Motivation is an activated state that energizes what is already there. Therefore, it is easier to enhance performance when interpersonal and organizational goals are in-sync, and job assignments are compatible with individual preferences and types.

Motivation is not intelligence; it is driven by emotion. Motivation influences the force and persistence with which intellectual and other activities are pursued. Although motivation cannot substitute for skill, training, or education in complex technical subjects, it can expand or reduce the value of training and affect the rate at which skills and knowledge are acquired.

Motivation is not happiness or satisfaction. Motivated individuals strive to achieve, often in spite of personal hardships. For this reason, supervisors should not expect employees to be motivated at work just because they are happy with their physical environment, pay, and other quality of life factors. Motivation is encouraged less by things that cause satisfaction and more by those that indicate progress toward important goals for both the organization and the individual.

Motivation is not inexhaustible. A large percentage of professional employees, particularly those with advanced degrees in the sciences, are significantly above average in terms of achievement and intrinsic motivation. However, managers who fail to recognize the things that motivate, often turn them off.

This makes the problem of motivation a difficult one: There is no management technique guaranteed to motivate toward a specific task. There are also many ways managers interact to demotivate professionals, no matter how high their initial interest.

Motivation is not performance. Performance is a complex outcome of many interacting factors. Motivation is only one. Among others are the difficulty of the task itself, luck, resources, appropriate skill and training, intelligence, and effective management.

WHY IS MOTIVATION IMPORTANT?

Those who manage technical activities in large organizations generally regard motivation as being among their top two or three management concerns.

There are several reasons for this.

- The motivated state allows people to work in a coherent, effective mode in spite of distraction. While many managers believe that they provide a working environment conductive to coherent work patterns, this is not always the case. Many technical specialists are faced with administrative duties, meetings, reports, and other peripheral activities that seriously detract from their primary tasks. Under these conditions, motivated individuals find ways of getting the job done in spite of the distractions.

- Motivation has special significance in problem solving. Solving complex technical problems requires not only an enormous personal knowledge base but also complex interaction with external knowledge, theory, and experiment. This can easily overload human information processing ability. In highly motivated individuals, however, much problem solving takes place at the edge of consciousness when apparently engaged in other tasks. In many cases, problem solving happens at a preconscious level, for example, when sleeping or daydreaming.

• Motivation has high leverage on total performance. This is particularly true for individuals whose success depends on high levels of training. There are several reasons for this. Motivated individuals spend more time working on problems than unmotivated individuals. Second, motivated individuals work more efficiently, and with greater concentration, than those who are unmotivated; and third, motivated individuals actively seek feedback on performance, which provides ongoing guidance toward verbal goals.

DIAGNOSING MOTIVATION

To begin, recognize those who are highly motivated and learn how best to use them. It is also important to recognize those who are not motivated and consider what steps you might take. For managers who are highly motivated themselves, it can be difficult to accept that others may simply want a defined job that they can leave behind when they head for home. Having a full life outside of work is their source of energy.

Generate a climate that encourages motivation toward organizationally valuable goals. Highly motivated individuals who want to pursue their own interests not only waste their time, from the organization's perspective, but yours as well. A key skill is managing day-to-day activities for such individuals without negative effects on motivation.

APPLYING THEORIES ABOUT MOTIVATION

Abraham Maslow, a leader of the humanistic psychology movement, assumed that human beings constantly strive toward the goals they need. He categorized these into a hierarchy of motivators, with physiological needs at the bottom and self-actualization at the top.

Security/safety, social, and ego/esteem needs are in between. He also observed that only unsatisfied needs motivate and that lower level needs are filled first. Once a set of needs is fulfilled, it no longer motivates.

Motivational theory can be difficult to apply; learning about it can seem pointless. However, interpreting general principles, in terms of an individual's "local" environment, can help create a more productive workforce. Maslow's general categories are of greatest value when applied appropriately in a technical environment. For example:

Self-actualization	Continuing technical growth, understanding, self-motivation
Ego	Knowledge, important problems, peer recognition
Social	Peers, colleagues, outside experts, professional societies
Security	Credit for results, freedom to explore, technical expertise
Physiological	Facilities, supplies, appropriate basic education

Note that credit for results is at the lower level (security) need, not at the ego level where many place it. Without credit for results, a technical professional's ability to seek a new job or advance in his or her career is severely limited, affecting his/her fundamental security. This means that higher level ego needs coming from peer recognition will be difficult to fulfill outside a very limited group of colleagues at work.

In extrapolating Maslow's work, Frederick Herzberg studied on-the-job aspects contributing to job satisfaction and dissatisfaction. Rarely were the same events sources of both satisfaction and dissatisfaction. He suggested that the opposite of dissatisfaction is no dissatisfaction (not satisfaction) and that the opposite of satisfaction is no satisfaction (not dissatisfaction). His theory is known as the Herzberg two-factor theory of job satisfaction or the motivation-hygiene theory. Satisfiers are integral to job performance and are job content factors, while dissatisfiers have to do with the environment and are called job context factors. In general, dissatisfiers, or hygiene factors, correspond to the lower needs on Maslow's hierarchy, and satisfiers, or motivators, are roughly analogous to upper level needs.

Expectancy theory, described by Lawler, Nadler, and others, reflects specific assumptions about the causes of behavior in organizations:

- There are both internal (individual) and environmental (organizational) forces.
- Conscious decisions, and the effort an individual is willing to use in performing the job, drive behavior.
- People differ in their needs, goals, and the rewards they desire.
- People base their decisions and behaviors on their expectations of the outcomes (rewards or punishments) and their perception of how hard the effort will be.

The impact of expectations on performance is well known. The classic Pygmalion story teaches us that you get what you expect. Expectancy is an attitude that is communicated, largely nonverbally, by a manager. It can be positive or negative. When it is positive, it generates a powerful motivating climate. Communicating this attitude is almost impossible to fake. Over 90% of the feeling is conveyed by tone of voice and facial expression.

Positive expectations are a proven motivator. Studies show that entry-level professionals do better immediately and over time when put with positive managers. Also, improvements in student performance correlate with teacher expectancy.

Expectations are an external motivation factor, which is present, whether you want it to be or not. In general, high expectations produce high performance, and low expectations produce poor performance. Expectations influence individuals and groups across all personality types, ranges of ability, and organizational levels.

We communicate our attitudes of expectation both verbally and nonverbally through tone of voice, facial expressions, and other forms of body language. In fact, studies show that when there is a discrepancy between spoken words and nonverbal attitudes, more than 90% of the emotional content communicated (the feelings) comes from the nonverbal component (Mehrabian). For this reason, feelings always come across; sending mixed messages leads to loss of trust and morale. If you want to communicate something positive, be in a positive mood to do it.

This effect shows itself in many ways. New employees who start with a supervisor who expects great things and who supports individual initiative and risk-taking have a real advantage. Not only do they do better immediately, but the effect lasts for years. The same is true for the classroom; research shows that teachers' expectations of their students are self-fulfilling.

The important difference between positive and negative expectations relates to the difference between assertiveness and aggressiveness. The assertive supervisor expects great things from subordinates without threatening. She or he simply believes that good things will happen and this attitude is readily perceived. The aggressive supervisor, on the other hand, generally expects the worst and believes that some level of coercion is required. Not only does an employee sense the lack of confidence, implied threats often lead to defensiveness. This usually limits willingness to take the initiative on assignments.

Supervisors with high levels of technical training often have difficulty in expecting the positive. In the first place, our educational system is based on correcting errors. Few teachers ever grade a paper without using a red pencil. Technical supervisors have an additional liability. Research and development projects are high-risk ventures. Projects that produce no tangible results are the rule, not the exception. Supervisors may seem to interpret project failure as human failure, leading to a negative, demotivating climate.

Another framework is Theory X–Theory Y. Formulated by Douglas McGregor, he proposes a Theory X that is a negativistic set of beliefs such as "People have an inherent dislike for work and will avoid it when possible" and "People must be coerced, controlled, directed, or threatened to get them to work toward organizational objectives." In contrast, Theory Y is an optimistic view of human nature and says, "People will exercise self-direction and self-control if they are committed to the objectives," "People not only learn to accept, they also seek, responsibility."

David C. McClelland is known for his studies on the degree of need for achievement (nAch). The nAch is influenced by many factors, including culture, relationships, life experiences, and the like. People with high nAch typically prefer to take personal responsibility for finding solutions to problems. They tend to set moderate and realistic goals, take calculated risks, and appreciate concrete feedback on how well they are doing. Those with high nAch tend to go on to other challenges once the nAch is satisfied. Those with low nAch tend to repeat tasks after success rather than after failure.

A need for achievement is the prime motivator in solving problems. Those with high achievement needs typically want to excel in all they do and get bored by routine tasks. They appreciate objective feedback on their progress and tend to set challenging but reasonable goals. They may seek out expert opinion but like to make decisions and will take responsibility for failure.

The Myers–Briggs Type Indicator®, developed by Katherine Briggs and Isabel Briggs Myers, is based on Carl Jung's theory of personality. The theory postulates that people's apparently random behavior is not random at all but actually consistent when it comes to how they prefer to get information, make decisions, and orient their lives. No one pattern is better than any other, but it is important for people to understand the preferences that underlie their motivation, and how those preferences affect their choices and behaviors.

A sense of competence, the feeling that one has the tools and ability to perform important job tasks, is another motivating factor of great importance for technical professionals. Studies suggest that self-confidence is a strong motivator and is partially responsible for the long periods of study, learning, and skill building required by professionals in both athletics and in science and engineering disciplines.

There are several reasons for the importance of the sense of competence as a motivating factor. The personal satisfaction of developing new skills and upgrading old ones is a motivating factor, which encourages individual growth. Competence is usually more easily judged among scientific and engineering specialists than it is among those who manage them, for several reasons. Technical specialists are generally responsible for their own efforts; blaming poor work on assistants is seldom effective for long. Also, the traditions of science expose one's work to the criticism of peers through seminars, internal reports, and other publications, a process that quickly reveals incompetence. In contrast, the work of managers is "getting things done through others." Unlike technical procedures, managerial decisions can seldom be validated by any quantitative procedure. In this respect, managers are less vulnerable than the specialists that report to them.

For these reasons, inadequate training or the loss of skills through obsolescence is a double threat. Not only does it reduce both capacity for performance and a sense of competence, but worse, it leads to demotivation and loss of interest, energy, and the ability to learn and grow. Thus, obsolescence starts a vicious cycle. If not recognized and treated early, this starts a downward spiral, which can end in career failure. Although personal competence is fundamentally an individual responsibility, managers have a responsibility to assign work that keeps basic skills from deteriorating and to provide opportunities through continuing education to develop new skills.

Supervisors have an obligation to both their employees and their organizations to assess competence and take prompt, supportive action when development appears to be needed. Those who promote high standards of performance and work on their own personal development set the right climate and provide powerful role models.

Motivation Checklist

- ☐ Learn what motivates those who report to you.
- ☐ Expect success.
- ☐ Provide opportunities for personal and professional growth.
- ☐ Recognize accomplishments formally and informally.
- ☐ Provide honest feedback.
- ☐ Identify and challenge those with high nAch.

What are some ways you can recognize those whom you supervise?

What opportunities do you have to create a motivating environment for each person you manage?

The Myers–Briggs Type Indicator is a useful framework from which to think about motivation. For each of the 16 types you can identify likely motivators. In Table 2.1 four specific types of preferences are paired. These pairs are snapshots of how motivation might be affected by differences and are listed along with things each appreciates and does not appreciate.

TABLE 2.1   Motivating by Type

Motivates	Demotivates
Sensing–Judging	
• Praise for product orientation	• Lack of deadlines
• Carefulness, caution, accuracy	• Vague instructions
• Dependability, loyalty, responsibility, industriousness	• Ignored or broken rules
Sensing–Perceiving	
• Praise for style and ability	• Lots of rules and regulations
• Flexibility to proceed as they choose	• Lots of planning or waiting to start
• Appreciation for cleverness	• Being told how to do a job or rush through it
Intuitive–Thinking	
• Appreciation for their ideas and capabilities	• Routine
• Challenging projects	• Rules or traditions that get in the way
• Recognition from those seen as competent	• Things that aren't logical or reasonable
Intuitive–Feeling	
• Recognized for their contributions	• Impersonal treatment
• Sharing feelings and ideas with others	• Being ignored
• Being acknowledged and feeling appreciated	• Not feeling supported

MOTIVATION SITUATION—SOLUTION

Jack

Jack first needs to meet with the individual to discuss how to best work together. Asking questions will help identify the individual's current level of motivation and plans for the future. Is he in fact a "disgruntled" employee as Jessi says? It is also important to find out why he wasn't offered the job Jack took. Comparing his perspective with that of Jack's manager will give insight into how best to coach him for future success.

Actual   During the first meeting, Jack learned that this individual had applied for the job but had never been told why he wasn't given the opportunity. Once Jack found out the reason, the two of them discussed it. Together they talked about how to ensure that he would be ready when the next opportunity arose. Several years later he was offered the job when Jack left the company.

REFERENCES

Domhoff, G. W. *The Scientific Study of Dreams: Neural Networks, Cognitive Development, and Content Analysis.* American Psychological Association (APA), Washington, D.C., 2003.

Goleman, D. *Emotional Intelligence: Why It Can Matter More Than IQ.* Bantam Books, New York, 1995.

Hallowell, E. *CrazyBusy: Overstretched, Overbooked and About to Snap.* Ballantine Books, New York, 2006.

Klein, G. *Intuition At Work.* Doubleday, New York, 2003.

Locke, E. A., and Latham, G. *Goal Setting: A Motivational Technique That Works.* Prentice Hall, Englewood Cliffs, NJ, 1984.

Stone, L. "Living with Continuous Partial Attention." From the article "The Harvard Business Review List of Breakthrough Ideas for 2007." *Harvard Business Review*, Vol. 85, No. 2, February 2007, pp. 28–29.

Wiseman, R. *The Luck Factor: The Four Essential Principles.* Miramax Books/ Hyperion, New York, 2003.

BIBLIOGRAPHY

Herzberg, F. "One More Time: How Do You Motivate Employees?" *Harvard Business Review*, Vol. 81, No. 1, January, 2003, pp. 87–96.

Hirsh, E., Hirsh, K. W., and Hirsh, S. L. *Introduction to Type and Teams.* Consulting Psychologists Press, Palo Alto, CA, 2003.

Maccoby, M. "Understanding the People You Manage." *Research Technology Management*, May–June, 2005, pp. 58–60.

Maccoby, M. "Why People Follow the Leader: The Power of Transference." *Harvard Business Review*, Vol. 82, No. 9, September, 2004, pp. 76–85.

McGregor, D. *The Human Side of Enterprise.* McGraw-Hill, New York, 1960.

McClelland, D. C. "Achievement Motivation Can Be Developed" in *Harvard Business Review*, Nov–Dec 1965, pp. 6–24, 178.

Mehrabian, A. *Silent Messages* (1st ed.). Wadsworth, Belmont, CA, 1971; Mehrabian, A. *Nonverbal Communication.* Aldine-Atherton, Chicago, IL, 1972.

Myers, I. B., and McCaulley, M. *A Guide to the Development and Use of the Myers-Briggs Type Indicator.* Consulting Psychologists Press, Inc., Palo Alto, CA, 1985 (8th printing 1992).

Nadler, D., and Lawler III, E. "Motivation: A Diagnostic Approach" in Hackman, R., Lawler III, E., Porter, L. *Perspectives on Behavior in Organizations.* McGraw-Hill, New York, 1977, pp. 26–34, and Vroom, V. *Work and Motivation.* John Wiley & Sons, New York, 1964; Lawler III, E. *Motivation in Work Organizations.* Brooks/Cole Publishing Company, Monterey, CA, 1973.

Pearman, R. R., and Albritton, S. C. *I'm Not Crazy, I'm Just Not You: The Real Meaning of the 16 Personality Types.* Davies-Black Publishing, Palo Alto, CA, 1997.

Treher, E. N. "Creating a Motivating Climate." *Managing in R&D, A Program for Technical Managers.* The Learning Key, Inc., Washington Crossing, PA, 1992, 2006.

CHAPTER 3

HINTS TO INCREASE INTERPERSONAL EFFECTIVENESS

INTERPERSONAL EFFECTIVENESS—MY STORY (ELIZABETH TREHER)

Leaving a career leading R&D in nuclear and radiochemistry and radiopharmaceuticals was not one I anticipated when I was in graduate school, or doing a post doc, or even in the early years of my career. I loved science. I loved my work. I was successful, and I had no good reason to want to change anything. I didn't initially volunteer to manage others, you might even say I was coerced, but I found I enjoyed it immensely. What led me to eventually leave the realm of doing and leading science was a pattern I saw more and more, particularly after I moved from a national laboratory to industry. A large percent of the scientists and R&D managers and executives to whom I was exposed, or with whom I worked, had neither interest nor ability to work well in teams, to communicate openly with colleagues, or to manage others effectively. Having worked with some extraordinary individuals who were very good at managing and collaborating with others, I strongly saw and felt the difference.

I might have lived with that, but I saw the impact this attitude had on friends and others. I saw a huge turnover in some departments because of the department heads. I saw people who spent their time complaining rather than working. Having a sympathetic ear, I listened to more than my share of stories. When I suggested that someone take a coaching course or a program to improve supervisory skills the answer was often the same—it's a waste of time; they don't know my world. Those with natural skills, who were the

A Guide to Success for Technical Managers: Supervising in Research, Development, & Engineering, by Elizabeth Treher, David Piltz and Steven Jacobs
Copyright © 2011 John Wiley & Sons, Inc.

least in need of the training, could extrapolate from sports meta-phors or other examples they commonly encountered in training, but most could not. I tried to meet with trainers and consultants hired by my employer to help them better understand the individuals and the work of those who attended their training. I was anxious for them to be successful so I wrote cases, I gave them examples. It probably helped a bit. Unfortunately, I continued to hear, "They don't understand my world."

After a couple of years of deliberating, I left R&D to focus on helping those in the technical world improve their interpersonal communication, team, and management skills. My first step was to set up and run a corporate university for an organization with 22,000 employees and next to create a center for science education (where we included programs for managing in R&D, managing IT profes-sionals, and others.) This led to co-founding The Learning Key, Inc., where I remain today, almost 20 years later. Developing effective interpersonal skills are essential if you want to be a good supervisor or manager—not only will you be far more productive, you will have a lot more fun and so will those with whom you work.

Most of us who choose to study and take up careers in engi-neering, science, and technology have a passion for the topics we pursue. Understanding others can seem impossible or unimportant. Some would claim it's even a waste of time. However, once you transition from an individual contributor to a supervisory role, this attitude can have a big impact. Your ability to understand and work with others grows in importance. One organization we worked with hired 18 individuals with master's degrees from schools they con-sidered to be "best." Two years later, only one person remained employed. The others had not been able to work in a team environ-ment and communicate effectively with their colleagues. This chapter explores a variety of elements that can impact how effec-tively we manage ourselves from an interpersonal perspective. It also includes information about the Myers–Briggs Type Indicator——a wonderfully helpful resource along the journey toward inter-personal effectiveness that may even change your life.

THE MYERS–BRIGGS TYPE INDICATOR

As we learn the terms and acronyms for our professions—chemis-try, biology, anatomy, physics, electronics, engineering, or other technical fields or programming languages—we develop the ability to communicate with and understand others who speak that same "language." The Myers–Briggs Type Indicator (MBTI®) gives us the vocabulary to discuss our preferences and the ways we are similar or different from others. It provides an objective framework from which to begin. The MBTI helps us to both value and to expect differences.

Developed by Katherine Briggs and Isabel Briggs Myers, the MBTI is a preference indicator based on Carl Jung's theory of psychological Types. Jung published *Psychological Types* in 1923. Based on the premise that people's apparently random behavior isn't random but is consistent when it comes to how they prefer to get information, make decisions, and orient their lives, it provides a sound foundation for better understanding ourselves, our colleagues, and our differences.

A number of resources are available to take the MBTI online. A free report is also available based on four temperaments, SJ, SP, NF, and NT, using another instrument with a similar foundation, the Keirsey Temperament Sorter II (see www.keirsey.com). Although it doesn't have the research and validation that supports the MBTI, there is a good correlation with MBTI results for those who have clear preferences. The first edition of the book *Please Understand Me*, by Keirsey and Bates (1998), also contains a short instrument that can be helpful to begin a dialogue about differences.

With the MBTI, four preferences are scored. The four pairs, or dichotomies, are:

- *E-I, extraversion and introversion*, our orientation toward the outer and inner world, respectively
- *S-N, sensing and intuition*, the two kinds of perception—the kind of information we prefer
- *T-F, thinking and feeling*, the two kinds of judgment
- *J-P, judging and perceiving*, the two attitudes for dealing with the environment and associated with how we like to live our lives

Remember, these don't tell us about skills; they speak to our preferences. Sixteen personality types result by combining one preference from each scale. The result is known as a type table as shown in Table 3.1.

TABLE 3.1 Type Table: Sixteen Types

ISTJ	ISFJ	INFJ	INTJ
ISTP	ISFP	INFP	INTP
ESTP	ESFP	ENFP	ENTP
ESTJ	ESFJ	ENFJ	ENTJ

USING TYPE EFFECTIVELY

Understanding psychological type preferences gives us a highly valuable guide for managing and communicating with others. Experience with type clearly shows that different types prefer to interact and communicate in differing ways. Working in organizations and on projects generally provides exposure to all types. Appreciation of others and their perspectives, as well as acceptance of your own preferences, is a positive energy source for working effectively with others. To maximize the benefits, we need to learn to develop type flexibility.

Type flexibility is a strategy to make a conscious choice in response to specific situations. It means the skill to choose a new approach or behavior. If we are type flexible, we can draw on a broader range of behaviors. Imagine, if you can identify another's type preferences and tailor your approach to her, it makes it easier for her to understand you. It also means you are more likely to be heard. This doesn't mean trying to change your natural style. It means recognizing your automatic approaches and learning to adjust them.

Developing type flexibility requires awareness, acceptance, and appreciation. Become aware of your own preferences and what they mean; accept your strengths and blind spots and those of others; and appreciate that other's preferences are equally valuable.

Try the following suggestions for approaching others from Thinking, Feeling, Sensing, and iNtuitive perspectives. Use them also as behavioral clues to provide insight into type preferences of those you supervise.

To communicate with thinkers, remember they prefer organized approaches and tend to be precise and to the point; like introverts, they often want time to think things through.

- Plan and organize your presentation.
- Divide your comments into sections, "The implementation phase will involve three ..."
- Be specific and use ranges, if you can't be precise. Instead of saying "In general, we find ..." try "More than seventy percent of the time, we find ..."

- Show you've considered alternatives; give pros and cons.
- Provide graphs, charts, or other summaries to support your data.
- Use bullets or outlines and don't make thinkers wade through a lot of extraneous data or material.
- Generate attention with phrases such as: "Before we start, let me describe the new procedure." Or "Let's look at the reasons behind this approach." "The evidence increasingly shows ..."

To communicate with feelers, remember that they often pick up on things that haven't actually been said and respond to body language and emotion.

- Be informal.
- Use small talk and approach on a personal level.
- Show how others will use or benefit from what you are presenting.
- Generate attention with:
  - "Our experience feedback shows ..."
  - "We recommend analyzing the needs by ..."
  - "The engineering group has been very supportive in ..."

To communicate with a sensor use specifics and a structured, step-by-step approach.

- Be brief, focus on your main points, and avoid extraneous/side bar comments.
- Emphasize the impact of your approach.
- Use visual aids in presentations.
- Generate attention with:
    - "This practical approach will ..."
    - "We will see immediate results so ..."
    - "We can realistically implement. ..."
    - "Let's focus on what we can accomplish now ..."

To communicate with an intuitive, remember to give an overview that provides a broader context or give a brief summary.

- Be open to suggestions and new ideas; seek their input (and plan extra time for this).
- Describe possibilities and the future value.
- Use trends.
- Generate attention with:
  - "We have developed a highly innovative approach that ..."
  - "This new perspective will give us long-term ..."
  - "We'd like your ideas on ..."
  - "This is a strategy that really hasn't been tried before."

Unfortunately, we often don't know the type preferences of those with whom we work. As you work with and observe your employees, you will gain clues and insights. Using references such as Keirsey and Bate's *Please Understand Me* or *Please Understand Me II*, gives a common understanding and helps generate discussions.

Plan for communication by developing an approach that honors all preferences by balancing the needs of sensors, intuitives, thinkers, and feelers.

- Start with a brief overview or conclusion.
- Present your information.

- Provide details only in supporting documents you can distribute later or put in the appendix of a written report.
- Offer your conclusions, describe the benefits to others, and share how you expect to gain approval, if you haven't already done so.

Sensing types prefer standard ways to solve problems and established ways of doing things. They typically enjoy using skills they have already mastered, more than learning new ones, and they are patient with routine and with details. Their work patterns tend to be steady, and they have a realistic idea of how long a job will take. Linear thinkers, sensors usually go step by step.

Intuitive types like solving new problems rather than doing the same thing repeatedly. This means they often enjoy learning a new skill more than using it. Unlike the steadier pace of a sensor (particularly an SJ), intuitives work in bursts of inspiration, with slack periods in between. They tend to reach a conclusion quickly and enjoy complicated situations. Their impatience with details and eagerness to look to the future can get in the way of being thorough and accurate.

Judging types like to get things settled. They typically work best when they can plan their work and follow the plan. In their desire to finish, they may decide things too quickly and go down the wrong road too fast. They enjoy coming to a conclusion about their work, a situation, or person. Often Js like to finish one project before starting another and may not appreciate interruptions.

Perceiving types tend to be polyactive and restless. They adapt well to changing situations and are willing to leave things open. Good at starting things, they may have too many projects going at once and have difficulty in finishing them. At odds with those who prefer judging, they may have trouble making decisions—or sticking with them.

APPLYING CHARACTERISTICS OF TYPE

Table 3.2 lists characteristics that come from our experience and numerous references. Place a check mark (✓) before those that most apply to you. Circle those that seem to fit an individual you supervise or your own manager.

TABLE 3.2 Type Characteristics Table

Extraversion	Introversion
• Enthusiastic	• Intimate
• Sociable; gregarious	• Territorial
• Interactive; initiator	• Concentration
• External focus	• Internal focus; quiet
• Breadth of interest	• Depth of interest
• Talk to understand their own thinking	• Intensive; contains feelings
• Multiple relationships	• Limited relationships

Sensing	Intuition
• Experience based	• Hunches
• Observant—senses draw them to the present	• Need variety
• Oriented to the past and present	• Oriented to the future; tomorrow
• Realistic and concrete	• Speculative and abstract
• Down to earth	• Head in clouds
• Facts, data, details	• Theories, ideas, meanings, possibilities
• Actual	• Fantasy
• Utility and practicality	• Ingenuity
• Sensible; traditional	• Imaginative
• Okay with repetition	• Seeks novel approaches

Thinking	Feeling
• Logical	• Social values
• Objective; analytical	• Extenuating circumstances
• Principles	• Humane
• Policy	• Good or bad
• Laws and standards	• Appreciate; accommodate
• Justice	• Affective: human values and motives
• Critical questioning	• Subjective

Judging	Perceiving
• Fixed	• Flexible
• Settled	• Pending
• Decided	• Gather more data, let's wait and see
• Closure	• Keep options open; emergent
• Plan ahead	• Adapt as you go
• Systematic; methodical "Let's wrap it up"	• Spontaneous, open to change; casual
• Get the show on the road	• "Tell me more"
• Scheduled	• Let life happen
• Run one's life	• Polyactive

Personal Awareness

Developing management skills and effective interpersonal communication start with increasing personal awareness. The MBTI is one of many tools for developing personal awareness. Personal awareness is the ability to "see within" and realize your own personal biases, judgments, preferences, thought patterns, and paradigms. It is the ability to realize that your own world of perceptions is not the same for those around you. It's not an admission of right or wrong but one of difference. Differences can create chasms or build bridges between people. Personal awareness means that you are able to:

✓ *Reflect*   Reflection is taking the time, energy, and dedication to stop and think about how individuals, situations, circumstances, events make you feel or react. What emotions do you experience? How long do they last? Is there a pattern for experiencing specific emotions? If so, what is the pattern? Reflection means taking the time to recognize personal characteristics that may be undesirable to others.

Reflection cannot happen in a short walk from the parking lot to your office or traveling between meetings. Of course those are opportunities to reflect for a moment, but reflection needs more than a moment. It needs enough time to let you "get out" what you need to get out. Taking 20 minutes to reflect may be minimal, but it is realistic in a typical workday.

Consider this suggestion. Close your office door or, if you are in an open-space environment, schedule a closed room. Ensure no one will interrupt you. That may mean asking an assistant to answer calls, turning off your cell phone and your computer monitor, and so forth. If you enjoy and relax to background music, turn it on low. It should not distract but focus you on the task.

- Take a paper and pen and to jot down answers.
- What situations, circumstances, individuals, or events make you feel or react?
- Describe your thoughts or emotions during the times you react.
- Look for patterns that cause strong reactions. Jot down your thoughts.
- Review what you wrote, what conclusions can you draw?

✓ *Avoid Judging*   We are constantly judging everything around us. Sometimes our judging helps us classify information, make a decision, or ignore useless information; for example, typically we don't notice the air we breathe. Without recognizing it, we apply these same types of judging to others.

If we experience a person being late for a meeting once, we may judge him or her as usually late, even when that is not the case. If someone reminds us of a good friend who is particularly clever, we may decide that person is clever as well—with little evidence to support our judgment. This unconscious habit can cause a lot of trouble as we deal with those we supervise. Reflect on judgments you have made. Where might you need to broaden your perspective?

✓ *Avoid Blame*   Blaming others seems to be a trend in today's world. It can be easier to blame someone else, rather than reflect and recognize the part you may have played. Blame seldom solves anything. Instead of seeking to blame, look for solutions. Face forward and find remedies to ensure the problem isn't repeated. Planning for the future, rather than looking to the past, helps to reduce a tendency to blame.

✓ *Seek Collaborations*   In conflict management, collaboration is called a win–win approach. In the context of personal awareness, collaboration is a chance for you as a supervisor to take the time to consider your perspectives, paradigms, and judgments and your part in a situation. From this foundation, you can work to understand the perspectives of others. Collaborations happen when there is:

- Clarity in perspectives
- Communication without judgment or blame
- A willingness to acknowledge your part

Application

To Increase Personal Awareness

- Take the time to *reflect* on a situation or event. What did you think or feel during it? After it? What impact does it have? What could have been different?
- Avoid *judging* the situation or others as good or bad. Realize things are the way they are, and the moment you add judgment you limit your personal awareness.

- Avoid *blame*, in terms of why something happened or who may have caused it to happen. When you blame, you live in the past and worry about something that has already happened. Recognize what happened, deal with it in the moment, and focus on the future without blaming.

- Seek *collaborations* to generate solutions, find resources, and solve issues positively. When you engage others in the solution, you learn more about yourself and the situation than if you try it alone.

ROLE OF EMOTIONS AND TRUST

Other elements that impact interpersonal effectiveness are emotions and trust. Emotions provide the context to explain the events we experience. In the workplace, emotions can be a double-edged sword for the manager. Expressing too much emotion can seem unprofessional; expressing too little emotion can appear detached and uncaring.

Emotions have a tendency to hijack the rational side of thought. Without realizing it, managers can very easily communicate from a frame of emotions rather than objectivity. Triggers are situations that can cause emotions to take over and responses to be reactionary. Reactionary responses are directly connected to our fears, biases, judgments, and feelings of safety. They interfere with effectively listening and sharing interests. The times when emotions are active can be very challenging for managers in any environment.

There are two aspects to which you should pay attention—the first is when you are emotional, and the second is when another person is emotional. In the first situation, the goal is to control your own emotions; the goal of the second situation is to help facilitate another to manage his or her emotions. In either situation, use the **RACES** technique.

RECOGNIZE THE EMOTION
ACKNOWLEDGE THE EMOTION
CALM DOWN
EXPECTATION CHALLENGE
SHARE INSIGHTS

This technique can be used before a tough discussion as a way to prepare ahead, used in the moment when necessary, or used after a discussion as a reflection guide. Use any or all of RACES before, during, or after a tough conversation. Over time, you will begin to integrate the technique into your daily conversations, and it will become second nature. Let's examine the technique.

Recognize the Emotion

This may seem easy, even common sense, but it's a step that is rarely considered. We tend to not realize we are having an emotion but instead jump into expressing our positions and opinions. Taking the time to recognize an emotion provides you with an enormous advantage. Before continuing, ask yourself the following questions: What am I experiencing? Why am I experiencing this? What are the physical manifestations? How is my breathing? What is my heart rate?

Taking the time to identify the emotion is essential to improving communication with others. Students of emotional intelligence discuss the fact that human beings are the only creatures that can have emotions about their emotions. Many clients we have worked with will say they are upset at a situation when instead they are angry and cannot recognize that.

Acknowledge the Emotion

Once an emotion is recognized, the next step is to acknowledge it exists. This may seem redundant, but it is very easy to say you are having an emotion and a very different experience to own the emotion. Acknowledging the emotion means owning the good and bad of the emotion. It provides a context that is affecting the situation. This is not suggesting that emotion is good or bad, just that it is present. Acknowledging the emotion means saying things such as: "This is my emotion. No one has caused me to feel this way, but I am feeling this way because ..." Or "I am experiencing [insert emotion] whether I like it or not." Or "I am [insert emotion]." No matter what statement above resonates with you, it is important to acknowledge the emotion you recognize.

Calm Down

Once you have recognized and acknowledged what you are experiencing, it is time to calm down. Yes, calm down! Calming down suggests that the emotion(s) you are experiencing is(are) causing metabolic and physiological responses that are reactionary. To effectively communicate, one needs to create an environment in which responses are not reactionary but thoughtful and meaningful to move the conversation forward instead of creating an adversarial one. Calming down can mean taking a few deep breaths or taking a walk. It doesn't have to take a lot of time, but taking the time to breathe and allow the current flood of emotions to dissipate can mean the difference between a fruitful discussion and a meaningless one.

Expectations Challenge

At this point in the process, you should be at a place mentally and emotionally where you can challenge your expectations. Challenging your expectations ensures you are not entering into a conversation from a position of wants but from a position of needs. Ask yourself, "What am I expecting from myself? Others? What is my motivation? Do I want to win? Do I want to collaborate?" Challenging your hidden motives allows you to create a dialogue that isn't defensive but one that builds understanding.

Share Insights

You are now finally ready to enter into the communication process. You've taken the time to recognize your emotion(s), acknowledge them, calm down, and challenge expectations. The only thing left to do is to share your insights with others.

As management, one outcome of effective communication is creating trust among others. Trust seems to be the elusive "holy grail" of managers. Always searching for it and sometimes experiencing it with others but rarely working in an environment in which trust is central to how people think about and interact with others. So, what is trust? It comes in many forms, such as the trust that someone will finish a task, or the trust that someone will not talk "bad" about you, or the trust that someone is telling the truth. No matter what trust means to you, creating trust as a manager creates an environment in which others think the best of each other first before thinking the worst. How often does that happen?

In our experience of working with a variety of groups, not often enough. In fact many times the exact opposite happens where a situation occurs and someone automatically jumps to a negative conclusion about the intent of someone's actions. That conclusion creates an atmosphere of distrust and conflict. The effective manager creates an environment in which trust is part of any conversation. It means that each person will:

- Accept the other person is not being malicious.
- Challenge his/her conclusions and ask questions to clarify the intent.
- Think the best of the other person.

As a manager, when you practice and implement the techniques in this chapter, you build the conditions for trust. Trust provides the framework to create effective working relationships.

REFERENCES

Domhoff, G. W. *The Scientific Study of Dreams: Neural Networks, Cognitive Development, and Content Analysis.* American Psychological Association (APA), Washington, D.C., 2003.
Goleman, D. *Emotional Intelligence: Why It Can Matter More Than IQ.* Bantam Books, New York, 1995.
Hallowell, E. *CrazyBusy: Overstretched, Overbooked and About to Snap.* Ballantine Books, New York, 2006.
Jung, C. G. *Psychological Types.* Harcourt & Brace, New York, 1923.
Klein, G. *Intuition At Work.* Doubleday, New York, 2003.
Locke, E. A., and Latham, G. *Goal Setting: A Motivational Technique That Works.* Prentice Hall, Englewood Cliffs, NJ, 1984.
Stone, L. "Living with Continuous Partial Attention." From the article "The Harvard Business Review List of Breakthrough Ideas for 2007." *Harvard Business Review*, Vol. 85, No. 2, February 2007, pp. 28–29.
Wiseman, R. *The Luck Factor: The Four Essential Principles.* Miramax Books/ Hyperion, New York, 2003.

BIBLIOGRAPHY

Barr, L., and Barr, N. *The Leadership Equation.* Eakin Press, Austin, TX, 1989.
Bates, M., and Keirsey, D. W. *Please Understand Me.* Prometheus Nemesis, Del Mar, CA, 1978.
Brownsword, A. W. *It Takes All Types!* Baytree Publication, San Anselmo, CA, 1987.
Keirsey, D., and Bates, M. *Please Understand Me: Character and Temperament Types.* 5th Ed., Gnosology Books, Ltd./ Prometheus Nemesis Book Company, Del Mar, CA, 1984.

Kroeger, O., and Thuesen, J. *Type Talk at Work*. Bantam Doubleday Dell, New York, 1992.

Myers, I. B. *Gifts Differing*. Consulting Psychologists Press, Palo Alto, CA, 1980.

Myers, I. B., McCaulley, M. H., Quenk, N. L., and Hammer, A. L. *MBTI® Manual: A Guide to the Development and the Use of the Myers–Briggs Type Indicator®*, 3rd Ed. Consulting Psychologists, Palo Alto, CA, 1998.

Quenk, N. L. *Essentials of Myer–Briggs Type Indicator® Assessment*. Wiley, New York, 2000.

Reina, D. S., and Reina, M. L. *Trust and Betrayal in the Workplace*. Berrett-Koehler, San Francisco, 1999.

Treher, E. N. "Managing for Interpersonal Effectiveness." *Managing in R&D, A Program for Technical Managers*. The Learning Key, Inc., Washington Crossing, PA, 1992, 2006.

CHAPTER 4

CLUES ABOUT COMMUNICATION PITFALLS AND STRATEGIES

COMMUNICATION SITUATION

Gwen saw herself as someone who was productive, a good listener, creative, and proactive. After graduating in chemical engineering, she had begun working in industry and also finished her advanced degrees. She worked on several major projects before she was hired as a team leader responsible for a staff of five.

Initially, she was seen as a strong team leader and her staff liked her. Soon, however, the lines of communication became strained. She did, however, have a great relationship with her boss, so her responsibilities kept increasing. She was also on several committees. From Gwen's perspective the work was enjoyable. She found some of her staff difficult to work with, and they sometimes viewed her the same way, but she decided that you can't please everyone all the time.

At the advice of her boss, Gwen attended a leadership course, which included a 360-degree assessment component. Gwen was excited to see the results and never imagined her report would change her perceptions of reality and herself. Instead of receiving the feedback she was expecting, she received a report that said she took risks without thinking of the consequences, was a poor communicator, seemed too rigid and structured, and didn't collaborate to achieve results.

Gwen was shocked, especially since she knew whom she had asked to participate in her 360 assessment. Not knowing what to

A Guide to Success for Technical Managers: Supervising in Research, Development, & Engineering, by Elizabeth Treher, David Piltz and Steven Jacobs
Copyright © 2011 John Wiley & Sons, Inc.

do, she had scheduled a meeting with her boss to discuss her performance and review her 360 results. What should Gwen do?

First, take a moment. Has anything similar happened to you?

What caused the differences in feedback?

How can Gwen improve her relationships going forward?

See the end of this chapter for suggestions.

Communication is critical to everything we do. We depend on communication for help, career growth, managing others, and for recognition. Communication affects us personally and it affects our organizations. From a supervisory perspective, it ties to motivation and morale, to skills and problem solving, to selection and promotion, and to the effectiveness of all research, development, and engineering functions. Most R&D executives rank communicating with other corporate groups as their most difficult nontechnical problem, and many technical professionals remain "invisible" and ineffective throughout their careers.

COMMUNICATION PATTERNS AND FACTORS

Communication patterns in many large organizations tend to be formal and hierarchical. Managers are responsible for efficiently using resources. In managing resources, information generally flows from supervisor to subordinate and authority flows from the top down. Communication is likely to be formal and structured in this context.

In the project environments typical of technical professionals, however, communication patterns need to be flexible and horizontal. Such "networking" communication requires the ability to bridge vocabulary (and functional) differences, learn new frames of reference, interact with people from other disciplines or specialties, and go beyond our areas of expertise—tasks many individuals find difficult.

Communication is often confused with information; they are not the same thing. The process of communicating involves transmitting and processing information between a source and a recipient. Studies of this process show that human beings have unique strengths and weaknesses. We are sensitive to an enormous range of signals through our five senses and our memory helps us learn and store information. However, the rate at which we process information is low, and the characteristics of memory constrain our communication with others. For these reasons, communication improves when using multiple senses.

Other important communication factors have to do with physical, functional, and cultural separation. Distances of 100 feet lead to a sixfold decrease in communication between managers and their employees. Allowing random meetings to spark communication doesn't work. Managers must plan to avoid physical isolation. Functional differentiation is another barrier. It requires effort to understand the needs of someone whose job, values, experience, and expectations are different. The same is true for those with a different cultural heritage.

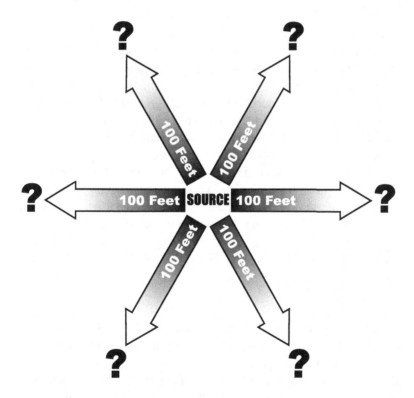

Defensive communication is easily provoked, as research with small groups has demonstrated. Since communication is essential to survival, we have strong psychological reactions to perceived threats, and as a result, they can almost completely block informative communication. Supervisors' attitudes, for example, are perceived as attempts to judge, evaluate, control, or manipulate, expressions of coldness or aloofness, or an air of superiority or certainty, can give rise to defensive reactions. *The greatest barrier to effective communication has been described as the tendency to evaluate what another person is saying* and therefore to misunderstand or to not really "hear" (Rogers and Roethlisberger, 1991). Many technical managers inadvertently create a defensive atmosphere, either through ignorance or bad habits.

A supportive climate, on the other hand, leads to much broader communication and facilitates transfer of new information. Such climates tend to be provisional, spontaneous, informal, and problem oriented. This is important because informal contact between colleagues is a powerful source of influence.

Informal and unstructured communication involves the "dance" between individuals using the spoken or written word, nonverbal signals and body language, tone, inflection, and volume. Assumptions, past experience, and backgrounds all play a part. Typically, managers "dance" by learning skills such as active and reflective listening and questioning; they challenge assumptions and adjust their communication for specific audiences.

Effective communication, an essential skill for supervisors, can be difficult to master. *What makes communication so difficult?* Let's examine several areas that together provide a framework for improving a technical supervisor's communication. They are listening actively, asking questions, challenging assumptions, and communicating by email.

Listen Actively

Effective listening provides the speaker with feedback that you are hearing the entire message, not just the words. Active listening means understanding the words, as well as what is meant by those words—the underlying expectations, biases, values, and attitudes. Gerard Egan (1994) suggests that people desire more than just a physical presence during the communication process; they want the listener to be present psychologically, socially, and emotionally.

Egan says that active, or complete listening, involves the skills of:

- Observing and reading the speaker's nonverbal behaviors such as posture, facial expressions, movement, and tone
- Understanding the verbal message
- Understanding the context of the message in terms of the person's background, experiences, culture, and so forth
- Challenging spoken words that seem not to align with the entire message

Interpretation Exercise: Applying Active Listening

We have said that active listening is more than hearing the words; it is paying attention to the nonverbals, body language, and tone. The following statements repeat with a different emphasis in bold. Read each and identify potential feelings or interpretations for the sentence. Suggested answers follow. For example:

a. **No one** seems to care when I provide input at staff meetings.

Potential Feelings: concerned, frustrated, worried, annoyed

b. No one seems to care when **I provide input** at staff meetings.

Potential Feelings: discouraged, doubtful, unimportant, unheard

1a. The current process still works, **why** do we have to change?
Potential Feelings:

1b. The **current process** still works, why do we have to change?
Potential Feelings:

2a. **Amazing**! You're asking me to recalculate the findings again?
Potential Feelings:

2b. Amazing! You're asking **me** to recalculate the findings again?
Potential Feelings:

3a. Nice thinking. **Your** idea may just be the thing we need for the project.
Potential Feelings:

3b. **Nice thinking**. Your idea may just be the thing we need for the project.
Potential Feelings:

4a. Until **I get** the report, there is nothing I can do. So I can't do my job.
Potential Feelings:

4b. Until I get the report, there is nothing I can do. So **I can't** do my job.
Potential Feelings:

Suggested Answers

1a. The current process still works, **why** do we have to change?
Potential Feelings: confused, overwhelmed, discouraged

1b. The **current process** still works, why do we have to change?
Potential Feelings: hopeful, confident, comfortable

2a. **Amazing**! You're asking me to recalculate the findings again?
Potential Feelings: exasperated, trapped, uncomfortable

2b. Amazing! You're asking **me** to recalculate the findings again?
Potential Feelings: relived, surprised, eager

3a. Nice thinking. **Your** idea may just be the thing we need for the project.

Potential Feelings: delighted, pleased, glad, recognized

3b. **Nice thinking**. Your idea may just be the thing we need for the project

Potential Feelings: doubtful, unsure, anxious or complemented, excited

4a. Until **I get** the report, there is nothing I can do. So I can't do my job.

Potential Feelings: frustrated, nervous, uncomfortable

4b. Until I get the report, there is nothing I can do. So **I can't** do my job.

Potential Feelings: secure, certain, relaxed or defensive, annoyed, frustrated

THE AIDR TECHNIQUE

A useful technique for active listening is **AIDR.** It is a take-off on the tool SOLER from Gerald Egan, which was created more for clinicians. **AIDR** works well in a technical manager's toolkit. *AIDR reminds us to be attentive, interested, demonstrate understanding, and reflect.*

*A***ttentive**

*I***nterested**

*D***emonstrate understanding**

*R***eflect**

Attentive   Attentive means to show, "I am with you." "My focus is on you." To do this, it helps to physically position yourself so you are face-to-face with the speaker to show your interest and that you are ready to listen actively. If you are speaking on the telephone, stand up and focus on listening.

Interest Interest means to show you are approachable and open to listening. Convey a nondefensive attitude by using eye contact, modifying your body position, whether by leaning forward slightly or uncrossing your arms.

Demonstrate Understanding This provides proof to the speaker that you have listened and heard. Paraphrase your understanding, ask questions for clarification, and show your understanding. Before expressing your own thoughts, begin by paraphrasing what was said and add a question such as, "Is that what you meant?" or "Is that accurate?"

As Covey stated (1989), "it is human nature to listen to respond instead of listening to listen." Taking the time to truly listen seems to take too much time. But as supervisors know, not taking the time can create an environment where greater conflict and more issues arise. This leads to using more time than if you had listened in the first place.

Reflect Once the speaker validates your understanding (*not your agreement*), you can move ahead to your own response, it might be your position, another's view, or contradicting data. You have proven you heard and understood the speaker, and you are likely to have a more open listener when you begin to speak.

The AIDR process ensures a listener understands, as clearly as possible, before responding with his/her own ideas. The process may appear to take longer, but it saves wasting time later trying to manage a miscommunication.

FOCUSING ON OTHERS— A DEVELOPMENT EXPERIMENT

One quick exercise to test your ability to focus on another is to monitor how often you use the word "I" in your communications. This is far more challenging for most of us than it sounds. Begin with a short communication. Call a friend and have a conversation without ever using the word "I." Once you can do this easily, attend a meeting or have a one-on-one conversation with an employee. Again, take the word "I" out of your vocabulary. This activity will quickly show you how much of your focus is truly on the other(s) and how much of the time you are thinking and responding with your opinions, your experiences, or your thoughts.

ASK QUESTIONS

Questions are another tool to improve communications with those we manage. Those of us with technical backgrounds spend a good portion of our lives asking questions and looking for the answers to solve technical problems. We tend to be less confident and skilled using questions to resolve interpersonal or communication issues, manage performance, or surface inappropriate assumptions. In a group that had worked together over several years, individuals held a one-hour meeting to share their perspectives. It finally became obvious that one staff member thought another had access to a specific area of a computer system, although he did not. The entire disconnect was created by not listening to what others said. Several times the person said he didn't have access to the system, but he wasn't heard. Eventually, after another member reiterated this point, the message finally registered, and the issue disappeared. Unfortunately, the significant energy and time devoted to the issue was wasted, and the entire process was draining.

Stop a conversation going in circles by asking questions to help others share their perspectives. In this situation, if someone asked, "Do you have access to the computer system?" the issue could have been avoided. Instead, lines were drawn and arguments began in a group of just six.

On the other hand, make sure your question doesn't reflect a hidden assumption on your part. For example, a new staff member hired to lead a research project in an area about which she was unfamiliar, spent her first few weeks on the job reading in her office or at the library. Her manager stopped in one day, while she was reading. His question? "When are you going to do some work around here?"

Her conclusions were that it was most important to look busy and that thinking didn't qualify as work. Surely, this was not the message he wanted to convey. He might have asked any number of different questions to begin a dialogue—"How are your plans coming for the new project?" or "What do you expect to be the biggest challenge in the project?" Instead, he offered a conclusion that neither improved communication nor began a dialogue about her work. Her answer, "I'll start working when I figure out what I am doing," conveyed her annoyance. Questions should be helpful to both the listener and the speaker and provide insight into the assumptions and experience each person brings to the conversation. Questions can help redirect the conversation, so it stays professional. They also change the balance of power. When you begin asking questions, you take control of the interaction.

CHALLENGE ASSUMPTIONS

The technique of challenging assumptions is another important tool in the effective supervisor's tool kit. To challenge assumptions, both the speaker and listener clarify and reiterate what is being discussed. Stop, think, clarify, and surface assumptions to improve your communications.

One approach is to list all the assumptions about a situation, problem, or individual. After the list is complete, discuss each assumption, asking why others think or feel the assumption is valid. Then ask, "What would happen if the assumption was false?" What would change? Challenging assumptions helps to minimize and resolve miscommunications.

EMAIL

Communication by email can have disadvantages as well as advantages. Assumptions and misinterpretations are two ways email can create problems. Rarely do we question what was meant; instead we make assumptions and accept them as accurate and true. To minimize creating conflict where none need exist, we suggest that you take your emails as seriously as your other communication. Emails can also be a good way to build your verbal communication skills. They have several advantages: You can take the words back before you send it, you can modify the language to improve your message, and you can rearrange how you present items to make sure you are "heard."

Karen is a good example. A highly respected executive responsible for several hundred statisticians, she had particular problems with one individual, Joe. They were not communicating at all. He said that she never listened and wasn't interested in his or others' views. She considered herself a good listener, although she had received similar feedback in the past. She didn't know what to do differently. Since face-to-face communication is rather impossible to undo, she began with their frequent written communications by email. In this way, she could revise and rewrite until she thought the message said what she wanted to convey. After looking at her prior emails, we devised a series of steps to serve as a guide. We have used similar steps in coaching many others and suggest you add them to your own managerial toolbox.

EMAIL GUIDE

1. *Start with a comment tied to the interests or prior message of the person* you are addressing. This is easy, if you are responding to an email. Make a comment about their message—"It looks like you have collected quite a bit of data" or "It sounds as if you are concerned that we might not meet our deadline." If you are starting a new email series, you might say "You mentioned X in the meeting the other day, and as I have thought about your comments, I believe that the file I am sending. ..."

2. Once you have acknowledged the person (their communication, interest, frustration)—*present your own comments*, again trying to relate to their needs/interests. If you have a different view, say so—"I have thought quite a bit about your presentation and, although I looked at it differently to begin with, I agree ...", or "... I still believe that we would be better off using Sarah's approach."

3. *Provide your conclusion*—"Perhaps the three of us can meet to further discuss the two options and make a decision." Or "After considering all the information, I have decided that. ..."

4. *Close.* This can be as simple as your name or an expansion of your conclusion.

Karen, like many of us, had been writing "efficient" emails. She had seen no reason to state what she considered to be obvious; she started and ended by simply sharing her conclusion. She found she needed to revise her emails quite a lot at the beginning, mostly to rearrange the order in which she presented her thoughts. One day she called excitedly to say "It worked. I sent Joe an email and the next thing I knew, he was standing in my office holding the printed email." He said, "This is the first time you have ever listened to me." They spent a good portion of the next hour talking. After a rather short time, Karen was able to convert her learning via email to her verbal communications.

APPLYING THE MBTI

We have already mentioned the MBTI and its role in interpersonal effectiveness and communication. In their book, *The Leadership Equation,* Lee and Norma Barr descriptively outline how to use the MBTI effectively in communication. Consider the following descriptions adapted from *The Leadership Equation* that are associated with extraversion and introversion, sensing and intuition, thinking and feeling, and judging and perceiving. Each influences our communication approaches. Can you recognize how your typical approach effects your communications with others?

Extraverts and Introverts

Extraverts tend to respond to situations with speed and spontaneity. Thus, they easily begin conversations, show enthusiasm, and jump into action. Introverts tend to respond to situations with reflection. They prefer calm and quiet so they easily can filter their conversations, stay focused longer, and develop their ideas. Introverts may think through something so clearly that later they mistakenly believe they have communicated their thoughts to others.

Potential strategies for extraverts to communicate more effectively with introverts are:

- Provide space and time for introverts to develop their thoughts.
- Give them advance notice so they can be thinking about a topic.
- Focus on the topic and minimize unrelated small talk.
- Try to avoid talking out ideas; instead take a moment and try to talk it out in your head before sharing. If you find yourself talking and thinking out loud, let others know that you are extraverting and to give you some time.

Potential strategies for introverts to communicate more effectively with extraverts are:

- Provide feedback enthusiastically and often.
- Talk about multiple ideas for short periods.
- After you think something through, say it!
- Engage in small talk more often.
- Ask extraverts about themselves and their thoughts or ideas.

Sensing and Intuition

Sensors tend to communicate with and rely on written methods such as notes, outlines, and lists. They gravitate to details and facts. Intuitives tend to communicate through images and symbols, relationships, body language, and ideas or concepts. Intuitives get bored and restless with a lot of detail, while sensors get annoyed if they can't see a connection to something feasible.

Potential strategies for sensors to communicate more effectively with intuitives are:

- Be open to additional ideas and methods that may at first seem to contradict your concrete facts.
- Start with the big picture or overall issue before jumping in with a lot of detail.

- Create discussions about issues and seek ideas, rather than use only one-way communication.

Potential strategies for intuitives to communicate more effectively with sensors are:

- Focus more on concrete, specific data instead of connections between thoughts and ideas.
- Include ways to implement an idea instead of just creating it.
- Anticipate problems with an idea and consider solutions.
- Focus more on routine methods and provide consistent follow through.

Thinking and Feeling

Thinkers tend to communicate using logic, formality, and objective analysis. Feelers tend to communicate using emotions, informality, and subjectivity. They may ultimately consider the same information but will probably communicate it in a reverse order.

Potential strategies for thinkers to communicate more effectively with feelers are:

- Provide verbal and nonverbal support to ideas and feelings.
- Early in your discussion, address how individuals are affected.
- Have frequent informal discussions to provide the feeler a chance just to talk.

Strategies for feelers to communicate more effectively with thinkers are:

- Be logical and objective when you present your views.
- Talk about the subject in depth without making unnecessary connections.
- Use more formal structures, such as agendas.
- Present any impact on others last, rather than first, in your presentation.

Judging and Perceiving

Judgers tend to structure their communication using plans, schedules, and time-dependent actions. Perceivers tend to structure their communication with spontaneity, open-ended meetings, and multiple options.

Strategies for judgers to communicate more effectively with perceivers are:

- Relax and suspend judgments about time and closure; allow the process to happen as needed.
- Limit planning and provide opportunities for change.
- Increase variety in meetings and discussions.

Potential strategies for perceivers to communicate more effectively with judgers are:

- Create timelines and milestones that you review frequently.
- Be concise and get to the point.
- Prioritize agenda discussion items and tasks.
- Once a decision is made, stick with it and move ahead; do not delay or go back to discuss it again, unless you have hard data that makes this advisable.

PLANNING A PERSONAL COMMUNICATION STRATEGY

Communication can and should be managed. Communication is such a critical factor in career and project success that it is important to examine and plan your own communication strategy.

Steps include:

- Identify specific communication targets among your subordinates, colleagues, managers, and other individuals at work. How can you broaden your network? As research at Bell Labs showed, star performers build their networks before they need them, and when they call someone for advice, they generally get a faster answer (Kelly and Caplan, 1993).
- Evaluate those relationships. Where do you need to build stronger partnerships through honest, consistent, and helpful communication? With whom do you spend the most time and is it effective?
- Assess your own listening and communication skills and work on their development.

- Decide specifically which relationships you will work on first and how you will proceed.

COMMUNICATION SITUATION—SUGGESTIONS

Gwen

What Caused the Differences in Feedback? Gwen had never previously asked for feedback or picked up on any of the subtle communications that might have provided some hints. Communication in her group was neither open nor honest. She realized that what seemed risky to others, and not to her, was likely due to the fact that she didn't often take the time to explain her reasoning or rationale and that the risks others perceived were probably far smaller than they realized. Her staff had made assumptions and so had she. She guessed that her limited communication was likely interpreted as a lack of collaboration. She knew she would have to have more input to be sure of that and to understand what others saw as rigid and structured.

How Can Gwen Improve Her Relationships Going Forward?

Actual During her performance review, Gwen felt comfortable talking openly and honestly with her manager about the results and possible differences in perception. Gwen's boss practiced listening actively, asking questions for clarification and understanding, and challenging assumptions. She modeled good communication practices and helped Gwen reflect on the process she used. At the end of the discussion, Gwen's boss challenged her to follow the same process with her staff. Reluctant at first, Gwen did so; she found that over time she was able to create new productive working relationships with her staff. She learned to surface and to discuss assumptions, and focused on more conscious communication practices such as active listening, using questions for clarification and understanding, and challenging assumptions.

REFERENCES

Covey, S. R. *The Seven Habits of Highly Effective People—Powerful Lessons in Personal Change.* Fireside/Simon and Schuster, New York, 1989.

Domhoff, G. W. *The Scientific Study of Dreams: Neural Networks, Cognitive Development, and Content Analysis.* American Psychological Association (APA), Washington, D.C., 2003.

Egan, G. *The Skilled Helper—A Problem-Management Approach to Helping,* 5th ed.. Brooks/Cole, Pacific Grove, CA, 1994, pp. 91–93.

Goleman, D. *Emotional Intelligence: Why It Can Matter More Than IQ.* Bantam Books, New York, 1995.

Hallowell, E. *CrazyBusy: Overstretched, Overbooked and About to Snap.* Ballantine Books, New York, 2006.

Kelley, R., and Caplan, J. "How Bell Labs Creates Star Performers." *Harvard Business Review,* Vol. 71, No. 4, July–August, 1993, pp. 128–139.

Klein, G. *Intuition At Work.* Doubleday, New York, 2003.

Locke, E. A., and Latham, G. *Goal Setting: A Motivational Technique That Works.* Prentice Hall, Englewood Cliffs, NJ, 1984.

Rogers, C. F., and Roethlisberger, F. J. "Barriers and Gateways to Communication." *Harvard Business Review Classic,* Vol. 69, No. 6, November–December, 1991, pp. 105–111.

Stone, L. "Living with Continuous Partial Attention." From the article "The Harvard Business Review List of Breakthrough Ideas for 2007." *Harvard Business Review,* Vol. 85, No. 2, February 2007, pp. 28–29.

Wiseman, R. *The Luck Factor: The Four Essential Principles.* Miramax Books/Hyperion, New York, 2003.

BIBLIOGRAPHY

Barr, L., and Barr, N. *The Leadership Equation—Leadership, Management, and Myers–Briggs®.* Eakin, Austin, TX, 1989.

Bridges, W. *The Character of Organizations.* Consulting Psychologists, Palo Alto, CA, 1992.

Bush, Jr., J. B., and Frohman, A. L. "Communications in a 'Network' Organization." *Organizational Dynamics,* Vol. 20, Issue 2, Autumn, 1991, pp. 23–36.

Goldberg, M. C. *The Art of the Question: A Guide to Short-Term Question-Centered Therapy.* Wiley, New York, 1998.

Hoke, C., Ed. *Around the Globe or Down the Hall: The Art of Distance Management,* The Learning Key, Inc., Washington Crossing, PA, 2008.

Lawrence, G. *People Types and Tiger Stripes,* 3rd. ed. Center for Applications of Psychological Type, Gainesville, FL, 2000.

Leeds, D. *The Seven Powers of Questions: Secrets to Successful Communication in Life and Work.* Berkley Publishing Group, New York, 2000.

Majchrzak, A., Malhotra, A., Stamps, J., and Lipnack, J. "Can Absence Make a Team Grow Stronger?" *Harvard Business Review,* Vol. 82, No. 5, May, 2004, pp. 131–137.

Mittleman, D. D., Briggs, R. O., Nunamaker, J. F., Jr., and Romano, N. C. "Best Practices from Experiences in Facilitating Virtual Meetings." [From *Around the Globe or Down the Hall: The Art of Distance Management* (Hoke, C., Ed.), The Learning Key, Inc., Washington Crossing, PA, 2008, pp. 80–99.]

Pollitt, I. "Managing Differences in Industry." *Research in Psychological Type*, Vol. 5, 1982, pp. 4–19.

Quenk, N. L. "Benefits of Using the MBTI®—And What It Cannot Do." *APT Bulletin*, Fall, 2004, pp. 36–37.

Quenk, N. L. *Essentials of Myers–Briggs Type Indicator® Assessment*. Wiley, New York, 2000.

Sample, J., and Hoffman, J. "The MBTI® as a Management and Organizational Development Tool." *Journal of Psychological Type*, Vol. 11, 1986, pp. 47–50.

Treher, E. N. "Communication." *Managing in R&D, A Program for Technical Managers*. The Learning Key, Inc., Washington Crossing, PA, 1992, 2006.

Treher, E. N., and Noah, J. "Interpersonal Communication: Challenges and Solutions." *Lab Medicine*, Vol. 39, No. 5, May, 2008, pp. 261–264.

Walker, A. C. "Effective Technical Management." *American Chemical Society*. Washington D.C., 1989.

CHAPTER *5*

SECRETS TO MANAGING PERFORMANCE

PERFORMANCE SITUATION

Transferred Technician

Sally had been a technician in a large, global organization for 17 years when she was transferred, yet again, to a new supervisor, Connie. Connie had two other direct reports but was new to the organization. She was told that Sally was a marginal performer who lacked motivation and that she had had 12 managers in the past. As a new manager, Connie took a workshop to help her work with Sally. At that time she said that Sally seemed to do her job well; she knew many people in the organization, so she was a real help when it came to networking and had a better understanding of how things operated there.

The workshop included an interim assignment, where the participants held a goal planning session, a performance feedback discussion on a specific issue, or a development discussion. Four weeks later the participants returned to describe their success (or issues). Connie was adamant that she speak first. She said that she and Sally had met to have a goal-setting discussion. When she shared the team's goals and asked how she felt she could best contribute to accomplishing them, Sally had asked "Are you allowed to ask me this?" The manager said she presumed so since the company had just sponsored a management skills workshop where they had suggested she do this. Sally looked amazed and said that in her 17 years at the company, no supervisor had ever asked her what she thought. Connie said that Sally was a top performer and not marginal at all.

A Guide to Success for Technical Managers: Supervising in Research, Development, & Engineering, by Elizabeth Treher, David Piltz and Steven Jacobs
Copyright © 2011 John Wiley & Sons, Inc.

SETTING EXPECTATIONS AND GOALS

A colleague, Robert Saunders, used to tell the story of a consultant hired by a chief executive officer (CEO) to work with a new executive. The CEO was frustrated that the new executive wasn't taking appropriate action and moving the CEO's agenda forward. After a number of questions, the consultant was able to create a list of key expectations and goals for the executive. He was asked not to discuss them directly with the executive but to try to get an understanding of why his performance was poor.

The consultant met with the executive and found he was also frustrated. He said that every time he tried to speak with the CEO to understand his expectations and what he wanted to accomplish, the CEO chuckled and said he was a bright guy and would soon be on top of things. "I am bright and I see many approaches we could take, but every time I start with one, the CEO gets upset. I just don't know what he wants." The consultant mentioned he and the CEO had created a list of goals and objectives, but he wasn't supposed to discuss them. He then said he had to go to the men's room and left the list on his laptop.

Several weeks later the CEO called the consultant to ask how he'd been able to turn the situation around so quickly. The consultant confessed that he'd left the list of goals and objectives in the executive's office briefly, and he must have seen them. The CEO responded, "I knew it. He cheated!"

No one is a mind reader. Guessing at your objectives is at best inefficient, if not totally ineffective. How well do you communicate priorities and goals? For each question that follows, which best describes your situation? If you have no supervisory experience, answer assuming you are the supervisor. It is also useful to ask your employees how they would answer these statements to ensure you have the same views.

My Staff Have:	**Usually**	**Sometimes**	**Rarely**
Clear and specific goals			
Input on their goals			
Challenging but achievable goals			
Freedom to decide how to approach their goals			
Deadlines for accomplishing their goals			

For those items where you or an employee checked rarely or sometimes, what can you do to move to usually? What about your own goals? Can you choose usually for them? Have you and your manager used a goal setting process you can apply with your employees or do you need to make changes in your own situation?

Goal clarity, difficulty, specificity, and acceptance, the degree to which an individual takes a personal interest in a goal, all influence performance. Research shows that harder goals lead to higher levels of performance. Goals must be difficult enough to seem challenging but not so difficult that they seem unattainable. Specific, quantitative goals lead to higher performance levels than goals such as "do your best." This is true as well for goals where the endpoint is clear.

To enhance goal commitment and acceptance have employees participate in the goal-setting process. Participation encourages and generates self-confidence. When an employee assists in goal setting, you will develop more ideas and will usually find that the resulting goals are set at a higher level. It also helps to develop trust and ensure that goals are perceived as fair and reasonable.

Explicitly stating goals tends to increase commitment. If you have a group or team, sharing goals openly assists both commitment and clarification. Group norms impact performance. Others may raise questions that you hadn't considered and that can help to restate goals more clearly and concisely. Vague goals leave too much opportunity for alternative behaviors.

To set effective goals with your employee, remember to:

- Be specific.
- Set time limits.
- Specify how you will judge performance.
- Prioritize them.
- Consider and discuss the need to coordinate with other departments or organizations. If meeting a goal is contingent upon a subcontractor's delivery, how will you judge performance if the subcontractor doesn't deliver? Is managing the subcontractor to facilitate timely delivery part of your expectation?

Goal-setting systems fail when employees are not an active part of the goal setting. Keep lines of communication open so that people learn about changes that can impact performance. If communication is blocked, motivation drops, and goals are less likely to be met. This is also true if proper plans to achieve objectives are not developed, so that long-term goals are not translated into short-term objectives.

To involve employees in the goal-setting process begin with the employee's key job tasks and your own goals and objectives, and establish specific, challenging goals for your employee.

Then:

- Prioritize and specify deadlines for each goal.
- Rate goals for difficulty and importance.
- Build in feedback mechanisms to assess goal progress.
- Provide rewards contingent on goal attainment.

In addition to establishing clear goals, the ability to influence performance is key to being an effective technical manager. But what determines whether employees will have high levels of performance? The ability to perform one's job effectively is a function of many variables. It is not enough to be motivated and want to perform well; one must also have the necessary knowledge, skills, and ability.

Other factors that can impact the ability to perform are:

- Motivation
- Sufficient resources, such as equipment, budget, and staff
- Appropriate skills, including training and development
- Understanding of the task
- Supervisory support
- Feedback on performance

Recognize and eliminate any barriers to effective performance from the list above.

CONSIDER PERSONAL STYLES—BOTH YOURS AND YOUR EMPLOYEE'S

To manage performance, consider the personal characteristics of each employee. This provides insight into individual behaviors and motivations. Research shows that the need for achievement, endurance, perceived ability, past success, self-esteem, focus of control, organizational commitment, and job involvement are characteristic of those who remain committed to their goals. Consider individual Type preferences and differences and their impact on your approaches for setting goals and managing performance.

If you are an extravert, put high-level goals or assignments in writing, so introverts can reflect before a discussion. Distribute agendas and materials in advance, if possible. Practice your listening skills. Give others the chance to voice an opinion. When extraverts dominate, introverts may not speak up and silence doesn't mean consensus.

As the manager, be careful that an employee doesn't take comments you make when you are thinking out loud as a new assignment. If you are simply "extraverting," say so.

If you are an introvert, give extraverts "thinking space." Don't assume that their first comments are their final views. Extraverts think out loud and clarify ideas by sharing and refining them as they speak; introverts need to let this happen and may need to ask if they mean for you to act on their comments or are they just "thinking."

Create time to think, when you need it. For example, "Could we take just a couple of minutes so both (or all) of us can consider this?" Or "I'd like time to think about this; can we discuss it again later today?" An employee may not be willing to ask for time to think, and managers should suggest it. For example, "We went over this rather quickly. Why don't you take some time to think about it and any questions you may have? Could we meet briefly tomorrow to see what we may have forgotten?

It is helpful for introverts to practice difficult performance conversations with a colleague before trying it for real. In addition, if you have carefully considered a situation—follow through. Thinking about it is not enough; let the employees hear your perspectives and get theirs as well. Introverts can reflect deeply and clearly, and their thoughts can seem so real that sometimes they think they have actually communicated when they have not.

If you are a sensor, you may tend to go into too much detail when discussing a goal, an assignment, or performance issue. Try to ask questions to surface the employee's thoughts. Don't immediately dismiss ideas you consider unrealistic or impractical. Listen and use questions to understand and to help others see potential pros and cons. Since not everyone shares your preferences, check to see that you are not losing another's attention when you provide a lot of detail. Intuitives are unlikely to stay attentive. Begin with a brief "summary" of whatever you are presenting or want to discuss, before you go into details. Avoid getting bogged down with questions about details and move ahead; provide detailed information later for those who want it.

If you are an intuitive, practice patience. Sensors may have important data that will impact a project's goals. Hear them out. Don't ignore the present or situations that require immediate attention. As much as you enjoy brainstorming and generating new ideas or approaches, remember that others may prefer what they consider to be more practical approaches and may resist your contributions. If they don't participate in the brainstorming you like, ask them to point out the pros and cons they may see.

If your preference is for feeling, don't be afraid to give direct feedback or to disagree with others with whom you work. Rarely do performance issues solve themselves. Healthy disagreement can lead to many positive changes. When you present your perspectives, others may agree with you, having seen the situation in a new light. Remember not to take things personally. When others disagree, it doesn't mean personal dislike or criticism.

If you are a thinker, remember to consider the impact of your decision or approach others. In addition to focusing on the goals and task(s), consider how they will affect others. How will you or your employee or team manage that? You may need to help find approaches to win support.

If you are a judger, listen to other options. Set aside enough time to hear and consider alternatives. Your tendency to move ahead quickly with a decision is less likely to get you into trouble if you have heard others' thoughts and concerns.

When you hold others accountable for their assignments and goals, focus on the outcomes, not process. Allow others to pursue their own ways in which to accomplish the goals. Assuming there is no need to follow specific procedures, such as good laboratory practices (GLPs), good manufacturing practices (GMPs), or standard operating procedures (SOPs), let others accomplish a task as they see fit. They may not use your way, and it may increase your anxiety, but your responsibility is to hold employees accountable for delivering on their goals, not in how they accomplish them.

If you are a perceiver, focus more on closure. A decision may be necessary, however incomplete the available information. Pay attention to deadlines. Others may not have your gift of last-minute deliverables. Thus, if you are managing others, make sure they have a similar preference, so you don't miss a deadline because you assumed they operate as you do. Perceivers can find they collect more information or data than is necessary to move ahead. Aiming to miss nothing, perceivers may delay too long and miss a window of opportunity.

The single biggest driver of conflicts and challenges in manager–employee relationships that we have seen is due to differences between preferences in perceiving and judging. This is true especially in technical environments where new approaches or products are developed and tested. Managers need to be comfortable making decisions with partial information. Technology has provided us with many ways to test and collect information, but resource constraints make it impractical to do everything that might be possible.

Perceivers can feel stressed when asked to move on when their perceiving preference wants to collect more data or do additional experiments. (See Table 5.1.)

MANAGING PERFORMANCE

Managing performance is challenging for many reasons. Those of us educated in technical fields often are drawn to problem solving; we go straight to the problem (as we see it) to figure out what is wrong. We take the data available and interpret it through our many filters—education and training, experience, culture, generation, and gender. Unfortunately, those filters are not infallible and may differ substantially from those of our colleagues who see things in different ways.

This propensity to interpret information has unfortunate consequences when it comes to managing performance and giving feedback. Our interpretations can cause controversy and unnecessary conflict.

The best advice we can give on managing performance is to leave your interpretations at home. Forget them. They may or may not be accurate, but when you give an opinion, it's just your opinion. It is not fact, and others may have a different view.

There is a big difference between your interpretation or conclusion and a specific observation. Feedback that I have a bad attitude, lack initiative, or am a poor communicator is not specific and is your conclusion. You have, perhaps, seen me do something that led to your conclusion, but to assist my improvement you have to help me to:

1. Hear what you have to say.

2. Recognize what I am doing specifically that you see as the problem.

Pelz and Andrews (1966) found that the performance of research labs correlated with the extent of communication. For Ph.D. levels there was a clear correlation between the number of

TABLE 5.1   Performance Checklist

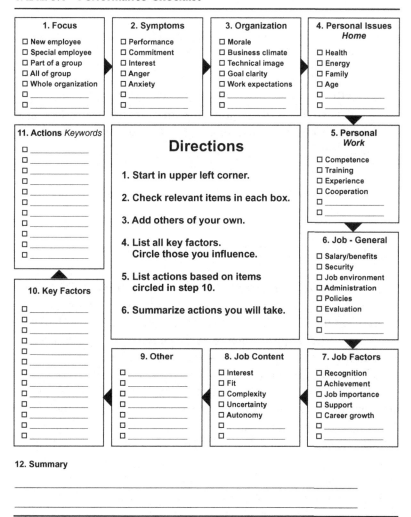

1. Focus	2. Symptoms	3. Organization	4. Personal Issues *Home*
☐ New employee ☐ Special employee ☐ Part of a group ☐ All of group ☐ Whole organization ☐ _____ ☐ _____	☐ Performance ☐ Commitment ☐ Interest ☐ Anger ☐ Anxiety ☐ _____ ☐ _____	☐ Morale ☐ Business climate ☐ Technical image ☐ Goal clarity ☐ Work expectations ☐ _____ ☐ _____	☐ Health ☐ Energy ☐ Family ☐ Age ☐ _____ ☐ _____

11. Actions *Keywords*

☐ _____
☐ _____
☐ _____
☐ _____
☐ _____
☐ _____
☐ _____
☐ _____
☐ _____
☐ _____
☐ _____

Directions

1. Start in upper left corner.

2. Check relevant items in each box.

3. Add others of your own.

4. List all key factors.
   Circle those you influence.

5. List actions based on items
   circled in step 10.

6. Summarize actions you will take.

5. Personal *Work*

☐ Competence
☐ Training
☐ Experience
☐ Cooperation
☐ _____
☐ _____

6. Job - General

☐ Salary/benefits
☐ Security
☐ Job environment
☐ Administration
☐ Policies
☐ Evaluation
☐ _____
☐ _____

10. Key Factors

☐ _____
☐ _____
☐ _____
☐ _____
☐ _____
☐ _____
☐ _____
☐ _____
☐ _____
☐ _____
☐ _____
☐ _____
☐ _____

9. Other	8. Job Content	7. Job Factors
☐ _____ ☐ _____ ☐ _____ ☐ _____ ☐ _____ ☐ _____ ☐ _____	☐ Interest ☐ Fit ☐ Complexity ☐ Uncertainty ☐ Autonomy ☐ _____ ☐ _____	☐ Recognition ☐ Achievement ☐ Job importance ☐ Support ☐ Career growth ☐ _____ ☐ _____

12. Summary

_____

_____

contacts and performance. For the groups with assistant scientists and non-Ph.Ds in labs generally dominated by Ph.Ds, performance peaked at one contact and then fell off. Pelz and Andrews didn't explain these results, but one explanation is that the assistants saw communication as a source of control rather than helpful information. Thus, performance is impacted positively by "informative" communication and negatively if it results in a defensive climate.

PERFORMANCE PROBLEM SOLVING

Once you have analyzed the performance issue(s), use the following steps as guidelines for talking with your employee:

- Plan before you have the discussion so that you can clearly describe your observations and expectations.
- Ask questions to explore reasons for the situation and generate potential solutions; evaluate solutions and agree on next steps.
- After you meet, remember to follow-up.
- When you see things improving, acknowledge and encourage the improvement.

DEALING WITH PERFORMANCE ISSUES

Often we realize that something is wrong but find it difficult to discuss the issue. Perhaps we want to avoid having an argument or creating conflict. We may expect that the situation won't occur again, so it's better just to ignore it. Regardless, have the conversation. Don't delay or assume the problem will go away on its own.

To have a performance discussion or provide feedback on a specific situation, remember not to communicate your interpretations or conclusions—focus on your observations. It can be easier to make a general statement such as "poor attitude" or "poor performance" than it is to be specific. However, these are conclusions and give no information about the behavior you want to see changed. Stop and ask yourself: "Why do I think this employee has a poor attitude?" "What has she or he said or done to make me feel that way?" Questions such as these can lead to understanding employee behavior. Behavior is what an employee says or does. Defining the specific behavior, rather than communicating your conclusions, is a key step to solving a performance problem.

Plan for the discussion by asking yourself questions:

Is the employee aware of the issue?

Could I be contributing to the problem?

Are there circumstances beyond the employee's control?

Does the employee have the skills and ability?

What are my expectations and does the employee understand them?

What is the gap between what I see and what I expect?

Remember, we aren't likely to continue a behavior unless we see a personal benefit. So, can you think of something that could be contributing to this?

MANAGING A PERFORMANCE ISSUE

Describe your observation clearly in an open way. Be specific and describe the performance. Remember to focus on the changeable. For example, social behaviors can be altered, whereas intellectual abilities probably cannot. Avoid saying things such as "you don't work fast enough" or "you have a bad attitude." *Fast enough* is not specific. *Bad attitude* is your interpretation, not an observation.

"You really need to work harder" or "Change your attitude" or "Be a team player" are not specific, and they are conclusions that may not be accurate. Even if accurate, they say nothing about what you'd really like me to do differently. I may think I am a great team player because I step in to help others and am willing to share my ideas. Your conclusion may be based on the observation that I come to team meetings late or don't brainstorm with the group. That conclusion won't tell me about those issues or help generate an appropriate solution. However, "I've noticed you don't volunteer ideas in our brainstorming sessions. The team would really benefit from your input" is a far better starting point than "You aren't a team player." If I think my other behaviors show that I am a team player, I may become defensive or angry before we really begin our discussion.

Look at the accompanying figure and jot down two or three sentences about what you see. Be as descriptive as possible. If you were to write a story about the characters in the drawing, what would you say?

Now look at your comments. Did you include any interpretations? For example, did you say a man and woman at work or a boss and subordinate? Often when we ask individuals in a group to do this, they almost universally describe the individuals in work scenarios, sometimes quite imaginative ones, and rarely, if ever, stick to observations. When you think about performance issues, and particularly when you plan to give feedback to someone— write down what you "see" and look to see if in fact you have listed an interpretation rather than something objective and verifiable. In the examples here, decide if the statement is an observation (O) or a conclusion (C). Next, try to revise the comments. Rewrite those statements to reflect what might have been observed?

See suggestions at the end of the chapter.

DISTINGUISHING BETWEEN OBSERVATIONS AND CONCLUSIONS

Response O or C	Statement
_____	His methods were sloppy.
_____	When giving a summary of the results, you failed to understand their true importance.
_____	She wasted the group's time in the meeting.
_____	She is a poor communicator.
_____	In spite of the stacks of papers and apparent disarray, she was able to pull the critical information we needed quite easily.
_____	You were rude and disruptive.

Describe Your Expectations

It isn't enough simply to describe your observations. Explain what you expect. This defines the performance gap. For example, "I expect everyone to take an active role in our meetings. You present your work, but are not generating suggestions or input when we need to brainstorm," is a statement that more clearly defines one expectation.

Explore the Cause(s)

What is the problem really about? Ask "Who/What/When/How" questions to gather information. Avoid "why" questions. Why questions often come across as judgments and make others defensive. What questions tend to invite factual responses and keep the discussion moving. For example:

> "*What* keeps you from giving your ideas when we brainstorm?"
>
> "I don't know."
>
> "You come up with good solutions to our programming challenges, what's the difference?"
>
> "I guess I just need to work at my own pace—not have a bunch of ideas shouted out without any time to think."
>
> "What might help you participate more?"
>
> "It might help if I knew what we were going to talk about ahead of time, so I could do some thinking."

Generate and Evaluate Solutions

Generate Solutions   Rather than give your own ideas, start with the employee's suggestions for handling the problem. Ask for ideas and have the employee generate solutions. The first idea generated is rarely the best, so push for alternatives. "What else might you do?" "How else could you approach this?" She or he may think of a solution you hadn't and will be more apt to change behavior if it is her or his idea. This also builds trust and better relations.

Asking for ideas will work some of the time, but since unexpected issues can arise, it won't work all the time. So how can you continue to get additional suggestions? It may be that you need to discuss new brainstorming approaches and use a technique where an individual writes specific ideas on Post-Its® for a few minutes before sharing ideas.

Evaluate Solutions   Ask questions to improve the quality of a solution. "How to" kinds of questions can help. Questions such as "What are the advantages of that?" "How would that resolve the issue?" or "What can you do to make sure this happens?" help the employee think through the solution. Before stating the problems

you see with any suggested solution, try to help the employee identify the possible pitfalls.

Decide on Specific Actions and Timelines

Either sum up the specific action to be taken or ask the employee
to do so. This reduces further misunderstandings by making sure
you and the employee agree on what each will do. After the meeting,
make informal written notes of agreed-to actions, so you will have
a record for later follow-up.

   Later, if the problem is corrected, reinforce the improvement.
Specifically describe the improvement and your appreciation, and
explain how the improvement is important.

- Listen and discuss issues the employee raises.
- Offer your support and commit to action, if appropriate.
- Thank the employee: "I noticed you gave a number of new
  ideas during our meeting today. Thanks, I'm glad we found a
  solution. How did you think it went?"

PERFORMANCE CONVERSATION CHECKLIST

Consider a conversation you have had with an employee. Which
of the following steps did you use? Which, if any, did you
omit?

- ☐ Described specific observations, not conclusions.
- ☐ Described my expectations.
- ☐ Checked that the employee was clear about expectations.
- ☐ Asked the employee for reasons and causes.
- ☐ Probed and asked questions to understand the employee's
  perspective.
- ☐ Discussed alternative solutions; asked first for the employee's
  ideas, without giving mine.
- ☐ Evaluated solutions through questions to help the employee
  think through advantages and disadvantages of specific
  approaches, if appropriate.
- ☐ Agreed on actions to take and the timeline.
- ☐ Followed up and gave the employee supportive feedback on
  improvement.

TACKLING RECURRING PROBLEMS

If you've taken these steps and performance does not improve, think through your approach. Does the employee need coaching or did you miss the real cause of the problem? Look over your notes from earlier meetings; be able to summarize them when you speak again.

Have you considered whether the employee is benefiting from the current situation? Does the employee have incentives NOT to improve? Is there a way to change the balance of consequences so the employee has more motivation to correct the situation? If you have had more than one discussion about an issue and you don't see improvement, speak with your own manager for his/her recommendations. Consider practicing the conversation you will hold with your employee. Ask your manager, a colleague, a family member, or friend to help. Role playing can be a safe way to practice, and, if you ask for and apply the feedback you get, your skills will improve. Try also to take the employees perspective and see how someone else might handle the conversation.

When you meet again, if the performance issue has not improved:

- Ask your employee to describe his/her understanding of prior agreements.
- Share your goal for the meeting. Express your support and confidence.
- Describe your observation, the performance gap, and your expectations.
- Ask the employee for input. Is she/he clear about the expectations? Listen.
- Ask questions to generate potential solutions. Have new ones emerged? If not, what got in the way the last time? Work together to resolve any issues.
- Describe the consequences of not correcting the situation.
- Agree on next steps and schedule a time to meet again.

PERFORMANCE ISSUE LINKED TO TECHNICAL PROBLEMS

Managing others with technical backgrounds means that they too want to problem solve and may have different views of a situation. This ability to contribute to problem solving is not a matter of training or an advanced degree, as many seem to believe. Some of the most talented professionals we have worked with had no advanced degrees. They were however, curious, clever, and motivated. In some technical organizations there tends to be a divide between those with a Ph.D. or M.D. and others. This creates an unfortunate environment where degrees are more highly valued than experience or capability. It also means that those with advanced degrees are more likely to become managers.

Their training to solve problems can lead to being overly directing—wanting to jump in and solve a problem themselves. *A good supervisor practices using questions to help others think through a problem and potential solutions themselves.*

One of the assumptions we tend to make in managing others with advanced degrees, or a high level of technical experience, is that we can't do much to help them improve their technical performance. In some cases, this is true. Occasionally, you may find yourself with an employee who is not capable of doing the job for which he/she was hired. In this case, at least in larger organizations, as an R, D or E manager you may have the luxury to change an employee's responsibilities to ones with a better fit. We once helped a chemist become an accomplished technical writer after he proved numerous times that he could be a hazard in the lab and had few natural gifts to be a successful synthetic chemist. Although he could generally repeat a literature prep without too much assistance, teaching him how to create something totally new proved, at least in his case, to be an impossible chore. He did, however, become a first-rate technical writer.

In other situations, with careful observation and discussion, you can turn an unproductive scientist into one who is highly productive. Don't assume that graduate school has taught everyone how to design good experiments!

How would you handle the following situation?

Keith, a synthetic inorganic chemist, spent many extra hours at work—nights, weekends, holidays. Unfortunately, that activity did not pay off in terms of results. The chemist was frustrated and felt unappreciated for all his work. His manager felt he couldn't reward someone who didn't produce.

How would you coach Keith? Where would you begin? What would you ask or say to Keith?

Some assume Keith either does or doesn't know how to do his work. Nothing could be less true. In managing technical professionals, we have tools that aren't available to managers in other disciplines. We typically have lab notebooks and other written records to explore in order to evaluate what might be getting in the way of successful performance. This doesn't apply just in situations where we share similar training and experience. As trained problem solvers, we should be able to look at an approach and generate questions to help the individual consider his/her approach.

Actual Situation

For 5 years Keith got no help from his manager, and the friction between them was high. When a new manager began to supervise him, she was puzzled by his lack of productivity, in spite of long hours and lots of effort. When he could provide no explanation, she asked to review his lab records. Although she wasn't a synthetic chemist herself, she could see that this individual did not know how to design experiments. Every experiment was done three times, so clearly a lot of effort was leading to no new knowledge. She didn't have to understand the chemistry to coach Keith on how to design a good experiment, and shortly afterward Keith became a productive contributor—one who could enjoy his weekends and time off.

MANAGING MANAGERS

As your managerial responsibilities grow, you will undoubtedly supervise others who are supervisors themselves. Let's assume you have been managing for some time and need to coach a new manager, Stan. Unfortunately, a valuable member of your team who had reported to Stan just left the organization.

Stan's Perspective

Stan liked his work and stayed late or worked on weekends when his projects required it. In 4 years he had paid off his student loans and was well on his way toward his goal of buying and living on a sailboat. He was proud of his accomplishments and was soon to present some of his results on the SY420 project at a national meeting.

In spite of this, Stan had begun to feel more and more uncertain about his job. Six months ago, when he received his promotion, he was pleased. It meant a pay raise and the support of two bachelor-level scientists. However, Stan didn't feel comfortable as a manager. He recently concluded that he might not want to manage anyone, even if the pay raise would help get that sailboat sooner.

Several weeks ago, his manager told him that one of his two technicians, Carlos, had asked for a transfer. Today he learned that Carlos had quit his job, even though he'd worked in the organization for almost 10 years. Stan's first thought was good riddance, but he said nothing. Carlos had been rather vocal, complaining that Stan treated him like a moron and gave him no interesting work. He thought Carlos was a capable guy, but Stan just didn't have the time to teach him new methods or bring him up to speed on his own projects so that Carlos could help. Months ago, Stan's manager suggested that he turn over the SY420 project to Carlos. Since it was an interesting project and one Stan had worked hard to get going, he'd decided to keep it himself.

Stan had never talked much with Carlos to understand what he wanted, especially after he heard he was trying to leave. He also didn't see why Carlos should get the interesting work, especially as it looked so promising, and leave him to write up results or start something else. Stan was just beginning his career and he felt he needed to build his reputation. He thought that maybe he just wasn't ready to supervise anyone, although having an extra pair of hands was useful sometimes. His other tech, Ann, never complained about her routine work. He assumed she was happy with her job.

> What are the key issues?
>
> What could Stan's manager have done when she/he first heard that Carlos wanted a transfer?
>
> How could you help Stan improve his supervisory skills?
>
> If you were Stan's manager, how would you have coached him?
>
> How might Carlos have managed his issues better with Stan?
>
> How could Stan manage Ann to ensure he doesn't lose her as well?

See the end of this chapter for suggestions to help Stan, his manager, and Carlos.

Coaching Stan, the New Manager

What Are the Key Issues?   Stan seems to be holding on to the behaviors of an independent contributor. He needs help transitioning to his new role. He may be afraid of losing his skills and credibility and seems to view his staff as competition. Have him take the Manager–Scientist Inventory in Chapter 1. His responses will give you both insight into some of his motivations and open discussion. It may be that Stan isn't motivated or ready to supervise others, or it may be that he is doesn't know how and is afraid to try. He appears to have a strong preference for introversion since he so clearly likes to work alone and seems to avoid communicating with his staff.

How Could You Help Stan Improve His Supervisory Skills?   As Stan's manager, once you are clear he should stay in a supervisory role, you need to spend more time coaching him. To begin, talk with him about what he sees as the benefits and disadvantages in managing others. Discuss the disadvantages and how to look at them in a positive way. Help him understand how his behavior is impacting his staff and work with him on what to do about it. Talk about his communication with Carlos. What got in the way? How might he have handled it differently? What were his concerns about delegating the project? Talk with him about Ann and how he can increase his communication with her. Coach him to work with her.

If You Were Stan's Manager, How Would You Have Coached Him?   Help Stan think through the benefits of an assistant—someone who can provide a sounding board, a source of new ideas, a way to progress more quickly in his own work. Consider how you and Stan work together. Do you meet one on one and do you listen to his work problems and help him think through his approaches? Can you use your relationship with him as a model for him to consider with his staff?

Certainly coach Stan on how to delegate and the benefits of delegation. Teach him a process for delegation. He lost a valuable employee, partially through a lack of understanding how to delegate. Had he delegated parts of his project to Carlos, he might have seen that his fears of being relegated to a report writer were exaggerated.

How Might Carlos Have Handled His Issues with Stan before Carlos Decided to Leave and Take Another Job? From what we know, Carlos did not manage his manager. By being proactive, asking questions about the project, he might have found opportunities to help Stan without Stan's needing to spend a lot of time with him. Since Stan didn't appear to initiate communication, Carlos should have requested that they meet briefly each morning, or once a week, or whatever was appropriate for the work he was doing. This would have given them an opportunity to get to know each other, be more comfortable talking, and to discuss the work they were each doing.

How Could You Help Stan Manage Ann to Ensure He Doesn't Lose Her as Well? Help him think through opportunities he has to delegate to Ann. Then he should meet with Ann to discuss her work, her experience, her goals, and the ways she thinks she can best contribute. He should share his own project goals and together they should discuss how she can support them. If Ann wants additional responsibilities, Stan should look for a more challenging assignment he could delegate and discuss it with her.

SUGGESTED ANSWERS FOR DISTINGUISHING BETWEEN OBSERVATIONS AND CONCLUSIONS

Response	Statement
O or C	*Possible, more specific, observation*
C	His methods were sloppy. *He failed to set up adequate controls and did not rule out alternative explanations for the results.*
C	When giving a summary of the results, you failed to understand their true importance. *When giving a summary of the results, you didn't report their significance.*
C	She wasted the group's time in the meeting. *She reintroduced the decision we made earlier, and the group spent 20 minutes rehashing our original comments.*
C	She is a poor communicator. *She speaks quietly and in a monotone so that few of us can hear what she says.*

Response	Statement
O or C	*Possible, more specific, observation*
O	In spite of the stacks of papers and apparent disarray, she was able to pull the critical information we needed quite easily.
C	You were rude and disruptive. *You interrupted Sam three times as he tried to describe the project's goals and key deliverables.*

REFERENCES

Domhoff, G. W. *The Scientific Study of Dreams: Neural Networks, Cognitive Development, and Content Analysis.* American Psychological Association (APA), Washington, D.C., 2003.

Goleman, D. *Emotional Intelligence: Why It Can Matter More Than IQ.* Bantam Books, New York, 1995.

Hallowell, E. *CrazyBusy: Overstretched, Overbooked and About to Snap.* Ballantine Books, New York, 2006.

Klein, G. *Intuition At Work.* Doubleday, New York, 2003.

Locke, E. A., and Latham, G. *Goal Setting: A Motivational Technique That Works.* Prentice Hall, Englewood Cliffs, NJ, 1984.

Pelz, D., and Andrews, A. *Scientists in Organizations: Productive Climates for Research and Development.* Wiley, New York, 1966.

Stone, L. "Living with Continuous Partial Attention." From the article "The Harvard Business Review List of Breakthrough Ideas for 2007." *Harvard Business Review*, Vol. 85, No. 2, February 2007, pp. 28–29.

Wiseman, R. *The Luck Factor: The Four Essential Principles.* Miramax Books/Hyperion, New York, 2003.

BIBLIOGRAPHY

Egan, G. *The Skilled Helper: A Problem Management Approach to Helping.* Brooks/Cole, Pacific Grove, CA, 1994.

Gratton, L., and Erickson, T. J. "Eight Ways to Build Collaborative Teams." *Harvard Business Review*, Vol. 85, No. 11, November, 2007, pp. 2–11.

Maccoby, M. "Is There a Best Way to Lead Scientists and Engineers?" *Research Technology Management*, January–February, 2006, pp. 60–61.

Maccoby, M. "Understanding the People You Manage." *Research Technology Management*, May–June, 2005, pp. 58–60.

Maccoby, M. "Needed: Managers Who Are Leaders." *Research Technology Management*, March–April, 2009, pp. 58–60.

Maxwell, J. C. *Winning with People.* Nelson Books, Orange, CA, 2004.

Prather, C. W. "The Dumb Thing about Smart Goals for Innovation." *Research Technology Management*, September–October, 2005, pp. 14–15.

Stayer, R. "How I Learned to Let My Workers Lead." *Harvard Business Review. OnPoint Best of HBR Leadership: It's Hard Being Soft*, Product #8172, 2001, pp. 29–41. (Article originally published in *Harvard Business Review*, Vol. 68, No. 6, November–December, 1990, pp. 66–83.)

Szakonyi, R. "101 Tips for Managing R&D More Effectively—II." *Research Technology Management*, November–December, 1990, pp. 41–46.

Treher, E. N. "Managing Performance." *Managing in R&D, A Program for Technical Managers*. The Learning Key, Inc., Washington Crossing, PA, 1992, 2006.

Walck, C. "Psychological Type and Management Research: A Review." *Journal of Psychological Type*, Vol. 24, 1992, pp. 13–23.

CHAPTER 6

INCREASING EFFECTIVENESS THROUGH DELEGATION

DELEGATION SITUATION

Carlos recently took a new job. He had quit a job he loved because he was assigned to work with a new manager who gave him no responsibility or interesting work. His long-time manager had retired; Carlos was accustomed to being trusted and liked and had been taught many new techniques, helping him to broaden his skills and knowledge. He might not have a graduate degree, but he was clever, learned quickly, and had always done well.

DELEGATION PLANNING

Best Person?

Time Available?

Level of Risk?

Experience?

How involved should I be?

Three months into his new job he had developed a good working relationship with his manager, a very young Ph.D. named Sherrie. She gave him lots of responsibility and participation on interesting projects. She seemed to trust him and pretty much left

A Guide to Success for Technical Managers: Supervising in Research, Development, & Engineering, by Elizabeth Treher, David Piltz and Steven Jacobs
Copyright © 2011 John Wiley & Sons, Inc.

him on his own to do his work and the assignments she gave him. He liked the independence.

Sherrie recently asked him to lead an important project. It called for collaboration with two other departments—customer service and development. They were to do an assessment and make recommendations that could have significant impact. As a technician he had never worked on a project with this kind of visibility and he was pleased about it.

The folks in development were great to work with and provided the data and perspectives he needed. Customer service, on the other hand, was the opposite. The department head never had time to meet and wouldn't delegate the project to anyone else. Carlos tried once to get help from his manager, but she was always too busy. As time went on, he and the development group ended up making all the recommendations that went into the report. When he handed the report to Sherrie as he left on Thursday afternoon, he thought he'd done a good job.

Friday morning Sherrie emailed him to see her immediately after her meeting. When he showed up, she was visibly angry. She had missed her daughter's soccer game the day before and spent most of the night revising his recommendations and rewriting the report to meet today's deadline. Apparently, omitting input from customer service had had a major impact. Carlos was also upset because Sherrie had a great relationship with the customer service department and she hadn't offered him any help.

What are the key issues?

Who is responsible for the situation? Explain.

How would you coach Sherrie?

What style of delegation did she use?

How should she have managed the assignment differently?

See the end of this chapter for how the situation was resolved.

DELEGATION CHOICES

Rita supervised three individuals in the quality assurance (QA) department. Chuck, the youngest, had recently graduated with a degree in materials science. He seemed to spend most of his time using his mobile phone—texting—yet he seemed to get his work done on time. Benje had been in the department years longer than Rita and was a steady, reliable worker. He willingly did what Rita asked but rarely sought out additional work. Rita's go-to person was Ivy. Whenever anyone needed help, Ivy pitched in. Whenever they took on a new project, Ivy was the first to come up with useful ideas. Consequently, Ivy had more than enough work to do—probably more than either of the other two could handle on their own. Nevertheless, Rita almost always delegated to Ivy.

A recent reorganization had caused Rita's workload to increase substantially. She knew she had to delegate the stress testing of their newest product, the question was—who should she pick? Although their work styles differed, their technical abilities, if not their paces, were generally equivalent.

Would you select Chuck, Benje, or Ivy? Explain.

What would you advise Rita, if she said she planned to delegate the project to Ivy?

See the end of this chapter for how the situation was handled.

DELEGATION BENEFITS

Delegation is one of the most useful management tools available. Learning to delegate is an important step in learning to manage effectively, but it tends not to be an easy skill to develop. Most technical professionals who assume supervisory roles have trouble delegating. The reason is simple—personal technical skills are often the reason for a professional's first promotion. Fear of losing those skills, or of giving up something one truly enjoys, is a powerful deterrent to delegation. Concern that mistakes will occur, or that others just cannot do something as well as a manager thinks she/he can, are other reasons new managers often cite as reasons not to delegate.

In fact, failure to be consistently sensitive to opportunities for delegating, and to react to them when they arise, is a major factor in poor management at all levels. Delegation requires both knowledge and skills, and these develop with practice. To become an effective supervisor, looking for delegation opportunities should be high on your priority list.

Delegation is facilitated by:

- Recognizing and respecting others' capabilities
- Evaluating tasks and communicating how they fit in the big picture
- Matching people and assignments
- Providing support and encouragement
- Tolerating ambiguity and uncertainty; interpreting failure as a key to learning

Delegation has many advantages. Delegation increases long-term effectiveness and short-term efficiency. It gives insight into current strengths and weaknesses, provides ways to improve performance, and creates opportunities for growth. Appropriate delegation empowers employees through sharing of a supervisor's power. It provides positive reinforcement of your role, builds morale, and generates trust. It is an important way to increase our abilities as managers to get things done.

Delegation has advantages for both supervisor and employee. By demonstrating your confidence, you build staff trust and self-confidence. It rewards, recognizes, and makes individuals more visible to colleagues, managers, and other groups and provides growth by on-the-job experience. It also helps to satisfy an employee's needs for responsibility, authority, and influence. Delegation can surface unexpected or unused abilities and help assess individual skills and potential for promotion and responsibility. Using an effective process for delegation reduces risk.

The key to remember is that delegation provides you time to do other things. It increases your authority through a legitimate use of power. Delegation can also increase the depth of an organization's capacity to respond. It improves communication when assignments cross normal communication channels and can build bridges between departments.

In managing technical problems, delegation offers significant benefits, providing opportunities to get different perspectives. Use it to build a team to concentrate on a special problem or project.

To delegate effectively it is important to understand both the concept of delegation and basic guidelines for successful delegation. Delegation depends strongly on the ability to motivate and communicate and to understand individual differences and preferences. A delegation protocol assumes that a task and appropriate individual have been selected. Delegation is a process. It requires preparation, initiation, implementation, and closure. When a review follows these four steps, it is also a learning process.

Delegation does not mean assigning tasks that are traditional parts of an individual's job. While you can delegate authority to carry out an assignment, the ultimate responsibility for performance is never transferred. Delegation always involves sharing. This may be authority, power, influence, information, knowledge, or risk. Such sharing builds morale and trust with an employee.

The environment often has many interfering factors, such as too much urgency, inexperience, and lack of trust. To minimize the influence of these variables, develop and follow a protocol to ensure that you plan and carry out each step of the delegation process.

DELEGATION ANALYSIS

To understand your own approaches to delegation, read the following situations and decide how you would handle them. Rank the answers from 1 to 4, with 1 being your first choice and 4 your last. You may prefer another response, but choose the one that best fits how you would handle the situation.

1. Your lab does the testing for a discovery research group. You have been doing one of the assays for a number of years. You generally run about four each week and they take about two full days of your time. You decide that it could be delegated to one of your staff to give you more development time. You decide to give one of the older techs the opportunity. He is reliable but slow, and it takes him a while to catch on. You meet to discuss the assay with him and he says, "It sounds like it would be interesting. But I am not sure I could handle it. I know it's important."

Assume that you begin by assuring him you are confident he can learn it. Then, you most likely would:

_____ A.   Show him exactly how you do the assay and what to look for.

_____ B.   Let him know you are available if he has questions, but you would like him to try it first on his own.

_____ C.   Show him results of prior assays and your notes; ask him questions to get him thinking about how to run the assay.

_____ D.   Watch him while he runs the assay so you can make suggestions or correct him if needed.

2. You receive a distraught call from a young engineer who reports to you. She is the company representative on a new project with one of your subcontractors. She was to have sent a report by yesterday detailing the project status and change requests. You have to present the information to your board tomorrow. She is asking you to call the subcontractor because he won't give her any information and she can't tell if it is an oversight or he hasn't completed it.

Assume that you ask her a few questions to better understand what is going on. You would then:

_____ A.   Remind her that she is responsible, and you are sure she can manage it.

_____ B   Ask her what she thought she should do to get the report, and help her think through how to approach the subcontractor.

_____ C.   Tell her exactly how to resolve the situation and give her leverage to use.

_____ D.   Explain approaches you have used in similar situations and let her handle it.

3. You are behind in your work and have a presentation to put together for an important meeting. One of your staff has not done well with her technical work, and you aren't in a position to hire a replacement or additional staff. You think she might be able to put the presentation together for you while you get caught up on some other things. After getting her buy-in to the assignment, she says she has a number of ideas to create a great presentation. You would most likely:

_____ A.   Tell her you also have some ideas and would like to work with her. Coach her as you go along and eliminate any unworkable ideas.

_____ B.   Show enthusiasm for her ideas, and then show her the approach you think would be best.

_____ C.   Ask her questions to see how clearly she understands the presentation. If you are satisfied, ask her to proceed and to show you her initial slides.

_____ D.   Commend her for her idea and tell her to go ahead with her approach. Tell her you are available if she wants any assistance and tell her you would like to see the first draft in 3 days.

4. Sanje is an experienced, dependable employee. He works very quickly and asked you if he could revamp the department's technical newsletter. He said he had a lot of ideas to improve the look and functionality and was anxious to give it a try. You had been interested in doing something similar for some time but had never gotten around to it. You and Sanje meet and agree that he should proceed. You would likely:

_____ A.   Ask him what he had in mind, offer some suggestions, and ask to see his concept when it is ready.

_____ B.   Show him the general approach you had been considering and ask him to meet those specifications.

_____ C.   Ask him to design the newsletter he thinks would be best for the department.

_____ D.   Explain your ideas and ask him to make sure that his redesign uses this format.

DELEGATION PROFILE

Transfer the numbers you assigned to the situations to the boxes on the next page. For the first situation, if you assigned A your first choice, 1, you would put a 1 in the box with the letter A on line 1. If your second choice was D, you would put a 2 in the box with the letter D. Fill in the grid and add the columns. At the bottom of a column is your score, at the top is the delegation style. **The lowest score is your preferred style of delegation, the highest score is your least preferred approach.** Which is your preferred style? Does it fit what you had expected? Do you have two styles you use fairly equally? As you learn more about each style, you will see that there are circumstances when each is appropriate.

Often, if you have a clear preference about how you prefer someone to delegate to you, you will find yourself using that style with others. Consider if perhaps you overuse your preferred style(s).

Situation	Directing	Advising	Partnering	Conferring
1.	A ____	C ____	D ____	B ____
2.	C ____	D ____	B ____	A ____
3.	B ____	A ____	C ____	D ____
4.	D ____	B ____	A ____	C ____
TOTALS				

PLANNING FOR DELEGATION

Before you begin, consider the following:

- What is the appropriate level of delegation? The appropriate level of delegation depends on the relative capabilities of you and your employee, as well as task difficulty, risk, time available, resources, and organizational constraints. Consider your own time and the interaction (control) you will need. How will you balance autonomy with the need for some control over outcomes?

- Who might be best for this assignment? How involved should you be?

- What is the appropriate follow-up? How often and what type of check points will you need?

Making the Assignment

For all but the simplest assignment, ensure understanding by giving the individual time to consider the assignment and then to discuss it later. This gives a chance to internalize and review understanding and make sure you are both on the same page. There may be elements you had not considered. Discuss the appropriate follow-up you want to use during the delegation process.

Following-up

Since the level of authority delegated can vary from almost none to nearly all, the frequency and nature of check points also varies.

Delegation is not a one-time discussion of a project with a review at the end. Depending on the complexity of the assignment, the experience of the individual to whom you have delegated, and the time available, you may need to meet and review status a number of times.

Ending the Process

When the delegated assignment has been completed, meet to evaluate both the task and delegation process. Get feedback on your role and how you can improve your delegation the next time.

STYLES OF DELEGATION

Directing is the delegation style with the most interaction and control. Feedback is immediate. This is appropriate for helping someone inexperienced learn a new technique or assist in complex and unfamiliar operations. Typically, the focus is on activities and how to do things. In addition to being available to answer questions, you may need to demonstrate a process or closely observe a process. Using a directing style in situations where more freedom is warranted can lead to a reputation of micromanaging.

Advising works best when your employee knows the basics, and the goal is to reach a higher standard of performance or to accomplish a related assignment. While the employee carries out the task(s), you provide guidance and intervene as needed. Focus on identifying and correcting specific difficulties that limit performance. Establish checkpoints to permit early intervention and ensure success.

Partnering is helpful with employees who are competent to accomplish an assigned task but may need assistance, information, or other limited guidance and support. As supervisor, make yourself available for assistance, if requested. Hands-on experience with little direction builds self-confidence and capability. Feedback is based on overall performance rather than on specific activities. Checkpoints are minimal and designed to catch unexpected problems while action is still possible.

Conferring assumes the employee is fully able to complete the task. Your involvement is minimal; there may be no more than one interim check point. This demonstrates trust and frees you for other tasks. If you find the employee needs more of your help than you anticipated, talk about it and discuss moving to a partnering approach.

Danger can come in letting frustration build or not allowing sufficient time for discussion and review, so that you step in and take over. This helps neither you nor the employee. Focus on the issues to let the employee be successful. If you have misjudged and allowed too much freedom to do an assignment, meet with the employee to guide him/her in making revisions to complete the assignment appropriately.

The managerial transitions discussed in the first chapter also influence options for delegation. From a transition perspective, consider your ability as a manager to perform a task, U, and that of your employee's, E. Some values of U/E have a disproportionate effect on the difficulty of delegating.

Often greater skill, training, or experience in one area (U >> E) generates a halo effect that leads to underdelegation and overmanaging. For this reason, delegated tasks should start by focusing on activities to increase growth in capabilities and autonomy. Also, look to delegate tasks that use an individual's non-technical skills and interests.

When U ≈ E, there can be a sense of competition. As a manager, you may have Es who see themselves as fully capable of doing your job. They may resist or resent U's decision-making power. For this reason it is valuable to focus on the problem-solving elements in delegation where U ≈ E.

Ways to do this include:

- Discuss a problem or task without imposing your ideas. Encourage contributions and the free flow of ideas. Ask questions to surface both ideas and to help surface the most appropriate paths.

- After you clarify the issues, complete the delegation process by considering the appropriate level of involvement. Remember that close direction, focused on specific activities and ways to achieve goals, should be minimal in most of the situations you face. Apply control and support to nontechnical matters such as time and resource constraints, priorities, and assistance with outsiders. When technical difficulties arise, discuss them in a collaborative problem-solving context. Probe and ask questions to help the individual consider options. Compared to the U >> E domain, shift the focus to discuss outcomes rather than activities. Areas of interaction, control, and support should be nontechnical. They include time and resource constraints, priorities, and assistance with outsiders. The level of involvement varies from advising to conferring when U ≈ E.

RELATION OF U/E TO DELEGATION STYLE

Decreasing Control (Interaction)

The relation of U/E to the level of involvement and interaction is shown in the continuum of delegation.

The Impact of U/E on Delegation

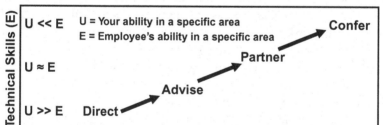

Independence (E)

The level of control changes most rapidly when U ≈ E. This reflects a greater need for managerial adaptability and understanding. Learning to delegate effectively in the U ≈ E domain is a critical test of managerial aptitude. It has proven to be an obstacle for many technical managers.

While U/E is a key concept where highly specialized knowledge and techniques are the rule, it is too simple for many situations. Knowledge and experience are not single-valued functions that can be cleanly captured in quantities such as U and E. Solving organizational problems requires information and political judgment that an employee may not have. This information is always difficult to communicate, and it is impossible to anticipate the insights that may be necessary. The delegation process establishes a flexible link between you and your employee that permits information sharing as needed, without diluting delegated authority and responsibility.

Although the number and type of checkpoints vary with delegated assignments and individuals, there are other considerations. For example, an early checkpoint is always useful. To clarify any confusion, relieve doubts, confirm understanding and constraints, plan to meet after you present the assignment. It is important because most people need to think through and digest an assignment before being able to ask sensible questions. This may be more typical of those with a preference for introversion but is useful for all. However, most employees feel they should understand everything immediately and may say that they do understand, assuming they will figure it out later. They will seldom request such a meeting so you, as manager, should do it.

Consider also a point of no return. Establish this by working backward from the most critical date (often the due date) to a time at which major revisions are still possible in a worst-case scenario. If the level of control requires additional interactions, tie them to completing critical stages. Other considerations include the importance of the task, individual's experience and ability, elements of risk, and organizational constraints. For example, a high-risk, important assignment typically requires increased involvement and perhaps more frequent checkpoints. A task delegated to a new, inexperienced employee versus someone with demonstrated competence and reliability will require more oversight. Review the delegation checklist to ensure you consider the major steps: preparing, initiating, implementing, closing, and reviewing.

DELEGATION CHECKLIST

Preparing

☐ Select a task and individual. Consider the individual, how the task fits into the broad picture, and the need for reliability and dependability or for independent judgment.

☐ Decide on how involved you will need to be.

☐ Define the goal in operational terms to make it possible for you to track progress and know when the task is complete.

☐ Identify what you need to communicate to the employee: critical information, data, constraints, resources, and sources of help or resistance.

☐ Identify deadlines, checkpoints along the way, and your expectations at each.

Initiating

☐ Introduce the topic and get an idea of the employee's interest.

☐ Stress your personal interest and support.

☐ Provide a broad definition of the task. How do you see it? Encourage questions to further define and clarify the problem. Plan for a second meeting to review the task, if the task is complex.

☐ Review sources of information. Who may be able to help or needs to be part of the problem-solving process? Describe how you can assist.

☐ Indicate special challenges, constraints, or opportunities.

☐ Describe what you expect and when. Will it be summarized in a report, written or verbal recommendations, or something else? Don't be vague; make it concrete.

☐ Define the level of control (directing, advising, partnering, or conferring) you are proposing. What decisions, activities, and authority, if any, are you retaining?

☐ Specify the resources and assistance available. Discuss how to publicize the assignment to those who will need to know about the task.

☐ Define the endpoint and checkpoints, if any, and what you expect at each of them.

☐ Discuss what to do if something does not go as planned.

Implementing

☐ If the task involves the cooperation of others, facilitate the employee's task by publicizing it and requesting cooperation.

☐ Follow the protocol defined in the initiation phase. Review progress at each checkpoint.

☐ If problems or misunderstandings occur, provide support and encouragement, but do not take over. Rescuing employees will not facilitate growth.

Closing

☐ Review the assignment and how you worked together. Thank your employee and see that the employee gets his/her share of the credit. Reviewing the assignment and process is an important part of your own development. Each time you delegate provides an opportunity to learn about your management style.

☐ Consider the following questions and get feedback from the employee. What seemed to work particularly well? Were you clear about which actions and decisions were yours and theirs?

☐ Did you delegate expected outcomes or prescribe activities to be performed?

☐ Did the employee have a clear picture of the goal and what was required?

☐ Did you provide the information for the assignment, or did the employee have to ask for it?

☐ Did you share information and influence? Was there a feeling of mutual trust?

☐ When problems occurred, how did you get involved? Did you take over or rescue your employee? Did you support and encourage but leave the challenge with the employee?

☐ Did you treat mistakes, confusion, or error as part of the learning process?

☐ Would you be happy to delegate another task to this person?

☐ Would she/he be happy to take the assignment?

☐ If you were to repeat this assignment, what would you do differently? Why?

DELEGATION USING TYPE

Each of us has a "natural" approach to delegation, and responds in different ways to U/E shown in the figure. We tend to perceive the needs of employees from our own perspectives and temperaments. This can create obstacles to communication as well as other problems.

The SJ traditionalists like responsibility and structure. They are conservative, with a strong sense of duty, and tend to be practical and well organized. They focus on establishing and maintaining their place in the world. Goals are short rather than long range, and they are more likely to resist change, unless they clearly see a benefit.

If you are an SJ, your delegation strengths are likely to be:

- Step-by-step planning and preparing for an assignment
- Organization and following a delegation protocol

Your delegation shortcomings may include:

- Performing best at either end of the delegation continuum (directing or conferring) where little flexibility is required.
- Neglecting to delegate due to a sense of urgency and an "I can do it better" feeling. This feeling may be correct, but it is usually not relevant in the context of delegation.
- Focusing on power and control that can interfere with sharing and empowering others.
- Tending to take over when problems occur.
- Being uncomfortable in the collaborative role necessary in the $U \approx E$ domain.
- Tending to dominate others.

The SP sensing-perceivers value personal freedom above rules and regulations and are flexible and able to adapt to change but not interested in routine. Focus tends to be on things rather than ideas. They are great in crises and troubleshooting but have a short-term outlook.

Delegation strengths include:

- Spotting opportunities
- Willing to delegate
- Getting people moving

Delegation shortcomings may include:

- Ability to "wing it" may mean they are less likely to follow a delegation protocol.
- Competence in spotting and handling crises may lead to rescuing an employee at the first sign of difficulty.
- Dislike of planning may lead to inadequate preparation and support.
- Losing interest in an extended problem.

The NT visionaries are thoughtful, logical, and strongly motivated by professional and personal competence. They deal well with complex issues and dislike arbitrary rules and unearned authority. Focus is on ideas rather than things or people.

Delegation strengths include:

- Conceptual and analytical skills that provide an excellent basis for planning and goal setting, especially in complex situations.
- Future orientation and innovative nature can lead to creative and valuable delegation assignments.

Delegation shortcomings may include:

- Disliking routine can result in failure to follow protocol or provide sufficient feedback and control.
- Personal grasp of problems and analytic ability may appear negative and critical to others and may lead to nit picking and insufficient listening.
- Striving for perfection may impede decision making and create unnecessarily high standards.

The NF catalysts gain energy from others. NFs are idealistic and seek growth for themselves and others. They tend to focus on people and values, rather than on things or abstract ideas.

Delegation strengths include:

- Good communication skills
- Inspires trust, credible
- Strong commitment to human and organizational values
- Motivated by need to teach, see others grow

Delegation shortcomings may include:

- Interpersonal closeness, leading to off-hand delegation that ignores much of the formal process
- Trust resulting in drifting and loss of control in delegated tasks
- Concern for feelings delaying confronting poor performance or diminishing the sense of urgency required for high productivity

TEMPERAMENTS

Use type and temperament to enhance growth, not eliminate opportunities.

Consider the following questions when choosing an individual, a task, and providing backup support. Does this individual prefer freedom to work independently or will she/he have difficulty with:

- Too much freedom or uncertainty or projects that are based on new directions or unusual approaches?

    If so, provide structure.

- Projects that are routine or perceived as boring?

    If so, ask if he/she can find a more efficient or effective method or approach.

- Close control and with little room for initiative?

    If so, emphasize challenging elements and the need for special skills.

- Tasks that require working alone and little interaction with others?

    If so, discuss ways that the employee can present and discuss status reports with others to provide that social connection or look for elements that can be done within a team.

- Tasks without opportunity for growth?

    If so, emphasize opportunities for learning or ask the individual to share their learning with others.

- Little positive feedback?

    If so, consciously plan to provide more feedback.

- Sticking to protocols and norms that make no sense to them?

    If so, increase the feedback you provide and discuss the rationale for protocols.

APPLYING NEW CONCEPTS AND SKILLS

Develop a plan to apply new concepts and skills back on the job. No matter how useful the ideas and techniques in any book are, it is often difficult to remember them all when you need them. In addition, there may not be time to follow the steps of a recommended process in the "real world." However, if you have a specific strategy for implementation, you are much more likely to use the information to your advantage.

Getting into Action

- How many tasks have you delegated in the past 3 months?
- Do you have something that you could delegate now?
- Evaluate your current delegation opportunities. Select an individual, the task and objectives, and your delegation approach.
- Plan how you will frame the assignment and benefits.
- Identify specific benefits for the individual and describe these when you suggest the assignment.

DELEGATION SITUATION—SOLUTION

The issues with Carlos and Sherrie stemmed from laissez-faire delegation. There were no check-in periods or follow-up; Sherrie then took over the project without speaking with Carlos or giving him feedback to revise the report himself.

Carlos should have met with Sherrie to discuss the customer service issues, learned how critical their input was, and developed a way to work with them. When he had problems, Carlos should have gone to Sherrie to discuss them. If she seemed busy, he needed to get her attention to let her know he had an important issue to discuss with her and that without her input, he might miss the deadline.

Actual Resolution   Carlos and Sherrie discussed the events and how each could have handled the delegation differently. She recognized that taking over the project had not helped either her or Carlos. In the future, they met at least once again soon after Sherrie delegated a new assignment. In this way, they could review his questions or concerns. Carlos also realized it was okay to bring issues to Sherrie for her input, and he did so. They built a strong work relationship and he continued to learn about the organization.

DELEGATION CHOICES—SUGGESTIONS

Would You Select Chuck, Benje, or Ivy? Explain   It would depend on their relative work loads since it appears that both are able to handle the assignment without undue support from Rita. As a new member of the group, it might be wise to delegate to Chuck and ask him to go over his plans with Benje and get his advice before he begins. In that way, the assignment benefits from Benje's experience and he sees himself as a respected and valued member of your team. It can also help to build a strong work relationship between the two of them. You can speak with Benje about it privately to suggest that he let Chuck handle the project independently, but to meet with him initially to review his approach and then periodically to see he stays on track, since he is new to the group. This gives Benje a coaching role and frees your time for other things.

What Would You Advise Rita, If She Told You She Planned to Delegate the Project to Ivy?   Rita seems to rely too much on Ivy—something that can't continue forever. In many groups, one or two individuals stand out, and when we delegate, we need to remember the others as well. Our own comfort level and confidence in one individual can lead us in a direction that is not the best for the entire group or specific individuals. All of us have a limit. If Ivy expects each new assignment to go to her, Rita should speak with her about her other workload and why she is delegating to Chuck (or Benje).

REFERENCES

Domhoff, G. W. *The Scientific Study of Dreams: Neural Networks, Cognitive Development, and Content Analysis.* American Psychological Association (APA), Washington, D.C., 2003.
Goleman, D. *Emotional Intelligence: Why It Can Matter More Than IQ.* Bantam Books, New York, 1995.
Hallowell, E. *CrazyBusy: Overstretched, Overbooked and About to Snap.* Ballantine Books, New York, 2006.
Klein, G. *Intuition At Work.* Doubleday, New York, 2003.
Locke, E. A., and Latham, G. *Goal Setting: A Motivational Technique That Works.* Prentice Hall, Englewood Cliffs, NJ, 1984.
Stone, L. "Living with Continuous Partial Attention." From the article "The Harvard Business Review List of Breakthrough Ideas for 2007." *Harvard Business Review*, Vol. 85, No. 2, February 2007, pp. 28–29.
Wiseman, R. *The Luck Factor: The Four Essential Principles.* Miramax Books/ Hyperion, New York, 2003.

BIBLIOGRAPHY

Barr, L., and Barr, N. *The Leadership Equation.* Eakin, Austin, TX, 1989.
Demarest, L. *Looking at Type in the Workplace.* Center for Applications of Psychological Type. Gainesville, FL, 1997.

Fritz, R. "When Delegating, Don't Dump." *Communication Briefings*, Vol. VIII, No. IX, February, 1990.

Maddux, R. B. *Delegating for Results, An Action Plan for Success*. Crisp Publications, Los Altos, CA, 1990.

Nelson, R. B. *Empowering Employees through Delegation*. Irwin Professional, Burr Ridge, IL, 1993.

Oestreicher, M. *Youth Ministry 3.0: A Manifesto of Where We've Been, Where We Are, and Where We Need to Go*. Zondervan/Youth Specialties, Grand Rapids, MI, 2008.

Prager, A. "How to Delegate Better." *Boardroom Reports*, December 15, 1988, p. 14.

Quenk, N. L. *Was That Really Me?: How Everyday Stress Brings Out Our Hidden Personality*. Davies-Black, Palo Alto, CA, 2002.

Treher, E. N., and Walker, A. C. "Effective Delegation," in *Managing in R&D, A Program for Technical Managers*. The Learning Key, Inc., Washington Crossing, PA, 1992, 2006.

Wilson, S. B. "Are You an Effective Delegator?" *Executive Female*, November/ December, 1994, pp. 19–20.

Zuker, E. *The Seven Secrets of Influence*. McGraw-Hill, New York, 1991.

BIBLIOGRAPHY   373

CHAPTER 7

POINTS FOR SUCCEEDING AS A COACH

COACHING SUCCESS

Lisa was a senior scientist in charge of several projects. Friends described her as a no-nonsense woman who presented information objectively. She expected others to ask questions as needed and to follow the process she presented. Lisa was successful until she went to work for a different company. After a while, it was apparent that her no-nonsense approach didn't work. Many individuals provided feedback to her boss that she was aggressive, didn't explain processes well, blamed others, and didn't listen. Lisa and her boss experienced each other in much the same way. One day her boss suggested Lisa receive coaching to deal with the problem. She was reluctant but knew her job depended on it, so she acquiesced.

> If you were to coach Lisa, what issues would you deal with?
>
> How would you help her be successful with her co-workers and boss?
>
> *See the end of this chapter for how the situation was handled.*

What do you first think when you hear the word *coach*? Perhaps a sports coach comes to mind. We don't expect an individual or team to be successful without a coach in sports. Yet in some organizations, coaching has a negative connotation or is seen as a final attempt to "save" an individual or cover all bases before termination. Don't be pulled into this trap. Great managers are also great coaches. Coaching provides an opportunity to address a specific performance issue or help another with career development. Coaching can take time but is also highly rewarding. The substantial

A Guide to Success for Technical Managers: Supervising in Research, Development, & Engineering, by Elizabeth Treher, David Piltz and Steven Jacobs
Copyright © 2011 John Wiley & Sons, Inc.

benefits include increased return on investment, productivity, communication effectiveness, and accomplishing goals (Grom, 2010). These attributes increase dramatically when coaching is customized for the person's specific situation and work culture. Successful coaching relies on building connections, challenging the status quo, and looking ahead.

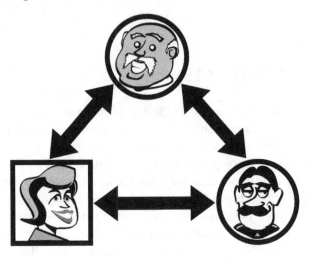

BUILDING CONNECTIONS

Connections, both professional and personal, are the foundation of sound, effective coaching relationships. Building connections begins with simple activities and information sharing, often by having lunch together, chatting over coffee, or walking together to meetings. These are informal opportunities to find out about work style, hobbies, successes, challenges, and professional goals.

This get-to-know-you phase of building connections provides you with information. Do you tend to see eye to eye or are you 180 degrees apart? Do you see openness or sense a shut down when you share your suggestions, thoughts, and feelings? Will you be compatible during a long-term coaching relationship?

Are you the best person to coach the employee? Will your relationship work better if you concentrate on short-term issues? Does the individual need coaching in the area(s) where you also need coaching and can't really help? If so, ask a colleague to coach or mentor that member of your staff. Remember that effective coaches spend more time listening and asking questions than telling and advising.

Building connections helps to expand both personal and professional networks. In any coaching process, opening doors and helping your employee expand his/her network is a valuable step. Kelly and Caplan (1993) break networking into three components:

- Be confident enough in your area of expertise to feel you have something to share with others.
- Inform others that you have something to share.
- Make yourself available to others.

HOW DO STAR PERFORMERS NETWORK?

Networking fosters development through new relationships and with individuals who are knowledgeable on a variety of subjects. However, the process is never one-sided. Networking is a process of give and take. Kelly and Caplan (1993) studied engineers and computer scientists at Bell Labs to understand the large differences between star performers and others (the majority of technical performers). They found a key difference in how each group approached networking. The stars built networks well before they needed them. For this reason, they rarely waited for responses to their calls for advice, as did the others, and received help with technical problems much more quickly.

GROUP SOCIAL NETWORKS

Singer and Helferich (2008) looked at networking at both group and individual levels and the ways social network analysis can help managers improve communication with customers. Although focused on support groups, the principles apply to all of us. Social networks help us see how we really get our work done, something that formal organization charts do not.

The Singer and Helferich (2008 p. 54) study showed the advice-seeking relationships among Ph.D. scientists from the analytical and formulation design departments in a pharmaceutical R&D organization. They used arrows to point to the source of advice. Both groups primarily sought help from within their own department. Although infrequent, the analytical group reached out to the formulation design group significantly more often than vice versa. Both groups lost significant opportunity to capitalize on their knowledge to solve technical problems. An example of such a communication network is shown in the social network illustration.

Social Network Illustration

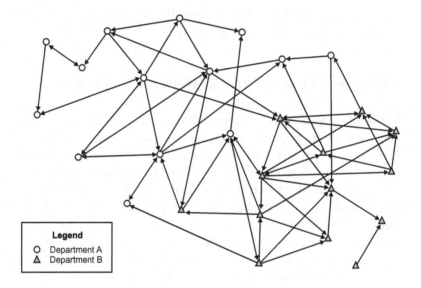

Application

Create a social network diagram for your own project, group, or department. Include the other groups or individuals with whom you do, or should, network. Draw arrows to show the typical direction of information flow both within your function and outside it. If you aren't sure, ask each person to identify those they call on for advice for a difficult scientific or technical problem. Software is available to analyze such data (Borgatti, et al., 2002), but for a general picture of communication strengths and opportunities, it isn't necessary. Use the visual picture to identify where you can improve networking—this will not only build new or stronger relationships for those whom you coach, it may help speed your innovation process or suggest new opportunities.

How Do Relationship Building and Networking Pay Off?

A pharmaceutical R&D manager asked a new employee to be the department liaison with the analytical department at another location. This required travel and a lot of time. The employee felt these activities wasted her time and should be done by a member of her team. When the manager insisted, she complied. There was no formal role of liaison, and she knew no one in the department, so she had to introduce herself and begin the communication process with members of the analytical department. This took planning and time away from her lab. The result, however, was that she met everyone in the analytical department and developed good personal relationships that lasted for years.

The outcome was that they had many excellent suggestions to support her team's work and became a true partner to solve technical problems. Had she drawn a diagram similar to the social networking diagram, it would have been obvious that she and each of the members of the analytical group were in frequent contact, due to the arrows going both ways while very few others in her own department were connected. It might also have explained why analytical didn't provide the same high level of service for her manager. What could have been the impact if others had built the same information-sharing relationship she did?

CHALLENGING THE STATUS QUO

The second key element of the coaching process is challenging the status quo. To coach for developing, improving, or enhancing needed skills, first determine the current situation and then challenge it. This requires that the individual you are coaching, the coachee, take stock of past and current challenges and successes. What are others' perceptions? Identify limitations and weaknesses, strengths, likes and dislikes, and hopes and fears. What is truly important? Trying to uncover and unpack all the related and unrelated issues so that you can clearly see the roadblocks is the key to coaching. Is the coachee ready to listen to a different opinion and be willing to accept new ideas? Does she or he feel stuck and motivated to work on solution(s)?

For example, the director of a department in a large pharmaceutical company had always considered himself as highly creative. Before attending a workshop, he completed both a 360-degree feedback instrument and an innovation survey. The reports showed others felt he was an excellent administrator but was rigid and not very creative. After the shock wore off, he decided to build on his administrative and management strengths and rely on others in his department to be the voices of creativity. Receiving feedback does not always mean we should act on it. His coaching focused on ways to improve his ability to support others' creativity and be a positive, supportive voice.

Surprises such as these are commonplace. Ted thought of himself as being skilled in visioning and being detail oriented. He also took a 360-degree feedback survey. Ted felt his management style worked, until he saw his feedback and found that others thought he was not good at visioning. Feedback said that he ignored long-term benefits for short-term gains and tended to ignore the future and focus on the present. This got Ted's attention, and he began to concentrate on the things that others saw as his strengths. His feedback also led to a process of evaluating his approaches and learning more about visioning. Challenging the status quo means being ready to grow and move forward.

This isn't always an easy step. In fact, many individuals never make the leap. Ralph, an engineer, scoured over blueprints from vendors who were proposing to handle a key phase of his project. He was to recommend the most cost-effective vendor with the highest quality. He rarely let others know what he was doing or how he did it. He was friendly but didn't work collaboratively. His boss, Virginia, kept challenging Ralph to involve others more. Nothing changed. Why? Satisfied with his approach, Ralph had no reason to behave differently. Virginia on the other hand, felt limited in her role and knew she didn't want to stay in the department forever. She began to present workshops on creating and maintaining a positive attitude. Her jovial and considerate nature led her to build new relationships in the organization. She eventually moved to another department to lead a large-scale project from inception to completion.

It is hard to help others move to where you'd like to see them. It demands their commitment. It means clearly knowing where they are, the opportunities that exist, what is important to them, and how to provide support to help them move forward. Ralph didn't want to evaluate where he was or consider new options. Virginia could easily describe her strengths, weaknesses, and worked to improve herself. She knew she didn't want to lead a maintenance engineering group forever and made the transition successfully.

An effective technical manager helps employees take stock of where they are and their aspirations. Sometimes, employees are unwilling to do either—if so, coaching isn't for them. Use the rest of the concepts in this book to manage their performance. An individual from another group may be able to help where you could not.

There is a tendency in the workplace not to talk about an employee's next job or position. In many technical organizations, career ladders have a limited number of rungs; in some, degrees rather than contributions are overemphasized. You may be restricted in giving promotions or providing new job titles, but there are many ways to create opportunities for employees to grow. Helping to broaden skills and knowledge is an important goal of any effective technical manager.

In your organization you may need to work somewhat independently to help employees with new development options. In others, formal processes can make this much easier. One example from a global R&D company was called an in-residence program. The in-residence program had three tiers (for executives, managers, and independent contributors including nonexempt staff), but the approach was the same in each. The three stages were:

1. Participate in an initial planning meeting and follow up on a career assessment process.
2. Write a proposal for the in-residence experience.
3. Implement the approved experience.

All participants first met with the person who ran the program. After that, stage 1 differed by level. Executives were provided an external coach or attended a multiday residential skills assessment program called the Total Role Assessment Center (TRAC) (McConnell and Simmons). After the TRAC program each participant received verbal and written feedback on about 20 to 25 leadership measures selected for the individual and the organization. Managers met with a professional on staff and occasionally attended TRAC. All others met with an internal career counselor. Stage 1 also included discussion and advice on the contemplated in-residence experience.

Stage 2 required that employees take initiative in formulating the what and the how of their assignments. They got help to make connections and network to find the right opportunity to fit their goals, and there were no real limitations on what they could do.

In stage 3, individuals used these experiences quite differently. Some sought occasional or regular meetings, while others went full time for 2 or 3 months to another department or division.

Some contemplated major career shifts, while others wanted to do their jobs better. For example, one senior director provided the same services to several operating units. He recognized they each were set up and worked differently and felt his department wasn't meeting anyone's needs as effectively as they could. He planned a program to spend time with each of the operating units, so that he could better understand and meet their needs.

A technician felt limited in her department. She was happy in her group and didn't want to leave but wanted to expand her skills. She designed her experience to spend time with the mass spectrometry group to learn to run samples for her own department. The mass spec group was willing to train her, and she became a more valuable resource in her own department. The mass spec group even borrowed her occasionally to help them. These are two of many successful examples.

An interesting part of this process was what didn't work. It proved the old adage "You can lead a horse to water, but you can't make it drink." Only about 10% of those who completed the first stage actually followed through with stages 2 and 3. Many asked if someone could write up their request because they didn't have the time. Those who did complete the program were universally enthusiastic; many went on to make successful career changes within the organization. Others improved skills or abilities for their current jobs. This is an important message for any of us who are inclined to coach or mentor others. You may see tremendous potential, and it may be quite real. The bottom line remains—the individual alone is responsible for making it happen. Although your organization may not have a formal program, you can still work with colleagues and those in other departments to create opportunities for your staff. Make sure they take a lead role in the process.

LOOKING FORWARD

The last phase of this coaching process is looking forward. Looking forward moves individuals beyond the present and focuses them on new goals and objectives and the changes necessary to meet them. Perhaps that change is as simple as identifying roadblocks or acknowledging conflict and displeasure with the communication style of a colleague.

Looking forward focuses conversations and discussions on achieving a goal. That goal may be to write emails more effectively, present ideas assertively in meetings, or train a line function to follow a procedure without making errors. Whatever the goals, coaching works best if you address one goal at a time before you move on to another. Depending on the goal and the employee, a coaching session may take one to six meetings. We are not suggesting you coach to rehash discussions, although this sometimes happens. Try to focus each discussion on one item and make progress on that item between discussions. It's motivating to both you and the individual you coach to experience progress.

A simple approach to begin coaching is to:

- Identify possible issues or topics for coaching.
- Discuss willingness and readiness to be coached.
- Discuss expectations in terms of confidentiality and ties to work performance. Consider if you want to coach for performance or for growth.

- Discuss expectations of both the coach and coachee in terms of sharing ideas, listening, and asking questions. Find out what the coachee considers helpful.
- Discuss current strengths, weaknesses, challenges, successes, hopes, and aspirations. If these aren't clear or you think that others' perceptions may differ, consider using a 360-degree feedback instrument to gather input from colleagues, direct reports, managers, and others.
- Review the feedback data to look for strengths from which to build and others that may be overused; look for surprises—the good or bad news that contradicts our self-perceptions and expectations. Consider your own perceptions of the individual you are coaching.
- Identify one or two items on which to focus coaching that will result in new skills, knowledge, or behavior.
- Draft a schedule for future meetings and close the meeting.

Follow-up meetings (30 to 60 minutes):

- Review expectations for the meeting.
- Review interim assignments and progress.
- Challenge the status quo by asking questions and keep the focus on the future and accomplishing the goal.
- Once a goal is reached, begin on the next goal.

There are many activities to consider as you coach to develop others. Adapt from the suggestions here and add to them as you coach. Try them yourself and select those that address skills you would like to develop.

The following list of development activities is categorized to coordinate with the topics and chapters of this book. In addition to these activities, see Lombardo and Eichinger (1989) and McCauley (2006) for more suggestions.

SUGGESTIONS FOR DEVELOPMENT ACTIVITIES

Roles, Issues, and Transitions

- Interview others with experience in your new role. If you know managers who also made the transition, meet with them. Ask others in departments whom you may not know as well to share their greatest challenges and successes in transitioning.

- Meet with your supervisor for advice based on his or her experience in prior transitions.
- Join social networking groups such as Linked-In, Fast Pitch, Twitter, and Facebook and create a network of others who are newly transitioning from R, D, & E into management.
- Read nontechnical books that are not necessarily on management to provide you with additional ways to be an effective manager. *How to Think Like Leonardo da Vinci* (Gelb, 1998) and *The Power of Full Engagement* (Loehr and Schwartz, 2003) are two examples.
- Become more familiar with your organization. How do the tech functions' strategic plans, goals, and activities interface with others? Who are the leaders of the major business units?
- Review your organization's literature to ensure you are aligned with the philosophy and can easily communicate it to your staff.
- Speak with managers outside the technical functions and discuss their approaches and challenges to see what you can apply.

Creating a Motivating Climate

- Search the Internet for resources on positive attitudes and optimism. Work on your own attitude and keep a positive outlook.
- Make an effort to celebrate successes, whether you have one employee or a team.
- Send personal thank you notes to staff. Even a hand-written line or two on a memo to congratulate or acknowledge an accomplishment can make a big impression.
- Help new staff members get to know each other by dedicating 10 to 15 minutes at several meetings for that purpose.
- Serve as a buffer for those you supervise. Protect your employees from busywork—unnecessary meetings, paperwork, or reports—so they can focus on their work.

- Create opportunities for staff members to "educate" others on topics that interest them. These could be work or non-work-related topics.

- Consider leaders you know who are good at building excitement and motivation in their groups. Ask to attend one of their meetings or talk to those they supervise to find out what they do.

- Recognition and a feeling of influence are both motivators for many people in technical jobs. Think about ways you can provide both and create a list and get to work on it.

Managing for Interpersonal Effectiveness

- Search the Myers & Briggs Foundation website (www.myersbriggs.org) and find at least one book or article to purchase and read.

- Consider your relationships. Make a list of interpersonal challenges at work or at home. Decide which are the important ones to work on improving.

- Make time to hold one-on-one meetings with your staff to discuss ways to improve communication based on individual Type preferences and interests.

- Keep a journal of times when your emotions "get in the way." Identify what caused the emotion and why. Identify one thing to do differently next time.

- Ask others to share one thing with you they would like you to do more of and one thing to do less. Be sure and thank them for the feedback.

- Smile frequently, especially when you greet or pass someone.

- Share simple stories or nonoffensive jokes if you can.

- When you see someone for the first time in a day, if your habit is to immediately ask about work, instead ask something about them, for example, about the weekend or a family member. Stop and listen to the response before continuing with your agenda.

Communication

- Draw a picture of a typical staff meeting and where each person sits. Insert lines of communication using colored pens to show who speaks to whom. Reflect on where the communication gaps are and what you can do to fill them. How can you involve those who rarely speak up?

- Enroll in an active listening seminar or workshop.

- Pause at least 5 seconds before responding in a conversation. Take that time to reflect and ensure you understand.

- Ask a trusted colleague to work with you. Identify a work subject and hold a conversation. Only respond with questions for the first 5 to 10 minutes of the conversation.

- During discussions with staff or colleagues, before sharing your insights reply with "I heard you say [fill in the blank]. Is that correct?"

- To expand your ability to ask important questions, those that get others thinking and lead to meaningful answers, watch TV interviewers. Pay attention to their questions. You will see some very skilled media professionals from whom you can learn. You will also find others whose questions actually lead only to "yes" or "no" answers rather than a useful dialogue.

- Concentrate on not using the word *but* in your communication during a meeting. Use only *and* or *or*.

- Ask three people for their suggestions on how you can communicate better with them. If each has a different response, ask a few more individuals until at least two people say the same thing. Then plan how you will improve in that area.

Managing Performance

- Review staff goals to ensure that each one is specific and has a clear endpoint. Revise as needed. For example, "Review the literature" could really be a life's work. How would you judge completion? "Review the literature and summarize key findings in a report" has a clear endpoint. To be even more specific, add a deadline, such as "by the first of next month."

- Write three lists to summarize expectations—how and why each staff member meets, does not meet, or exceeds expectations. Remove your interpretations and subjective words and use only observations and objective terms.

- Make a personal timeline of your greatest successes at work. Under each, write the elements that caused it to be successful. What can you apply to improve performance in other areas?

- Create a pie chart on how you use your time in a typical workday. Does the chart align with your values and goals? If not, what changes can you make? How can you use this activity with your employee(s) to talk about task deadlines?

- Take your current organizational chart and turn it on its side. Now assume this is reality. What would you do to be effective in accomplishing goals? What can you apply?

- Hold goal review meetings quarterly to ensure progress. If needed, revise goals and partner with your staff on how to accomplish the goals.

- Post these development suggestions at work. Ask colleagues to add their own ideas to the list.

Effective Delegation

- Make a list of tasks that you find easy to delegate. Make another list of those tasks that you tend to keep and think are difficult to delegate. Why are they difficult? Is there a relationship between the tasks that are easy to delegate and those you don't like? Are the tasks that you keep rather than delegate the ones you enjoy?

- Create a personal desktop reference with the steps of delegation. Put it in a spot you can see clearly to remind you to delegate.

- When delegating a task, ask the individual to reiterate what you are asking. For a complex assignment, wait a day or two before the employee talks about the assignment, so she or he has time to consider it and come up with questions. Answer any questions.

- Talk with your boss about how he or she delegates. Reflect on the process you have experienced. Determine if you can apply the same process to your staff.

- Decide which delegation style is the most comfortable for you. Challenge yourself to find delegation assignments that will require a different style each time you delegate.

- Make a list of the reasons you don't delegate. Find a way to overcome or balance each item on the list.
- List each individual who reports to you and come up with an assignment to delegate. Decide the style you will use and follow through on the delegation.

Coaching for Development

- Find someone outside your immediate unit/department and ask him or her to coach you on a specific area you would like to improve.
- Ask a trusted colleague to practice an upcoming coaching conversation by role playing with you. Describe what you would like to provide coaching on and take the role of the coachee yourself. Observe how the other person approaches the topic and manages the conversation.
- Take time to watch your favorite type of coach (sports, life, cooking) and identify three to five things she or he does that you like. Decide how you can apply them when you coach.
- Interview your customers (internal or external) and identify what a staff member does well and what can be improved. Use a coaching style when relaying this information to your staff.
- Feedback is important in coaching. During your next staff meeting, record the number of times you provide feedback that is negative or positive or constructive. Evaluate after the meeting. In what ways can you transform your feedback into feedforward?
- Identify an area in which you would like to grow or a position for which you would like to prepare. Ask someone you think could help to be your mentor. Remember that mentoring takes time and not everyone is able or willing to give that time. If you think she or he might be reluctant, begin first with asking to meet for lunch or for coffee or breakfast before work.

Managing Groups, Teams, and Meetings

- Ask other colleagues if you can observe their staff or project team meetings. Observe and make a list of what worked well and what did not. Compare with your own meetings. Determine what you can do differently in your next staff meeting.

- Using the Internet, search for a variety of team definitions. Create a definition of teams that works for you. Share the definition with your staff and ask for feedback. Revise as necessary. What elements are most important to you?

- Videotape a staff meeting and review it. Identify places where the conversation shuts down. What did you do or not do? What can you do in the future? Bookmark the tape or edit it to share with your team.

- Take a 360-degree assessment or meet with each of your employees and colleagues and ask for feedback in a specific area where you would like to improve.

- Pay attention to your patterns of response with others. Are you generally enthusiastic and open to others' ideas or do you first criticize and challenge? Practice delaying any immediate response. Ask questions if you feel you must reply immediately—"What do you see as the pros and cons? Do you have any other ideas? Would you let me think about it for a few minutes?"

- How do you and the team manage conflict? Do you spend time trying to understand a situation from everyone's perspective? Do you get to the bottom of what is really important to each person? Ask questions and listen to gain a better perspective of what others' think before you offer your own.

- Analyze team decisions. Are you clear as to which decisions are yours and which others will make or you will make as a group?

Creativity and Innovation

- Read an article from a discipline that is unlike yours. For example, if you are a biologist read an article from a interior decorating magazine. Determine how many connections you can make between the discipline and your science.

- Pick an object (e.g., a coffee mug) and determine at least 10 new uses for the object. Repeat this for a week, picking a different object each day. Record your objects and new uses and at the end of the week include your observations on being creative. Share and discuss with your staff.

- During staff meetings, if a problem needs to be solved, challenge the group to brainstorm and generate ideas for 10 minutes before analyzing any idea. Facilitate the brainstorming, ensuring only that ideas are generated and not analyzed.

- Have your staff define creativity and its elements. Hold yourself and your staff accountable for the definition on your current projects. At the end of 3 months, evaluate if problems are being solved more creatively. If not, examine the definition and modify it as needed.

- Learn the basics of a new language. After several weeks of learning, reflect on the challenges and successes. How are the challenges and successes similar to being creative in your work? Share with your staff.

- Select a book or article with tools for enhancing creativity and breaking context traps. Practice at least one new tool each week for a month.

- If you cook and use recipes, try creating a dish that you develop from scratch. If you drive the same way to work each day, take an alternative route.

- Cut out a dozen or more pictures from the newspaper or magazines (or use a set of Interpra® cards). Meet with family members or friends and ask each to select a picture that represents the best thing that happened to them that day. Have a discussion about the pictures they selected and their comments. Think of two opportunities to apply this at work. For example, "Choose a picture that best represents our team" or "Choose a picture that could hold the solution to this problem."

Managing Projects and Decisions

- Hold a conversation with your supervisor about decisions and agree on what are yours to make and what might be your supervisor's or others' decisions.

- Create a project status report form to provide status updates every other week. Practice using the form with your projects for the next 2 weeks. At the end of the 2 weeks, decide if the form needs revisions. Practice again, until you feel the form works. Share with your staff and ask them to use it. Revise as needed.

- Unless it is an emergency, delay a decision for 3 days and let your subconscious work on it. Wake up each morning asking yourself what the decision should be. Determine if letting your mind work on the problem helps or hinders you in making decisions. Share your experience with a colleague.

- Evaluate your electronic and paper filing systems. Can you file and retrieve project documents easily? What can you improve?

- Streamline your project meetings. Reflect on what gets in your way or where you waste time and ask for help so that you can manage this better. This doesn't mean another resource. Perhaps there is a better approach but you don't know what it is. Ask around and find someone to speak to about it.

Managing Up

- When meeting with your supervisor, note the times emotions run high. Identify the causes. What can you do to decrease the times emotions run high? Create two or three solutions. Practice them the next time you are meeting.

- Consider you are coaching a colleague who is having trouble with his or her supervisor. Name 10 things you would say to them to help them in the situation. How many do you do?

- Record all the goals and projects your supervisor is working on and identify which you can support. Share the list with your supervisor and ask for input. Listen more than talk during the meeting. Revise the list to reflect the meeting. Follow through by supporting those goals.

- Ask your supervisor to take any type of inventory with you, such as the MBTI or Manager–Scientist Inventory. Share results with each other and determine the ways you can complement each other and build a more effective working relationship.

- Search the Internet for quotes about effective supervisors. Create your own quote about your supervisor. Share and discuss your thoughts with her/him.

- Pay attention to others' perceptions about your supervisor. In what ways can you use their understanding to help you improve your relationship with your supervisor?

- If you don't have the best of relationships with your supervisor, ask yourself "How can I make him/her look great today?" Keep this in mind all day and you will find that your interactions are more positive.

In addition to the development suggestions provided, keep in mind the research done by the Center for Creative Leadership on factors that develop talent. Among them are a challenging boss and assignments, a variety of assignments, and a diversity of people with whom to interact. As a technical manager, you can directly influence each of these factors. Even if your own work group is not diverse, take opportunities to bring others from your organization together to help with idea generating or problem solving.

COACHING SUCCESS—SOLUTION

Lisa's coach worked with her to become aware of personal preferences and how those preferences may cause tension and conflict. They discussed how she can better present information to others based on their preferences and build connections with co-workers and her boss.

Lisa completed the MBTI. During a meeting to discuss the results, she realized how she was impacting others with styles different from hers. She and her coach examined how her current situation differed from her preferences. During the discussions, Lisa began to realize that her natural approach to presenting information didn't work for everyone. She began to see that her co-workers and boss were not intentionally being difficult. She agreed to try one simple thing the next time she needed to present a new process. After explaining the process, she asked the group to review it for 10 to 15 minutes. At that point, Lisa asked the group to teach her the process. As they taught the process themselves, she was able to clarify any misunderstandings. This simple technique helped build a connection between Lisa and others and eliminated the blaming culture. It also helped Lisa's boss recognize that the issue involved more than just Lisa. Everyone needed to consider how to communicate with each other and be willing to ask questions and make adjustments.

REFERENCES

Borgatti, S. P., Everett, M. G., and Freeman, L. C. *Ucinet for Windows: Software for Social Network Analysis.* Analytic Technologies, Harvard, MA. 2002.

Domhoff, G. W. *The Scientific Study of Dreams: Neural Networks, Cognitive Development, and Content Analysis.* American Psychological Association (APA), Washington, D.C., 2003.

Gelb, M. J. *How to Think Like Leonardo da Vinci.* Dell, New York, 1998.

Goleman, D. *Emotional Intelligence: Why It Can Matter More Than IQ.* Bantam Books, New York, 1995.

Grom, T. "Executive Coaching." *PharmaVoice,* Vol. 10, Issue 1, January, 2010, pp. 32–34.

Hallowell, E. *CrazyBusy: Overstretched, Overbooked and About to Snap.* Ballantine Books, New York, 2006.

Kelley, R., and Caplan, J. "How Bell Labs Creates Star Performers." *Harvard Business Review,* Vol. 71, No. 4, July–August, 1993, pp. 127–139.

Klein, G. *Intuition At Work.* Doubleday, New York, 2003.

Locke, E. A., and Latham, G. *Goal Setting: A Motivational Technique That Works.* Prentice Hall, Englewood Cliffs, NJ, 1984.

McCauley, C. D. *Developmental Assignments: Creating Learning Experiences without Changing Jobs.* Center for Creative Leadership, Greensboro, NC, 2006.

McConnell, J. H. *TRAC: An Accurate Evaluation of a Manager's Ability to Succeed in Your Organization.* McConnell-Simmons Co., Morristown, NJ 07960. Phone: (201) 859-5514; email: john@mcconnell-simmons.com.

Singer, J., and Helferich, J. "Supporting R&D Support Groups." *Research-Technology Management,* Vol. 51, Issue 1, January–February, 2008, pp. 49–57.

Stone, L. "Living with Continuous Partial Attention." From the article "The Harvard Business Review List of Breakthrough Ideas for 2007." *Harvard Business Review,* Vol. 85, No. 2, February 2007, pp. 28–29.

Wiseman, R. *The Luck Factor: The Four Essential Principles.* Miramax Books/Hyperion, New York, 2003.

BIBLIOGRAPHY

Corey, G. *Theory and Practice of Group Counseling,* 4th ed. Brooks/Cole, Pacific Grove, CA, 1995.

Douglas, C. A. and Morley, W. H. *Executive Coaching: An Annotated Bibliography.* Center for Creative Leadership, Greensboro, NC, 2001.

Egan, G. *The Skilled Helper—A Problem-Management Approach to Helping,* 5th ed. Brooks/Cole, Pacific Grove, CA, 1994, pp. 91–93.

Fournies, F. F. *Coaching for Improved Work Performance.* Van Nostrand Reinhold, New York, 1978.

Kaplan, R. E. *Internalizing Strengths: An Overlooked Way of Overcoming Weaknesses in Managers.* Center for Creative Leadership, Greensboro, NC, 2002.

Kinlaw, D. C. *Coaching for Commitment: Managerial Strategies for Obtaining Superior Performance.* Pfeiffer, San Diego, CA, 1993.

Lombardo, M. M., and Eichinger, R. W. *Eighty-eight Assignments for Development in Place: Enhancing the Developmental Challenge of Existing Jobs.* Center for Creative Leadership, Greensboro, NC, 1989. Reprinted 2004.

Loehr, J., and Schwartz, T. *The Power of Full Engagement—Managing Energy, Not Time, Is the Key to High Performance and Personal Renewal.* Free Press, New York, 2003.

Luderman, K., and Erlandson, E. "Coaching the Alpha Male." *Harvard Business Review*, Vol. 82, No. 5, May, 2004, pp. 58–67.

Maccoby, M. "Understanding the People You Manage." *Research Technology Management*, Vol. 48, No. 3, March–April, 2002, pp. 58–60.

McCauley, C. D. *Technical Report 26—Developmental Experiences in Managerial Work: A Literature Review.* Center for Creative Leadership, Greensboro, NC, January, 1986.

Minor, M. *Coaching and Counseling: A Practical Guide for Managers.* Crisp, Los Altos, CA, 1989.

Nadler, D. A. "Confessions of a Trusted Counselor." *Harvard Business Review*, Vol. 83, No. 9, September, 2005, pp. 68–77.

Wiger, D. E., and Harowski, K. J. *Essentials of Crisis Counseling and Intervention.* Wiley, Hoboken, NJ, 2003.

Witherspoon, R., and White, R. P. *Four Essential Ways That Coaching Can Help Executives.* Center for Creative Leadership, Greensboro, NC, 2002.

CHAPTER 8

TECHNIQUES TO MANAGE GROUPS, TEAMS, AND MEETINGS

FACILITATION SITUATION

Terri was in charge of a global project team whose members were co-located in North America and Europe. The group met frequently, and often some members could not make the meetings. In fact, Terri could count on one hand how many times the entire group met face to face over an entire year. Most meetings included teleconferencing members at distant sites. Occasionally, one senior individual was so dominant that the individuals dialing in never actually spoke after their initial greeting.

Terri's leadership was routinely usurped by one individual who clearly wanted to take charge and by another who typically dissented during decisions. It was also common in meetings to rehash decisions previously made. Meeting notes never seemed to work, either because no one read them before meetings or because those who hadn't attended an earlier meeting still wanted to have their say.

Frustrations mounted and team members formed small cliques. Terri seemed to become less and less of a leader and more and more of a "yes" person.

What is causing Terri's slip in leadership?

How could Terri more successfully lead this global team?

See the end of the chapter for suggested responses.

Individuals make up a group. That means a team will have the same challenges, successes, and frustrations that individuals

---

A Guide to Success for Technical Managers: Supervising in Research, Development, & Engineering, by Elizabeth Treher, David Piltz and Steven Jacobs
Copyright © 2011 John Wiley & Sons, Inc.

experience at work. Whether they operate as a group or as a team depends on a number of factors, which have been studied thoroughly and about which much has been written. Our emphasis here is less on how to build a team and more on how to lead a group to high productivity. Whether the group members report directly to you or are part of a project team where you have no direct authority, your goal is to help the members be successful.

BUILDING COLLABORATION

To move a group down the road toward collaboration, there are four *key elements about which all members need clarity*:

- Our individual roles versus the roles of other group members
- Operating principles
- Individual autonomy versus group interdependence
- Decision making; who will make what kinds of decisions?

Domestic and international groups all tend to struggle with these dichotomies. Cultural differences can play a role due to differing geography, ethnicity, age, gender, and personal preferences; for our purposes here, we will not explore them specifically but acknowledge they exist.

Some of us tend to be either individual or group oriented. This doesn't suggest you can't work well either way, but human beings seem to have a natural preference for one or the other. This connects as well to leading groups. Those of us who like the group interaction (and enjoy what can be a less efficient process) are more likely to find we are soon comfortable leading a group. Those of us who prefer the opportunity to reflect and quietly pursue individual objectives may need to work harder to feel comfortable in leading a group. Factors that can impact our comfort level include working with those who are experts outside our own fields (the U << E syndrome described in Chapter 1). Facilitating successful meetings where we are not the expert can feel threatening and may take practice.

Let's start exploring how to lead groups by examining the components of the first dichotomy—**Individual roles versus the roles of other group members**. In groups, every member has a role, although in large groups several may share a role. There are responsibilities tied to the functional area we represent. These relate to project content and outcomes. Other roles associated with group process and group dynamics include that of facilitator, and a third that deals with structure—roles such as timekeeper and recorder.

Each individual brings his/her own strengths, perceptions, and diversity to the group. Unfortunately, our experiences, perhaps on another team or in another organization, lead us to make assumptions about what our colleagues do or should do in their roles, based on their functions or job titles. If we don't have a chance to talk about our assumptions and expectations to verify that our views are in sync with those of the individual(s) filling a role, we are likely to be surprised and possibly disappointed when our expectations aren't met.

ROLE CLARIFICATION ACTIVITY

Use this activity with your teams to make sure everyone has a common understanding of each others' roles. Ask everyone to describe their own role and responsibilities. After that is completed, have each member do the same for every other role on the team. Use a separate document for each role. Sample questions are:

1. What are the primary roles and responsibilities of _____?
2. What should this role do more of?
3. What should this role do less of or not be doing at all?
4. How can this role best assist you and the team?

Collect the pages for each role and give them to the person(s) in that role. Groups of one, or more, can evaluate their roles simultaneously. If several individuals share a role, have them first review their own comments about their role and come to a consensus. Next, review the comments others have made. Highlight the parts of the role where you agree and look for areas of disagreement. For example, you believe that something is part of your role and others list a responsibility that you hadn't considered. Prepare to present a summary of this information. After your group discusses and comes to a consensus on each role, you will have a powerful foundation from which to develop your team. Remember, consensus is a solution that is acceptable enough for all members to support, and no one opposes it. In working with teams in trouble, even those that have been together several years, we often find that role clarity issues are behind many of their issues. Don't let that happen in your team!

GOAL CLARIFICATION ACTIVITY

An additional activity that can be very insightful is to ask each member of the group to write in his/her own words the purpose of the project. Even if you have the project purpose in writing and ask individuals to put it in their own words, you are likely to find there is not consensus on the goals. This again provides a valuable discussion to ensure everyone has a common understanding. Very rarely do all members see the goal in the same way and discussing those different perceptions is a valuable exercise. If you are working with only one other person, this can still be a useful exercise for you both.

Being clear on roles and goals is a great beginning, but it isn't the end of the game. Have you ever experienced a situation like this one? It's 9:05 AM and your meeting was supposed to start 5 minutes ago. As the group members enter, some are talkative, some look disgusted, and some haven't arrived and are late again. You sit back in your chair and say to yourself, "Dealing with this staff is impossible; they show no respect for others' time." If you can relate to this, you're not alone. Technical managers across the world experience this situation. What can you do?

GROUP OPERATING PRINCIPLES OR NORMS

One way is to establish agreed-upon operating principles, often called group norms. These are the behaviors that group members feel would help them and are willing to commit to using. Making a list doesn't mean everything will work perfectly at first, but it gives you a starting point against which to measure progress. Keep the list to no more than a dozen items on which the group can agree to work. Common items include come prepared to meetings, show up on time, show respect, and listen to others.

After the list is created, review it with the group. Everyone has the responsibility for ensuring the list is followed, which means anyone can ask for the conversation to stop momentarily to review the list. Often on lists such as these, people suggest items such as show respect, trust, and listen. These are fine goals; however, they are conceptual and the expected associated behaviors are likely to vary by team member and thus be hard to evaluate.

Concept Level (Our words)

Context Level (Our experiences)

We do not experience life at the conceptual level. We experience life at the context level. When we only use conceptual terms, it is hard to decide if we actually achieved the intended behavior. It's important that when people offer concepts such as trust, communication, listening, or respect that you encourage them to describe the associated behavior or action—the context. If someone suggests that a group norm should be "respect," ask what respect means to him/her. You may hear something such as "knowing I will not be criticized for my ideas" or "letting everyone contribute before jumping ahead." Asking group members to translate high-level principles into specific actions helps to foster openness and honesty and leads to specific behaviors everyone can see and work on.

INCREASING MEETING EFFECTIVENESS

At the end of every meeting, allow 1 to 2 minutes to review your list of norms. Highlight those you did well with and to select one for improving the next time. After a short series of meetings, your group is likely to have made significant improvement, and over time the operating principles will become second nature. At that point you might just ask members to name one thing they feel the group did well and one thing that could use further work.

There are organizations that seem to have a culture of lateness. When meetings typically don't start on time, more and more individuals begin to arrive late, so as not to waste their own time. If you want to start on time, discuss as a group what to do. Some groups add incentives for behaviors that are particularly tough to change. We've seen groups charge a dollar for each 5 minutes (or 1 minute) members come in late and reserve the funds for a group lunch or donuts at an early meeting; others make an individual sing a song on arriving late or even bar entry to the meeting. The latter probably won't help your group progress too well, but some insist that is the best approach. We suggest your group should decide together and help enforce the decision.

INDIVIDUAL AUTONOMY VERSUS GROUP INTERDEPENDENCE

Another dichotomy is to balance the tension between individual autonomy and group interdependence. Individuals need autonomy to function to accomplish their goals. At the end of the day, each person is paid to do a job. For some, this autonomy becomes a way of life. Technical professionals tend to like freedom to pursue their work and have control over how things are accomplished. This isn't a bad thing; we all need control over aspects of our daily lives. It becomes an issue when personal autonomy affects others.

Members of a project team are interconnected. If I don't meet my work commitment, others on the team are likely to be affected. All team members feel the effect in some way. Likewise, if a project succeeds, all celebrate. Therefore, group interaction suggests that at some level in a team, personal autonomy is sacrificed to create, sustain, and enhance connections between team members.

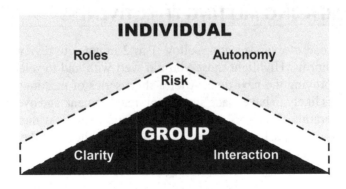

Groups interact in many ways. Whether in face-to-face or virtual settings, all groups deal with time and space. Rather than make assumptions, your group needs to come to consensus and include norms for areas that impact both the individuals and the group as a whole. A norm around time may develop without ever discussing it. For example:

- ☐ Is it okay to be late for meetings? What happens if I miss them?
- ☐ Is it okay to revisit decisions that have already been made?
- ☐ Is it okay to chitchat after a meeting begins?
- ☐ How often do we check email? During normal business hours or 24/7? What about returning calls? How quickly should we respond?
- ☐ What communication procedures should we use in an emergency?
- ☐ What happens when we miss deadlines?

Norms also develop for dealing with space. Space can be physical or emotional. Is the group physically located together? What is the physical relationship between office and lab space or between your group and your customers? How big or small are meeting rooms? How many are in the same office layout? Is it an open-space layout?

Do people feel comfortable sharing their thoughts and feelings? What about in brainstorming ideas, asking questions, and working together? If members operate with time and space restrictions that allow them to close off interactions with each other, they will act like a group of autonomous individuals rather than become a cohesive unit. However, when we use space and time constructively, it can help groups balance individual autonomy with group sharing, brainstorming, and problem solving.

Last, how does the group deal with challenges and successes? Are they perceived and dealt with as individual responsibilities, thus tipping the scale to the individual autonomy side, or are they perceived as team issues and consistently dealt with at the group level? It may not be just one or the other. However, most organizations and groups seem to make that delineation clearly. Instead, try to suggest an approach that includes both individual and group recognition.

Take advantage of small successes—acknowledge them and celebrate. One large team we worked with added a "standing ovation" to their group norms. When any individual or subgroup, for any reason—even just the fact that they'd had a bad day— needed support, they would stand up and say, "I need a standing ovation." All other group members would then stand and give them a rousing ovation and applause. As members of that team joined other teams, they brought with them the habit of standing ovations. With time it became part of the organization's culture.

As the manager, you have the privilege of creating an environment where standing ovations are possible. When sharing occurs at the concept *and* the context level, individuals have the autonomy to accomplish their own work, along with opportunities to interact with fellow team members to share challenges, celebrate successes, brainstorm, and solve problems.

DECISION MAKING

Once you strike a balance between individual autonomy and group interaction, your group also needs to *agree on when to make individual decisions versus group decisions*. Who will make what decisions? A simple but effective approach is to consider four buckets of decisions—theirs, yours, ours, and mine.

Bucket A—Theirs   These are the decisions the leader of the group (or more senior managers) will make independently.

Bucket B—Yours   These are the decisions the leader will make with input from the group.

Bucket C—Ours   These are the decisions the group will make as a whole. They are the decisions that are important enough to take the time to reach consensus.

Bucket D—Mine   These are the decisions that an individual or small subteam can make on its own and communicate back to the entire team.

Confusion and conflict around whose decision it is can undo many otherwise productive teams. When decisions are remade by others, or expectations about decisions are not met, it is hard to maintain team commitment. Frustration and anger often result. Avoid these problems by clarifying up front who will make what decisions. If the team will only provide information to influence a decision, make sure the members know this from the beginning. Use this same approach to work directly with individuals whom you supervise. If, in the end, the decision will not be yours, or you alone will make the decision, talk about it. Don't let frustrations about decisions impact a good working relationship.

MEETING MANAGEMENT TECHNIQUES

Among the elements to consider when establishing or improving a group or team, meeting management is high on the list. A simple technique is to consider meetings from the framework **PAAS** (**P**urpose, **A**genda , **A**ction, **S**tructure).

Purpose

What outcome(s) do you need from the meeting for each agenda topic? For example,

- ☐ Decision making
- ☐ Educational/informational
- ☐ Problem solving
- ☐ Planning
- ☐ Other

Sometimes we have meetings because we feel we must, or we think they are expected. Another common reason is to share progress. What percent of your meetings are used to provide status reports or updates to others? If you use your time this way, you have a wonderful opportunity to gain yourself and your team more time. *Stop* those meetings. Meetings today typically fall into that category, and they are a poor use of anyone's time. Meetings are costly and time is valuable. As a manager in R, D, &E, your job is to protect your staff's time so they can work productively. Ask individuals to review status and current reports on their own before a team meeting, not with the whole team. When they have questions, they can bring them to the meeting for discussion.

One of the best examples of this approach was managed by a colleague who ran as many as 100 technical projects at a time. He developed a simple online program where the project members on each of his projects completed short weekly online reports. He intentionally provided limited space in each section of the report, so being concise was essential, and it took little time to complete; the focus was on status, outcomes, concerns, and issues or problems to discuss at weekly meetings. Important data and documents were uploaded into the project archives. Before a meeting, team members could generate a summary of the team's progress and issues with one click.

They spent their meetings collaborating to brainstorm, trouble-shoot, and resolve project issues. The meetings were typically short and highly productive, so no one wanted to miss one. Those who couldn't attend, however, could go into the system and read a report of the meeting outcomes. That report was generated as the meeting progressed; thus, all members of the group could see and review it online. The time spent in many organizations writing, reviewing, and approving minutes was handled at the meeting, again saving time. The weekly summaries made project compliance (or lack of it) "visible." No one wanted to let the other team members down by not meeting their own commitments.

This illustrates the individual/group balance in meeting management. Meetings should provide opportunities for group problem solving, planning, decision making, and other areas where time for discussion and brainstorming will have an impact. Use written progress reports only for what is truly significant or new and the issues or questions for the group to know about and to help resolve.

Agenda

Whether you use a process similar to that described above or not, take the time to create an agenda. This should be more than a list of topics and times. Consider who is involved for each topic and their role (related to the outcomes you need). The agenda prescribes the intended context and helps to minimize time wasted on other topics.

The purpose(s) (intended outcomes) of a meeting need to be clearly stated on the agenda, so members can plan appropriately. For example, if I want Ethan to present and discuss highlights of a training he just attended (where the meeting outcome is education) versus present a summary and recommendations on whether we should bring the training in for our whole group (where the outcome is a decision), he and others are likely to prepare differently.

If the meeting has only one purpose, state it at the top. This can provide a sense of direction during the meeting. You can also minimize side conversations by referring to the purpose to bring things back on track.

However, in many meetings you will have multiple outcomes. If so, link them to each agenda item. Creating an environment with a clear path for discussions and outcomes provides focus and creates balance between individual and group issues.

Agendas should always include the:

1. Purpose or objective(s).
2. Date, time, and location.
3. Topics to cover, with the associated outcomes.
4. Participants involved and expectations for each. Will they present, recommend, and decide, or demonstrate?

Action

Facilitating a meeting is action oriented. It means using active listening to your advantage. It means creating a safe environment for members to express their ideas, share their needs, and critique ideas to create a better solution. It means creating an environment where team members challenge and support each other and deal with conflict head-on. It's actively supporting and expressing diversity to accomplish the stated meeting purpose. It means paying attention to who is sharing and who isn't and working to have all members participate. It means noticing who dominates and who discourages new ideas and solutions and managing those dynamics.

As facilitator your primary role is to ensure the meeting purpose and outcome(s) are achieved; however, facilitators often wear multiple hats at the same time. Other key roles are those of timekeeper, conflict manager, recorder, and administrator. It is most effective to assign and rotate these roles to other members at each meeting. This builds skills and helps the group so that it doesn't come to rely on you. Use Table 8.1, which lists team meeting roles and responsibilities for your next meeting. Before the meeting decide who will take each role. Don't feel that you must be the facilitator just because you are the manager or project team leader.

TABLE 8.1   Team Meeting Roles and Responsibilities

Role	Responsibilities
Timekeeper	Ensures the meeting begins and ends on time. Ensures time is devoted to each agenda item appropriately, adjusting as needed.
Recorder	Ensures important information, such as decisions made are kept for future reference.
Administrator	Ensures all meeting logistics are managed including sending out meeting reminders when appropriate, confirming meeting location, etc.
Facilitator	Creates and shares the purpose, intended outcome(s), and agenda of the meeting. Also leads the group through any appropriate decision-making models.
Team member	Stays actively involved and participates in discussions and brainstorming to help achieve the meeting's outcome(s).

APPLICATION: YOUR OWN MEETING

Take a moment and reflect on a recent meeting. Can you, in one sentence, state the purpose(s)? Did you have an agenda? Did it include topics, expected outcomes, participants, and their roles during the meeting? Did you achieve your purpose? Did participants leave with clear outcomes and next steps? Did you evaluate the meeting for improvement opportunities?

Structure

In addition to agendas, roles, and ground rules, which are formal structures, consider the informal structure of meetings such as who talks to whom, who most influences decisions, and how are discussions led. Informal structures are tied to the culture of the group and are the unwritten rules of a group.

What is the culture of leading discussions in your groups? Is it one in which only the subject expert speaks and fields questions, or do peers contribute and make suggestions? Is their input valued? In what ways is the culture reinforced? Do aspects need to be changed?

Substantial evidence supports the idea that creativity and problem solving benefit by combining the insights of those with different backgrounds and experiences. As we work longer and longer in a field, our views tend naturally to be directed by our experiences. Having others help us look at our work in different ways can lead to new perceptions and approaches.

To what extent does the manager influence the culture of the meetings? In your own meetings, is there a substantial difference when you are present versus when you can't attend? Do you lead all the meetings? Do you speak first? Technical managers can have significant personal impact on their staff. Look for opportunities where you can learn and model new behaviors. Try the feedforward technique proposed by executive coach Marshall Goldsmith. *Feedforward* means that rather than focus on the past and what has already occurred, provide suggestions for the future and work as a group to support the desired change.

Meeting management can seem daunting, but it doesn't have to be. Effective meetings are simple. They have a purpose, clear outcomes, active participation, and a structure that supports the meeting and the participants.

We started this chapter examining the dynamics of leading teams and then transitioned into meeting management. Effective technical managers realize the importance of managing both individual and group needs when leading groups. Creating effective environments helps members share their thoughts and feelings and builds a true collaborative spirit. When you hear members challenging ideas, adding their own, and openly discussing different perspectives, take the time to appreciate the culture of collaboration and teamwork you are building.

FACILITATION SITUATION—SUGGESTIONS

What Is Causing Terri's Slip in Leadership?

Terri seems to be facing several issues—group roles aren't clear, there is no clear process for how decisions are made or who has the ultimate decision authority, and she is not using effective meeting management. Terri has not raised the issue of team members' assumptions about roles and decisions. Nor does she seem to realize how she is supporting ineffective team behaviors.

How Could Terri More Successfully Lead This Global Team?

Does this seem like a simple problem to fix? Has this ever happened to you?

Terri could be more successful if she and the group:

- Create meeting norms to outline how members interact during meetings.

- Use their norms to begin each meeting and review at the end for group input on the group's effectiveness.
- Create and follow an agenda.
- Take time to clarify each member's role.
- Come to a consensus on their decision-making process and who must approve and what to do if that person is not available.
- Use meeting notes, record decisions, and how decisions are made.

Actual   Terri met with each team member to discuss that person's role, talk about individual needs and wants, and listen to feedback and recommendations about the meetings.

During those individual meetings, Terri realized that no one was intentionally trying to dominate or take over. Time constraints and other projects made it difficult to read notes between meetings, and people felt like others weren't listening to them.

Rather than tackle everything at once, the group decided that all meetings would start by reviewing notes and any questions from the previous meeting and work on better listening skills. Before sharing their own thoughts, they practiced providing their understanding of what the speaker had said. They also made a conscious effort to acknowledge and ask for input from those who were calling in.

These two simple actions helped tremendously and gave the group members incentive to continue improving their meetings.

REFERENCES

Domhoff, G. W. *The Scientific Study of Dreams: Neural Networks, Cognitive Development, and Content Analysis.* American Psychological Association (APA), Washington, D.C., 2003.

Goleman, D. *Emotional Intelligence: Why It Can Matter More Than IQ.* Bantam Books, New York, 1995.

Hallowell, E. *CrazyBusy: Overstretched, Overbooked and About to Snap.* Ballantine Books, New York, 2006.

Klein, G. *Intuition At Work.* Doubleday, New York, 2003.

Locke, E. A., and Latham, G. *Goal Setting: A Motivational Technique That Works.* Prentice Hall, Englewood Cliffs, NJ, 1984.

Stone, L. "Living with Continuous Partial Attention." From the article "The Harvard Business Review List of Breakthrough Ideas for 2007." *Harvard Business Review*, Vol. 85, No. 2, February 2007, pp. 28–29.

Wiseman, R. *The Luck Factor: The Four Essential Principles.* Miramax Books/ Hyperion, New York, 2003.

BIBLIOGRAPHY

Borman, E. G. *Discussion and Group Methods—Theory and Practice*, 2nd ed. Harper and Row, New York, 1975.

Coutu, D. "Why Teams Don't Work." *Harvard Business Review*, Vol. 87, No. 5, May 2009, pp. 99–105.

Davis, S. *This Meeting Sux—12 Acts of Courage to Change Meetings for Good.* Facilitator U.com Press, Arroyo Grande, CA, 2008.

Goldsmith, M. *Try Feedforward Instead of Feedback.* Marshal Goldsmith Leader to Leader Institute, www.marshallgoldsmithlibrary.com, Santa Fe, CA, 2002.

Hoke, C., Ed. *Around the Globe or Down the Hall: The Art of Distance Management.* The Learning Key, Washington Crossing, PA, 2008.

Hunter, D., Bailey, A., and Taylor, B. *The Art of Facilitation—How to Create Group Synergy.* Fisher Books, Tucson, AZ, 1995.

Luft, J. *Group Processes—An Introduction to Group Dynamics*, 3rd ed. Mayfield, Mountain View, CA, 1984.

Majchrzak, A., Malhotra, A., Stamps, J., and Lipnack, J. "Can Absence Make a Team Grow Stronger?" *Harvard Business Review*, Vol. 82, No. 5, May, 2004, pp. 131–137.

Monalisa, M., Diam, T., Mirani, F., Dash, P., Khamis, R., and Bhusari, V. "Managing Global Design Teams." *Research—Technology Management*, July–August, 2008, pp. 48–58.

Myshko, D. "The Softer Side of R&D." *PharmaVoice*, April, 2008, pp. 50–56.

Runde, C., and Flanagan, T. "Managing Team Performance." *Talent Management Magazine*, May 2006, pp. 26–29.

Schultz, B. G. *Communicating in the Small Group—Theory and Practice*, 2nd ed. Harper Collins College, New York, 1996.

Strohmeier, B. R. "Achieving Effective Technical Leadership in Today's R&D Organizations." *Journal of Leadership Studies*, 5.1, 1998, p. 27.

Zafft, C. R., Adams, S. G., and Matkin, G. S. "Measuring Leadership in Self-managed Teams Using the Competing Values Framework." *Journal of Engineering Education*, 98.3, 2009.

CHAPTER 9

CLUES TO FOSTER CREATIVITY AND INNOVATION

SAM'S DILEMMA

The long-standing practice at a major consumer pharmaceutical company was to only hire scientists and formulators with patents and publications. The assumption was that this was the only way to get new and innovative products. Yet the numbers of new, innovative products these people generated were minimal, compared to the larger number of line extensions they created. This only led to incremental innovation.

Sam, the head of R&D, was in a quandary. How could they develop groundbreaking products, not simple line extensions? The company president had come from marketing and invited Sam to many meetings to hear the latest and greatest new product idea from marketing. One idea, called Rise and Shine, was adapted from an old sci-fi theme. They wanted to take a core of caffeine, enteric coat it, and surround it with a thick layer of Benadryl. They suggested that consumers, when unable to get to sleep, would take one and drift off to sleep; 8 hours later the caffeine would be released, causing them to become wide awake. The technical challenges to this idea were staggering. It was not physically possible to create the compound so that dissolution timing could be sufficiently controlled. In addition, the physiology of everyone who took it would differ, causing some to wake up wired in the middle of the night and others to sleep well past the promised time. These were only a few of the problems he could see.

A Guide to Success for Technical Managers: Supervising in Research, Development, & Engineering, by Elizabeth Treher, David Piltz and Steven Jacobs
Copyright © 2011 John Wiley & Sons, Inc.

Sam also saw that marketing felt it was its job to be innovative and realized there was no reason his own scientists couldn't come up with ideas as cutting edge as these. Yet, they had not done so for a very long time.

Whether you lead R&D as Sam or have only one technician or associate, the principles are the same.

What would you suggest to Sam?

How can you foster creativity and innovation?

See the end of this chapter for the actual resolution.

SOCIAL AND EDUCATIONAL INPUT ON CREATIVITY

The future of the United States and the world lies in creativity and innovation. Technical managers are faced daily with creating an environment to foster creativity and innovation. In many technical settings, organizational rules and constraints can serve to inhibit or reduce creativity. In addition, our educational process, with few exceptions, often serves to drive out creativity as we seek to streamline and homogenize classes and schools and to simplify administration. Very few schools or companies actively foster and reinforce creativity or try to develop it in their students or employees.

Paul Torrance (1999) documented three developmental drops in creativity test scores of children. First, when they enter kindergarten, next in fourth grade, and again in seventh grade. These drops were all due to increasing conformity to behave in the ways they believed others expected and to the fear of being different.

Augustus Walker (1988) describes a similar effect in adults. Test results, including those with professional scientists, suggest that there is considerable and effective pressure to conform. Individuals, confronted with the unanimous opinions of their colleagues, go along with an obviously incorrect judgment about 40% of the time. That number rises to about 80% if the circumstances are uncertain or ambivalent, demonstrating the need for social support when in doubt. Although science values independent thinking, groups favor conformity, another factor leading to dysfunctional group decision making.

Imagination, the foundation of creativity, is one of the things we seem to lose the older we get, and it is tough to get it back again once it is lost. The research of Marjorie Taylor (1999), a psychology professor at the University of Oregon and author of the book *Imaginary Companions and the Children Who Create Them*, shows that preschool children, for example, those who have imaginary friends, are more creative. They also have greater social understanding and are better at incorporating the perspective of others.

Abraham Maslow, who developed the hierarchy of needs said, "the key question isn't, "what fosters creativity?" But it is, "why in God's name isn't everyone creative?" Where was the human potential lost? How was it crippled?" (Maslow, 1943, at http://wisdomquotes.com/quote/abraham-maslow.html). His quote brings to light an assumption common to many of us: You have to be born creative and innovative. This belief is supported by the fact that certain scientists or inventors have multiple patents, while others have few or none. Yet, the assumption is false. Yes, there are studies that show that creativity is linked to multiple genes (Li, 1987; Bouchard, 1993; Lykken, McGue, Tellegen, and Bouchard 1992), and, yes, certain individuals have an ability to take greater leaps. However, each of us has the potential to take creative steps and to innovate. From a Myers–Briggs perspective, all types are creative and may express that creativity in different ways. In our experience, intuitives are likely to make unusual leaps while sensors tend more to adapt existing ideas and innovations and apply their creativity by making incremental improvements.

RAISING THE BAR FOR CREATIVITY AND INNOVATION

Dow Chemical's polyolefin and elastomers business is reported (Stevens and Swogger, 2009) to have significantly increased the creativity index of its R&D leadership culture by strategically bringing in and placing starters (typically NTPs) and finishers (typically STJs) in appropriate roles. They found that R&D leadership responsible for new product development needed about 60% starters, while the business leadership overall needed finishers and only about 30% starters. Using the MBTI-based creativity index, they increased their creativity scores substantially as they moved people into jobs for which they were better suited. These efforts produced over $23 billion in total value from 1991 to 2001. During this time, the number of patents increased by a factor of 4, and the speed to launch was 3 to 4 times faster. They also launched 13 major new products.

DEFINITIONS: CREATIVITY AND INNOVATION

What is creativity? What is innovation? There are many, even contradictory, definitions of these terms. We define creativity and innovation in the following way:

Creativity is a process by which we generate something unique.

Innovation is implementation of a creative idea to develop a product or process; some limit innovation to be the change or improvement of an existing product.

We can be creative and not innovate, but can't innovate without creativity. This, in fact, is one of the management dilemmas technical managers face. It is not enough to use our intelligence and creativity in R&D; we must also be able to generate something new and useful.

Our colleague, Gus Walker, points out that working in R, D &E is a bit like fishing. Amateur fishermen enjoy the activity of fishing—the camaraderie of friends or the quiet of a time alone, the environment, and the experience. Catching fish is a bonus, but even if they don't catch any, they will probably continue to fish. Professional fisherman, on the other hand, can't stay in business if they don't catch fish. In managing technical professionals, we need to remember that activity (creativity) alone is not sufficient. To remain in business, we need to catch fish (innovate to develop products). This can be challenging to manage those who join industry from academia, where the activity of research is a sufficient reward in and of itself. That is not the case in most technology-based companies.

There are many things that technical managers can do to increase or decrease innovation and creativity in individuals and groups.

We can help others to:

- Increase self-awareness.
- Enhance the creative environment.
- Use collaboration, teamwork, and build a culture of trust.
- Use tools to foster creativity and get unstuck.

Increase Self-Awareness

It has become increasingly clear, thanks to Goleman's (2000) work with emotional intelligence, and others, that the most successful people have a very high level of self-awareness. This allows them to do two things well. First, it allows them to know what they are very good at and what they have a talent for and what they don't. Second, it spurs them to go after jobs where they can leverage what they do best. Have you seen individuals in a job that they aren't suited for or for which they don't have a talent? When we've asked this during presentations around the world, no less than 90% of those in the audience raise their hands to say they have.

To help others develop self-awareness, try the Cartoon Character exercise from Adele Lynn (2007). Ask each person to identify a cartoon character whose trait (not appearance) is most like his or her own. After they list the traits they think they share with the character, have the others on the team say if they agree or disagree with the cartoon character or trait and give the reasons why or why not. Decide first if the group is ready for this kind of feedback. This is a great exercise to get people to better understand themselves and others. If you have only one employee, do this together, sharing your perceptions.

Enhance the Creative Environment

Red or Blue? As you picture that most creative space, what colors do you see? Are there any reds or blues? Mehta and Zhu

(2009) studied the impact of red and blue colors and found that color enhanced performance. Test subjects, when given attention-demanding tasks, did best when primed with the color red. When asked to be creative, they responded best to blue. We all know red is a stimulating color. It is the color of stoplights and stop signs, emergency rooms, and danger. Mehta and Zhu speculated that people want to avoid those things and for that reason they do better on detail-oriented tasks. Blue on the other hand is a comfortable, safe color, the color of the sky and the ocean.

What about your work environment? Does it foster creativity? Is there a location you could modify to enhance creativity? Can you use red or blue accents with your staff?

Have your staff identify which is most important to them, red to focus or blue to be more creative. They may not know, in which case you should get pictures that are bright blue or bright red; have them hang them in a place staff members can see when trying to think of creative ideas. Ask them to try one for 2 days then switch to the other to see if they can distinguish trends in creativity.

Other aspects of our surrounding work environment can stimulate and suppress creativity. What are the labs, offices or cubes, and conference rooms like? How cluttered is your office? Are papers, articles, and journals scattered or piled, like land mines, all over? Studies have shown a correlation between clutter and creativity. Probably the most extreme example we can cite is the office of a highly creative university chemistry professor. The office was a relatively small space with one extra chair; every surface and the entire floor were covered with piles of paper. A visitor needed to allow extra time for stacks to be relocated and the chair uncovered. Some stacks were more than a couple of feet high. Yet, the professor had the uncanny ability to go directly to the proper place and find what he needed. Fortunately, he didn't share an office.

Impact of Pressure   Does the standard atmosphere in your organization support or undermine creativity and innovation? In many of today's corporations, we see a steady stream of mergers and acquisitions (M&As). What's the direct effect of M&As in most companies? If you answered downsizing, redeployment, right sizing, smart sizing, reduction in force, or layoffs, then you are right. What does this generate? Mostly fear—and pressure.

How does fear impact creativity and innovation at work? How comfortable would you or your employees be if you were worried that your jobs were about to be terminated (as you were just made redundant by the doubling of a workforce doing the same thing)? Teresa Amabile (1998), an explorer of business innovation at Harvard Business School, showed that innovation and creativity is positively associated with joy, and even love, and negatively associated with fear, stress, and anxiety. When people were happiest and loved their work, they were more likely to come up with innovative ideas. She affirmed previous research showing that generation of a creative idea is almost always preceded by an associated incubation period. One day's happiness seemed to prepare people who were ready to be creative with the ability to come up with an innovative concept the next day.

Where do most of your creative ideas occur? Many individuals wake from sleep having solved a problem or dreamed a solution, come up with great ideas in the shower, or are at their most productive as they commute to work. It differs from person to person. For those with a particular, physical place, some suggest looking at the surroundings and listing the things that make it comfortable for you to be creative.

Logic follows that in situations where fear, anxiety, and pressure reign supreme this innovative cycle and incubation period is greatly reduced. Amabile's research showed that people under stress or pressure not only lost their creative ability for the day they felt the pressure, but the impact lasted for the following 2 days. Stress is common in merging companies. Most people under stress are not innovative, they are not collaborative, they are not risk takers, and they are not boat rockers. They become survivalists. One of the highest stressors you can suffer is losing a job. The M&A trend, and the resulting stress, produces even greater challenges for technical managers and leaders.

As mentioned earlier in this chapter, Stevens and Swogger (2009) describe another type of organizational stress. In their example, a Dow Chemicals business had been doing so poorly that it was considered for divestiture. Significant gains in creativity and innovation were essential for survival. The process used to increase innovation included measuring the R&D leadership culture via a creativity index, using new selection criteria for leaders in specific jobs, and training and coaching business opportunity analysts. These efforts were successful by all measures of innovation—new products developed, sales, best in class for time to market, and total value delivered over about 10 years.

What Can You Do to Reduce Stress? Helping your staff focus on their own development, even if project work is uncertain, is one way to maintain momentum and motivation. You probably can't change your entire work environment, but you can try to decrease the stress in your sphere of influence. Taking your employees out to lunch and getting away from the area can decrease stress and increase team cohesion. Meeting after work has the same effect. Even those who are married or have kids can meet with the team occasionally, especially if you schedule ahead of time.

You can take walks at lunch and incorporate play into what you do every day. Read books to relax, laugh, or learn new perspectives. Humor is essential for de-stressing your staff. Use humor in the form of jokes, stories, puns, or anecdotes. Never target anyone in the group, although if you make fun of yourself, it can actually build trust in the team. So, what else can you do to decrease the stress? Find something that gives you comfort and balances your work activities. Whether by exercise, volunteerism, or a simple hug, each of us must find a way to reduce our own anxiety to support those we supervise. For those whose jobs call for focus on a lot of detail, try activities that draw on your imagination; if you deal with people all day and are generating ideas and using a lot of imagination, try more solitary, hands-on activities such as gardening or painting.

Once you have found ways to balance stress and created a comfortable, colorful environment, you have set the stage to be creative. How then can you develop new creativity and innovation skills? As Louis Pasteur said in a lecture at the University of Lille in 1854: "Chance favors only the prepared mind."

Change Perspectives One approach we heard about for coming up with innovative ideas took advantage of a busy travel schedule. This individual traveled all over the world giving presentations. He spent a lifetime in the air or in airports waiting to get up in the air. He made it a habit to go to the bookstore in every airport to buy different magazines to read. In this way, he was able to add pieces to his brain puzzle. The range of knowledge that he built this way allowed him to see innovative products, techniques, and tools that were useful in other disciplines and industries to help create major breakthroughs.

A classic example of this was a company that specialized in automotive lubrication and oil changes. The hoses that hung from the ceilings for engine-oil-reservoir filling constantly dripped. They brought in three engineers to solve the dilemma. One of the executives brought in an office cleaning woman whom they knew and respected to see what she might add. At the end of weeks of research, design, and development, the engineers came up with three very expensive, complex solutions that would take months of work to build, plus the time to mass produce and install them across the country. The cleaning woman brought a detergent bottle with a snap cap, opened the cap, and turned the bottle over to show nothing dripped out. In the end, the new design for the hoses was based off the simple design the cleaning woman suggested. Without her experience and perspective, the solution would have been expensive and time consuming.

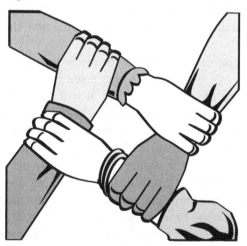

Use Collaboration, Teamwork, and Build an Environment of Trust

Differing perceptions, training, and experiences are known to produce higher levels of innovation in teams. Research using the MBTI has shown that teams with the greatest diversity of Types are the most creative, if they can work through and value their different perspectives. It takes longer for such a group to feel like a team, but if they do, they outshine teams with less diversity.

Another example, from an exercise we use in workshops about the pharmaceutical industry, compares individual and team solutions to rank order a number of pharmaceutical development steps. They first do the exercise individually and then work in small teams. Because it is relatively easy to make false assumptions, no individual has ever had a perfect score, and of the many hundreds of teams that have participated in the activity, only one failed to do better as a group than the average of the individual scores. All but a handful did better as a group than the best individual score on their team. More than 99.9% of the teams did better than their individual members did by themselves. For the most part these were individuals at public workshops who hadn't previously worked together, yet they came together and worked as an effective team.

There are many ways to develop a more collaborative team. Skills for doing this are included in this book and others. There are also easy, short activities you can use to help participants build relationships and learn more about each other. Many of us have interests and skills we use during our personal time that can help as well at work.

During one of your lunches or afternoons away from work with the team, ask each person to share something they've done or somewhere they have been. Discuss how it was unusual and the ways it affected them personally. Not only does this bring the group closer, it allows each of the team members to see the diversity of the group and to appreciate each member from a more personal perspective. Remember to ensure that one person doesn't monopolize the conversation, as many of us love talking about ourselves. Depending on the group, you may need to limit individual time. Give each a 5-minute timeline; tell them you'll indicate when they have 30 seconds and 15 seconds left before they start. Then keep time in a subtle way so you don't interrupt their thoughts, feelings, and candor.

The following simple activity has many variations. Ask each person to think of things about themselves—three true and one false. Other members then guess which is false. One individual we worked with indicated that he'd lived in a nudist colony for a couple of years. All guessed that was false. However, it was true. When his family immigrated to the United States, he was a small child and they had lived in a nudist colony, since they felt it was most affordable. This works even for groups that have worked together for a long time. There is always something new, and perhaps surprising, to learn about our colleagues.

Group Creativity versus Individual Creativity   Collaboration beats out individual creativity when groups work well together. Groups bring diversity via different perspectives, education, experience, and different knowledge. Teresa Amabile's (1998) surveys showed that the most creative teams are those with the confidence to share and debate ideas. When people compete for recognition, or worse, when they are incentivized to be creative, they stop sharing information and think less innovatively.

Tools to Foster Creativity and Get Unstuck

There are two competing views on the subject of creativity. One claims that with sufficient effort and tools to help, anyone can become creative. They feel the solution is to build creativity skills and use the many self-help books written by the De Bonos (1985, 1996, 2005) of the world. Others feel the genetic component is too significant and that it is preferable to target jobs based on preferences and creativity scores.

Whether you fall into one camp or the other, practicing using tools to break context traps and to expand the ways we view information or look at data seems to us a useful practice. Our minds are hot-wired so we can effectively categorize and interpret events, people, and things. This categorization is essential to our ability to think and function but can limit us and help us more easily fall into context traps that we are unlikely to recognize. Most of the creativity tools help us get unstuck—by changing our perceptions and helping us to see beyond our assumptions. They break a train of thought and help those thoughts diverge. Even the most creative of us benefit from this.

Tools to Increase Creativity

There are dozens of books and online resources that list and describe tools for increasing creativity. We don't intend to repeat them here. Several good ones are provided in the references bibliography.

Brainstorming is a common method to generate new ideas. Everyone is encouraged to call out ideas quickly without considering the value of the idea but emphasizing quantity. A recorder writes all ideas on a flip chart. In a virtual setting where participants are all online and use teleconferencing, the ideas are posted electronically for all to see.

Unfortunately, traditional brainstorming has a number of pitfalls, including:

- Any kind of feedback during a brainstorming session is detrimental to the process, whether positive or negative. Yes, we can ask people not to comment and review rules about brainstorm guidelines first, but this generally doesn't work for long.
- Contributions are usually uneven, where some provide many ideas and others few or none. Attempts to equalize contributions by going to each person successively can embarrass some and frustrate others.
- Introverts who prefer to think about things before speaking can be less productive with others speaking, sometimes more than one at a time.
- In discussing the ideas at the end of the brainstorming, technical groups tend to focus on the problems they see, so conflict easily results after another's ideas are criticized.

Brainstorming is still a powerful tool, and there are alternatives to overcome these problems. There are many names used for modified techniques, such as brainwriting, brainsketching, and nominal group techniques.

Nominal group technique is a form of brainstorming designed to generate multiple, divergent ideas by encouraging all members of the group to contribute. This tool supports introversion and extraversion and prevents dominant members from taking over.

To use this approach:

- Ask each member to write down as many ideas as possible on Post-Its® in 2 to 3 minutes.
- Have each person read his/her ideas, rotating among group members, and post the ideas.
- Group the ideas by topic and rearrange under each topic heading.
- Have group members use colored dots to mark the ideas or categories they most favor or want to expand on. Limit the number of dots per person. The key here is that it is easy to see where there is consensus and agreement with an idea and

no one goes through the experience of having a favorite idea attacked. The good ones come to light, the others quietly fall out. With so many ideas it is also less likely for anyone to become attached to a single one.

• Go back to the ideas/categories selected and continue idea generation or discussion before voting again as a group.

Similar to the process above, brainwriting also fosters equal contributions and minimizes the context traps of traditional brainstorming aloud. A broader array of ideas results. If members are gathered at a table, put one blank page per person, plus at least one more, in the center. Ask each person to write down three ideas on one page and then exchange it for another in the center. On the next page, either continue with the first ideas or build on those another has suggested. (The first person to complete his/her page will be drawing another blank one.) Once everyone has had a chance to add to several pages, stop the process and as a group review and categorize the ideas for discussion as with the nominal group technique.

For brainsketching, have each member draw a picture of a solution to a problem and as the page circulates, ask others to add to the drawing or create another. Visual metaphors are a powerful way to help us expand our thinking. Intepra® cards, a set of simple images, are useful for creating idea or connections on any subject. See http://www.thelearningkey.com/catalog/product_info.php?products_id=53.

When using any type of idea generation process, consider using Bob Eberle's **SCAMPER** technique (Michalko, 1991). Described in most creativity literature, it is a structured way to break the context traps that form quickly. The acronym breaks down to the following:

Substitute: What else? Who else? Other ingredients or materials? Other place?

Combine: Blend? Alloy? Combine purposes? Combine appeals? Combine benefits?

Adapt: What else is like this? What other idea does this suggest? What could I copy?

Minify/Magnify: Order, form, shape, size, time, frequency, dimensions, characteristics?

Put to other uses: How else to use? Where else? Who else?

Eliminate: Remove or condense elements, materials, streamline, understate?

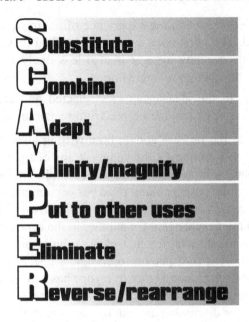

Substitute
Combine
Adapt
Minify/magnify
Put to other uses
Eliminate
Reverse/rearrange

Reverse/Rearrange: Can you interchange or exchange components or find other patterns, opposites, sequences?

You can use these tools effectively with just one employee. If you want more ideas, ask a colleague from another group or department to join you. The key to remember is that the first solution to a problem is rarely the best, and it *is* worth the time up front to explore alternatives. You don't save time in the long run by working on the wrong problem or tackling the wrong solution.

SAM'S DILEMMA—RESOLVED

Sam needed to turn his R&D group into an innovation "factory" to build on new and creative ideas. There had to be ways to foster innovation in each and every person in the department. He began a process to increase creativity and innovation in every member of R&D, from the chief scientists to the administrative assistants in each department. Everyone, not just the scientists.

They created six-person I-teams, or innovation teams, composed of everyone from within R&D, not only the scientists. These team members were given extra time to create innovative ideas that would improve R&D and allow them to do their job of creating the new product concepts for the company's future.

One innovation team of six people had two formulators, two analysts, one library assistant, and the leader who was a logistics and packaging manager. The formulators were Ph.D. scientists, one a woman about 6 feet tall from Ireland, the other a man from China. One of the analysts was a rock-and-roll drummer with tattoos and piercings and the library assistant was an Internet guru who lived to surf. The manager of logistics and packaging had graduated as a pharmacist and flown helicopters and airplanes in the military. The diversity on the team in backgrounds, perspectives, and experiences was vast and amazingly synergistic, leading to significant innovation. Not all groups evolved into high-performing teams. Some floundered as they continued to rely on old ways of coming up with new ideas.

They also set up creativity rooms in the R&D area, with reds and blues, soft lighting, and gentle fabric arcs to stimulate creativity. For many it was a safe harbor and sanctuary from the Dilbert-like cube cities that many lived in at work.

REFERENCES

Amabile, T. M. "How to Kill Creativity." *Harvard Business Review*, Vol. 76, No. 5, September–October, 1998, pp. 76–87.

De Bono, E. *De Bono's Thinking Course*. Barnes and Noble, New York, 2005.

De Bono, E. *Six Thinking Hats*. Little Brown, Boston, MA, 1985.

De Bono, E. *Teach Yourself to Think*. Penguin, New York, 1996.

Domhoff, G. W. *The Scientific Study of Dreams: Neural Networks, Cognitive Development, and Content Analysis*. American Psychological Association (APA), Washington, D.C., 2003.

Goleman, D. *Emotional Intelligence: Why It Can Matter More Than IQ*. Bantam Books, New York, 1995.

Goleman, D. *Working with Emotional Intelligence*. Bantam, New York, 2000.

Hallowell, E. *CrazyBusy: Overstretched, Overbooked and About to Snap*. Ballantine Books, New York, 2006.

Klein, G. *Intuition At Work*. Doubleday, New York, 2003.

Li, C. C. "A General Model for Emergenesis." *American Journal of Human Genetics*, Vol. 41, October, 1987, pp. 517–523.

Locke, E. A., and Latham, G. *Goal Setting: A Motivational Technique That Works*. Prentice Hall, Englewood Cliffs, NJ, 1984.

Lynn, A. *Quick Emotional Intelligence Activities for Busy Managers—50 Team Exercises That Get Results in Just 15 Minutes*. AMACOM (American Management Association), Broadway, New York, 2007.

Maslow, A. "A Theory of Human Motivation." *Psychological Review*, Vol. 50, 1943, pp. 370–396.

Michalko, M. *Thinkertoys*. Ten Speed Press, Berkeley, CA, 1991.

Stevens, G. A., and Swogger, K. "Creating a Winning R&D Culture—II." *Research-Technology Management*, Vol. 52, No. 3, April–May, 2009, pp. 22–28.

Stone, L. "Living with Continuous Partial Attention." From the article "The Harvard Business Review List of Breakthrough Ideas for 2007." *Harvard Business Review*, Vol. 85, No. 2, February 2007, pp. 28–29.

Taylor, M. *Imaginary Companions and the Children Who Create Them*. Oxford University Press, Oxford, NY, 1999.

Torrence, P., in Davis, G. A., "Barriers to Creativity and Creative Attitudes." *Encyclopedia of Creativity Vol. 1*, p. 168 (edited by M. A. Runco and S. R. Pritzker), Academic Press, San Diego, CA, 1999, pp. 165–174.

Walker, A. *Communication in Technical Organizations*. Effective Research, Pittsburgh, PA, 1988.

Wiseman, R. *The Luck Factor: The Four Essential Principles*. Miramax Books/Hyperion, New York, 2003.

BIBLIOGRAPHY

Adair, J. *The Art of Creative Thinking*. Kogan Page, London, 2007.

Bouchard, T. J., Jr. "The Genetic Architecture of Human Intelligence." from Vernon, P. A. (Ed.), *Biological Approaches to the Study of Human Intelligence*. Ablex, Norwood, NJ, 1993, pp. 33–93.

Bouchard, T. J., Lykken, D. T., McGue, M., Segal N. L., and Tellegen, A. "Sources of Human Psychological Differences: The Minnesota Study of Twins Reared Apart". *Science* 250(4978), October, 1990, pp. 223–228.

Bragdon, A. D., and Gamon, D. *Building Left-Brain Power*. Brainwaves Books, Bass River, MA, 1999.

Breen, B. "The Six Myths of Creativity." *Fast Company*, Issue 89, December, 2004, p. 75; http://www.fastcompany.com/magazine/89/creativity.html.

Buckingham, M., and Coffman, C. *First, Break All the Rules: What the World's Greatest Managers Do Differently*. Simon and Schuster, New York, 1999.

Diebold, J. *The Innovators—The Discoveries, Inventions, and Breakthroughs of Our Time*. Truman Talley Books/Plume, New York, 1991.

Fobes, R. *The Creative Problem Solvers Toolbox—A Complete Course in the Art of Creating Solutions to Problems of Any Kind*. Solutions Through Innovation, Corvallis, OR, 1993.

Hardy, E. E. *OOPS! I Never Thought of That—Creativity Is Just Common Sense*. E.K. Enterprises, San Diego, CA, 1975.

Henard, D. H., and McFadyen, A.M. "Making Knowledge Workers More Creative." *Research-Technology Management*, Vol. 51, No. 2, March–April, 2008, pp. 40–46.

Holmes, J. S., and Glass, J. T. "Internal R&D—Vital but only one Piece of the Innovation Puzzle." *Research-Technology Management*, September–October, 2004, pp. 7–10.

Jewett, D. L. "What's Wrong with Single Hypotheses? Why It Is Time for Strong-Inference-PLUS." *Scientist*, Vol. 19, No. 21, November, 2005, pp. 10–11.

Katz, L. C., and Rubin, M. *Keep Your Brain Alive*. Workman Publishing, New York, 1999.

Keim, B. "Seeing Red: Tweak Your Brain with Colors." *Wired.com*, February 5, 2009; http://www.wired.com/wiredscience/2009/02/coloreffects.

Lykken, D. T., McGue, M., Tellegen, A., and Bouchard, T. J., Jr. "Emergenesis—Genetic Traits That May Not Run in Families." *American Psychologist*, Vol. 47, No. 12, December, 1992, pp. 1565–1577.

MBTI® Activity Index, www.winovations.com/calculator.htm.

Mehta, R., and Zhu, R. "Blue or Red? Exploring the Effect of Color on Cognitive Task Performances." *Science*, Vol. 323, Issue 5918, February, 2009, pp. 1226–1229.

Osborn, A. *Applied Imagination: Principles and Procedures of Creative Problem-solving*. Charles Scribner's Sons, New York, 1963.

Parnes, S. J. *Optimize the Magic of Your Mind*. Creative Education Press, Buffalo, NY, 1997.

Parnes, S. J. *Visioning: State-of-the-Art Process for Encouraging Innovative Excellence*. DOK Publishers, East Aurora, NY, 1988.

Prather, C. W. "The Dumb Thing about Smart Goals for Innovation." *Research-Technology Management*, Vol. 48, Issue 5, September–October, 2005, pp. 14–15.

Rigby, D. K., Gruver, K., and James, A. "Innovation in Turbulent Times." *Harvard Business Review*, Vol. 87, No. 6, June, 2009, pp. 79–86.

Shallcross, D. J. *Teaching Creativity Behavior—How to Evoke Creativity in Children of All Ages*. Bearly Limited, Buffalo, NY, 1985.

Simon, E. S., McKeough, D. T., Ayers, A. D., Rinehart, E., and Alexia, B. "How Do You Best Organize for Radical Innovation?" *Research-Technology Management*, Vol. 46, No. 5, September–October, 2003, pp. 17–20.

Snyder, S. *Brainstorming—The Science and Politics of Opiate Research*. Harvard University Press, Cambridge, MA, 1989.

Stevens, G. A. and Swogger, K. "Creating a Winning R&D Culture—I." *Research-Technology Management*, Vol. 52, No. 1, January–February, 2009, pp. 35–49.

Vandemark, N. L. *Breaking Barriers to Everyday Creativity: A Practical Guide for Expanding Your Creative Horizons*. Creative Education Foundation Press, Buffalo, NY, 1991.

VanGundy, A. B., Jr. *Getting to Innovation: How Asking the Right Questions Generates the Great Ideas Your Company Needs*. American Management Association, New York, 2007.

VanGundy, A. B., Jr. *Techniques of Structured Problem Solving*, 2nd ed. Van Nostrand Reinhold, New York, 1988.

Von Oech, R. A. *A Whack on the Side of the Head: How You Can Be More Creaitve*. Warner Books, New York, 1983.

Waller, N. G., Bouchards, T. J., Lykken, D. T., Tellegen, A., and Blacker, D. M. "Creative, Heritability, Familiarity: Which Word Does Not Belong?" *Psychological Inquiry*, Vol. 4, 1993, pp. 235–237.

Wang, S. "The Power of Magical Thinking—Research Shows the Importance of Imagination in Children's Cognitive Development." *Wall Street Journal*, December 22, 2009.

Wolff, M. F. "Managing Large Egos in Best of Managers at Work." *Selected Papers from Research Management*, Industrial Research Institute, New York, 1981–1986.

CHAPTER 10

POINTERS ON MANAGING PROJECTS AND DECISIONS

PROJECT SUPPORT

Angela was chatting with her colleague Carolyn one day, when Carolyn excused herself and went to meet with another project leader who had just walked into the lab. He was apparently dropping off some samples, and Angela heard him say, "Hey, give me a call when you have the data—I need it at the latest by Friday."

As he walked out of the lab, Carolyn turned and rolled her eyes. She commented, "Don't worry Ang, your samples always come first." Surprised, Angela said she appreciated her support and asked why Carolyn ran her samples as a priority.

What might Carolyn have told her?

Have you been on a project where team members stayed motivated and helped each other? What about projects where this didn't happen? What were the differences?

Are you more likely to behave as Angela did with Carolyn—or like the guy who dropped off the samples? Have you experienced benefits or disadvantages of either?

See the end of this chapter for what Angela learned.

A Guide to Success for Technical Managers: Supervising in Research, Development, & Engineering, by Elizabeth Treher, David Piltz and Steven Jacobs
Copyright © 2011 John Wiley & Sons, Inc.

There are many excellent books on project management, resources from professional organizations such as the Project Management Institute, and successful simulations such as Foundations™—The Project Management Simulation to teach project management processes and tools. Having a basic understanding of project management benefits every technical manager, but the bottom line is—if you can't communicate, and work well with others, you will jeopardize your projects.

In most organizations today, certainly the larger ones, you can get help to use project management tools. Some companies assign individual project managers to project teams to handle administration and maintain project plans and updates. Others set up teams with co-leaders, one to deal with the project management aspects, the other to lead the science and technology. If you are lucky and have such support, work to develop your relationship and discuss how together you can best serve your project and the team by pooling your skills and interests. All those who work in a project environment need to develop skills in interpersonal communication, performance management, coaching, and the other topics addressed in this book. In fact, influencing project team members and their line management may well be your sole option. Most project teams are diverse, with members from many functions—individuals whom you are not likely to supervise or control directly. This carries with it new challenges stemming from a lot of responsibility and little authority.

It is tough to keep a team focused and maintain momentum and motivation given the other demands your team members are likely to face. Some may be on several projects or have major responsibilities to their line functions independent of their role on your project.

Helping to negotiate time and priorities is essential. Having taught project management to thousands of individuals and coached many project managers, it is clear that even those with Project Manager Professional (PMP) certification don't come guaranteed to be effective project managers. No matter how easy it is for you to use project planning tools—or figure out how a critical path may have changed—if you don't lead your team, influence stakeholders, and negotiate effectively, your project will suffer. It may die unnecessarily. It may also continue long after it should have been killed, which is perhaps even worse from an organizational point of view.

SO, WHAT CAN YOU DO?

The key points to remember are:

- Learn the basics of project management.
- Understand and take advantage of different approaches to project planning.
- Challenge what does not make sense.
- Consider the difference between risk and uncertainty.
- Look for ways to improve communication in your project.
- Use sound team decision-making principles.
- Avoid going for the "big bang" and prioritize and proceed incrementally.
- Be assertive, and work to kill a project that should die.
- Make timely decisions and use consensus wisely.

LEARN THE BASICS OF PROJECT MANAGEMENT

Understand the value and discipline of managing projects. Even if your role is that of a technical leader and you have an expert project manager's support on your projects, learn the principles, terms, and methodology of project management. Read at your leisure—lunch breaks or evenings. This isn't like saying learn quantum mechanics or nuclear physics in your spare time to understand and apply it. Start with the simple principles and processes of project management. Speak with project management experts in your organization or outside it and develop your project management network. Learn enough to know the benefits of project management and the ways it can help, or hinder, your projects.

UNDERSTAND AND TAKE ADVANTAGE OF DIFFERENT APPROACHES TO PROJECT PLANNING

Small, innovative organizations tend to have simple, informal planning systems that take ideas from anywhere in the organization. As technical organizations grow, planning systems get increasingly complex. Large organizations with mature product lines usually have formal, intricate systems that emphasize top-down, prescriptive planning.

There is no apparent correlation between complexity or formality of planning and future success. Evaluate your project plans considering the balance of prescriptive, contingent, adaptive approaches (Treher and Walker, 1996).

- *Prescriptive plans* give explicit instructions on how to reach an objective, providing little or no discretion.
- *Contingent plans* anticipate and devise a limited number of alternative subplans based on possible changes that could occur.
- *Adaptive or evolutionary plans* are useful when the number of possible forks down the road are so large that it is impractical or too costly, if not impossible, to plan for all of them. These plans postpone action until sufficient information is available to reduce future uncertainty.

Most plans contain elements of each. As uncertainty and rate of change increase, plans should move from prescriptive toward adaptive. High levels of uncertainty are most typical in discovery or exploratory research projects. Unfortunately, as pressure for results grows, managers in organizations of all sizes, with all types of projects, tend to rely on contingent or prescriptive plans. If your project has uncertainty, recognize it explicitly in the plan. Deal with it adaptively or with backup plans and help senior management understand that prescriptive planning in uncertain environments is not advantageous. It frequently causes unjustified speculation, wastes time, and gives a false sense of security. It also delays delivery of useful results and commits us publicly to a course of action that may be totally inappropriate to solve our problems. Adaptive planning allows us to modify our approaches and respond more rapidly as we learn.

We often use adaptive planning successfully in our personal lives but ignore its power in our work. For example, when developing a new recipe, you could carefully plan all the ingredients and their exact amounts or create a general approach and taste and modify according to the result of the previous step. This latter approach builds improvements on the spot—perhaps after getting feedback from family members.

Adaptive planning has several advantages. It includes many small objectives and:

- is results versus process oriented.
- provides earlier delivery and so earlier feedback.
- results in earlier detection of problem areas and minimizes wasted resources.
- builds in the expectation and a formal protocol of making modifications, reducing the likelihood of getting overly attached to an unworkable plan.

CHALLENGE WHAT DOES NOT MAKE SENSE

Be willing to speak up. This applies to all technical managers, project leaders, and team members. Those who have worked in basic research and discovery, working in uncharted territory, know the futility of presenting a complete project plan with defined milestones and dates—especially when they are several years away. Not only does this waste time, it has been clearly shown to significantly extend project time and costs.

Use project management planning that fits with the types of projects you work on. Consider and present alternative project management approaches that make sense for your project. Challenge plans that do not support your current project. Use active listening and other techniques described in this book to effectively make your point. For example, use an adaptive approach where you have high levels of uncertainty. This doesn't mean you don't plan. It means you plan based on what you now know and need to discover next. Once you have that data you'll be in a better position to evaluate options and decide on the next fork in the road. Again, plan for that.

CONSIDER THE DIFFERENCE BETWEEN RISK AND UNCERTAINTY

Be able to communicate those differences and explain how they impact your project. You can quantify risk but not uncertainty. Risk is represented by a normal Gaussian curve while a Cauchy (Lorentz) distribution is associated with uncertainty. Look for sources of uncertainty that you face on a project. If you are doing discovery research or working in early development, you are likely to be primarily in uncharted, uncertain territory. In other project areas there may be numerous sources of uncertainty, such as missing or unreliable data, conflicting results, and confusing information. Begin by identifying these sources and then explore tactics to handle them.

You might:

- Delay a decision until you have more information.
- Increase your monitoring.
- Make assumptions or accept the uncertainty and move ahead.
- Simplify your plan or modify your approach.

Application

Consider a project or one aspect of the project. First, list the areas of uncertainty. Then explore the tactics you might use to learn more and reduce the uncertainty.

Things with Uncertainty	Potential Tactics

LOOK FOR WAYS TO IMPROVE COMMUNICATION IN YOUR PROJECT

Although we include a chapter on managing groups, teams, and meetings, there are additional techniques useful for team management in other chapters. Of the many studies done with different types of technical projects and organizations, the major reasons for project failure always includes communication. In addition, Treher and Mead (2006) describe specific project launch and ongoing enhancement approaches to build effective project communication from the beginning.

Clues that there are potential communication issues include:

- Speaking in acronyms: Make your team a model for clear communication. Some companies speak almost exclusively in acronyms. If yours is one, set up an acronym database or post terms and phrases on a flip chart. Ask all members to explain their acronyms and jargon, so others will learn and understand; if after explanations you are still confused, seek help while at the meeting.

- You use active listening, and in spite of this others roll their eyes or stop to explain to you what you really mean. Reassure the experts that you respect their opinion and need them on the team for that expertise. Ask questions to engage them as to why they feel or think the way they do. Ask them to give a short presentation to the whole team describing the work they are doing on the project and some of their challenges. Validate their challenges and add comments as appropriate to support the project moving forward.

- People shake their heads in disagreement or frustration. Stop the discussion and ask each person to say a word or two about what she or he is feeling or thinking; then have each suggest a solution or another approach. Often a few minutes up front will surface issues you need to hear. Glossing over or ignoring them is unlikely to make them go away. This also forestalls erroneous assumptions. Again, your goal is openness; and if a team member strongly disagrees, you need to understand the reasoning and decide for yourself.

AVOID GOING FOR THE BIG BANG— PRIORITIZE AND PROCEED INCREMENTALLY

Learn as you go and incorporate feedback (Gilb and Finzi, 1988). Build that learning into a revised project plan. Design specific elements and test as you go. If customers are involved, seek their feedback early and often. Don't wait till you have perfected a solution to find out it wasn't what they needed or wanted and wasn't even necessary. The same advice goes for stakeholders. This will help you surface problems early and help to resolve them or end a project sooner.

Prioritize

Prioritization is part of this. Consider priorities from the perspectives of the team, senior management, and your customers. We've already discussed a simple prioritization technique using colored dots where each member "votes" for a selected number of options based on ideas generated with the nominal group technique.

Use this approach in multiple ways. For example:

- Prioritizing potential solutions to a technical problem
- Deciding among options when you have limited development time or resources
- Finding a way to get an early product version out for expanded testing and market input

Related to nominal group technique approaches (and often done in conjunction with them) is a form of Pareto analysis. If you have many different problems to solve—or potential solutions— first group them into similar categories, such as thermal properties, and compare the number of cases of each type of problem or solution to prioritize your efforts.

Distinguish between Urgent and Important Activities

Avoid the classic tradition of letting urgent matters take priority over important ones. In organizations today, even in technical functions where we most need concerted time to think and carry out experiments and testing, our time is more and more fragmented. Many otherwise capable professionals allow the urgent to drive out the important activities. Effective technical managers always differentiate between the urgent and the important.

If you have many goals or subgoals, list them with all your tasks and decide which are urgent, which are important, and which are both urgent and important, and use your time accordingly. Discard all that are unimportant, even when they are things you enjoy.

Leverage Your Time

You may also need to evaluate your activities considering the time each will take. Concentrate on those that will give you the greatest "reward" in the least amount of time and start there.

By managing priorities and focusing your efforts on activities that are most likely to provide useful information in the shortest time, you will progress more quickly. If you couple this with also getting early input and feedback on your progress, you are less likely to fall into the big-bang trap. You won't have waited until the project is near completion, or is complete, before you learn what your "customers" have to say.

One element of Foundations™, a project management simulation The Learning Key® designed, forces teams to run a 10-minute pilot to test their project plans for implementation. From the beginning, participants know there will be pilot and productions runs, and that they will have time to re-plan between the two. Interestingly, almost no team ever uses the pilot to test a few alternative approaches. Typically, they make a plan, follow it, see mistakes, and make corrections. Rarely do they even generate multiple options before deciding on their approach. Considering several approaches up front saves time and resources, and we can speculate it will result in more innovative and successful products.

Hundreds of teams have participated in this simulation, and each of them vastly improved their plan, their implementation of the project, or both as demonstrated in their accomplishments during the 20-minute "production" run. Afterwards, most of the participants are able to identify opportunities that they had never previously considered to generate similar, early feedback for their own projects.

The Trap of Experience

Others (Sengupta, et al., 2008) have found, using a computer-based software development game, that "If not explicitly required to evaluate objectives, managers will continue to pursue the targets set at the outset of a project even when events render the targets inappropriate."

These authors suggest that revising targets is:

- Seen as an admission of failure in many companies.
- So strong a bias that it effects our decision making, even if the overall outcome is worse.

Their recommendations include providing more insights into relationships among variables. They also discuss pitfalls and remedies for what they describe as the "experience trap."

BE ASSERTIVE AND WORK TO KILL A PROJECT THAT SHOULD DIE

A recent survey of 22 life science companies found scientists worked, or knew those who worked, on goals that they did not believe added value and felt were likely to fail downstream (Acton and Andrews, 2006). Every organization has stories of projects that should have died but kept a life of their own. Some persisted to the point where multi-million-dollar plants were built and scrapped, or products known to be inferior to the competition were launched and soon withdrawn.

Staw and Ross (1989) describe four major drivers of "escalation situations," which are those where there remains a possibility of turning a project or course of action around by persevering (adding time, money, or effort).

These are:

- *Psychological factors* that lead to information processing errors and sunk costs that continue to influence subsequent decisions. Unfortunately, experiments have shown that people commit more resources, not fewer, to losing causes to justify or rationalize their previous behavior (Staw, 1976, cited in Staw and Ross, 1989).
- *Project variables* impact persistence in several ways, including whether an issue is considered temporary or permanent and the size of the ultimate payoff. Long delays between expenditures and financial returns may delay action, since losses are expected at the beginning and unlikely to raise concerns.

- *Social phenomena* include persisting so as not to admit a mistake to others (or to themselves). Fox and Staw (1979, cited in Staw and Ross, 1989) found that those in administrative roles with low job security or management support allocated the most resources to losing courses of action.
- *Organizational determinants* of persistence generate many of the most costly examples. Breakdowns in communication, slowness to respond, difficulty in altering existing policies or goals, political forces, and even the values and identity of an organization can drive projects to continue regardless of the economics involved.

When leading a project, facilitate open discussions of concerns and problems. If your team can't discover a potential solution, bring the issue up early to the senior manager. Use managing up techniques to ensure a successful conversation. The longer a project continues, the more entrenched it becomes, making it even harder to kill later.

USE CONSENSUS WISELY AND MAKE TIMELY DECISIONS

The key to successfully managing a project is the ability to make decisions and clarify whose decision it is. Chapter 9 describes a simple framework of four buckets, A through D, to clarify whose decision it is. As a project leader you will need to make decisions— sometimes on your own and perhaps more frequently with input from your team and others.

It is also important to remember, that having a feeling of influence is a critical motivator. Most of us understand the realities of organizational life and that there are decisions that are not ours to make. Even if we don't necessarily agree, we still need to support them. If you are willing to consider input, let your team members know. In that case, soliciting other's perspectives and carefully listening is likely to help with your decision. If, on the other hand, you have already made a decision, are unlikely to change your mind, or a decision has been made for you and you can no longer influence it, you should let your team know. Pretending to seek advice and then ignoring it will backfire. After you do make a decision, share the reasons for it, especially if the decision is not in line with the recommendations others have provided.

Strategies to Build Consensus

When you need to reach team consensus, as we discussed in Chapter 5, remember to:

- Listen to others' ideas.
- Ask questions to surface and explore reasons and concerns.
- Consider different opinions as helpful and build on ideas from all team members.
- Explain your thinking and perspectives.
- Approach a decision with logic and reason.
- Select ideas for merit without critiquing those you don't like.
- Don't make a decision until you have resolved team members' concerns so that everyone can live with the decision.

Avoid Classic Group Decision-Making Traps

No area of team interactions is more vulnerable to failure than group decision making. Don't agree just to avoid conflict—take steps to prevent groupthink. The Abilene paradox is a form of groupthink. It refers to the tendency of groups to take action that none of their members truly support. It was first described by Jerry Harvey (1974) based on a personal family experience. A trip to Abilene is an expedition that a group makes against the unspoken wishes of its members. Even if you think you will be the lone voice, speak up if you disagree with a decision. Others may agree with you but lack the courage to be the first one to say so.

The term *groupthink* comes from psychologist Irving L. Janis (1971). He observed the thinking that occurs when people are part of a cohesive group, and the desire for unanimity overrides their motivation to assess alternatives realistically. Janis noted that the groups he studied were unable to see beyond their own narrow focus, to consider alternatives and to foresee how their course of action could seriously threaten, and in some cases destroy, the groups' own goals and principles. In each case there was an extreme desire to please one another and to be team players.

Symptoms of groupthink include self-censorship, creating pressure to convey that disagreement is not acceptable or perhaps disloyal, stereotyping other groups, and using "us versus them" arguments. A classic behavior is providing summarizing statements, assuming there is agreement, and no one speaks up.

Remember that some of the symptoms of groupthink may be common practices outside the United States or related to MBTI preferences. In Asian cultures, for example, behaviors such as not wanting the leader to lose face, preferring not to stick out in a crowd, and not sharing thoughts that might be construed as impolite can lead to groupthink. From a Type perspective, introverts also prefer not to stick out, and those with a preference for feeling often avoid saying things that could generate disharmony.

Suggestions for avoiding groupthink include maintaining an open climate and avoiding isolation. As a leader of the group, avoid being too directive. When you meet, have members play the role of devil's advocate or critical evaluator.

There are many, simple, structured decision-making tools. Examples to help look at problems and decisions from different perspectives are the MBTI Z-model and DeBono's six thinking hats. Since most of us have standard ways of approaching decisions, both techniques improve decision making by having us consider different elements.

The six hats each represent a different style of thinking:

- *White hat*: focuses on the data you have and the knowledge you are missing and past trends or historical data.
- *Red hat*: looks at a decision with intuition and emotion—how others will respond when they don't fully understand your perspective.
- *Black hat*: looks for flaws and reasons that something will not work.
- *Yellow hat*: promotes positive thinking and looking at the benefits and value of a decision.
- *Green hat*: is the creative, idea-generating process to develop possible solutions.
- *Blue hat*: is for facilitation and control; it helps to redirect to other hats as the situation warrants.

The Modified Z

An MBTI tool, the Z-model, also helps to broaden input for considering a decision by using our four preferences of sensing, intuition, thinking, and feeling. Since we each are typically biased toward our own two favorites (N or S) and (T or F), we tend not to use all four equally. In a group setting, we are more likely to have members whose preferences are different from ours. We recommend changing this model slightly to The Learning Key's approach by reordering the first two steps. We call it the modified Z.

Most problem-solving and decision-making approaches (as the white hat) begin by looking at what we know, the data we have or need to get, and the existing literature and information on the subject. This immediately puts us into a context of the past and can be a limitation in trying to come up with creative ideas and new solutions. By starting with the idea-generating step, regardless of the past, we are more likely to broaden our context and break free of historical constraints. To build on these differences in decision making, try the following approach.

The Learning Key's Modified Z

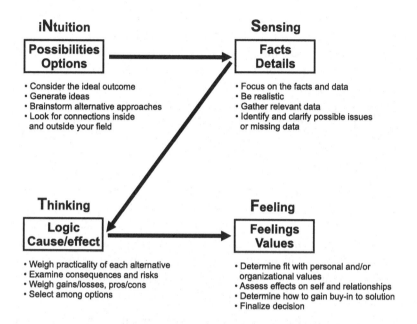

iNtuition

| Possibilities |
| Options |

• Consider the ideal outcome
• Generate ideas
• Brainstorm alternative approaches
• Look for connections inside
  and outside your field

Sensing

| Facts |
| Details |

• Focus on the facts and data
• Be realistic
• Gather relevant data
• Identify and clarify possible issues
  or missing data

Thinking

| Logic |
| Cause/effect |

• Weigh practicality of each alternative
• Examine consequences and risks
• Weigh gains/losses, pros/cons
• Select among options

Feeling

| Feelings |
| Values |

• Determine fit with personal and/or
  organizational values
• Assess effects on self and relationships
• Determine how to gain buy-in to solution
• Finalize decision

Start with Intuition

Using intuition and idea-generating techniques gives us a large pool from which to begin to analyze and evaluate. When you start with intuition, you are much more likely to generate ideas in an environment free of past experiences and issues so that you have a more positive orientation. There are several idea-generating techniques and references in Chapter 9 on innovation and creativity.

Apply Sensing

Next, our sensing helps us to focus on the current data. This is the information we have now. Then consider what you need to collect and review. By focusing on hard facts, current data, missing information, and resources, you bring reality to ideas generated by intuition in the first step. This grounds the process and sets the foundation for potential solutions to be evaluated next in the thinking step.

Use Thinking

Once we have spent time with sensing and intuition, we can move on to an objective analysis, look at pros and cons, risks and opportunities, and analyze the information. This is where many of us stop. We come to a decision based on the information we collect from sensing or intuition. Assuming we are able to carry out a plan, we begin implementation. Effective problem solvers do not fall into this trap—they go on to step 4.

Using Feeling

The fourth step, using our feeling function, is also critical. It will help us look at our decision early on from other viewpoints while we can consider their impact and plan an approach. What might be the perspective of the final customers, subcontractors, senior managers, the board of directors, and other groups and individuals? It helps to remind us we are likely to need to plan how we will influence those others to gain or keep their support.

This can help us avoid classic mistakes in influencing such as:

- Advising before understanding
- Attempting to build/rebuild relationships without changing our conduct or attitude
- Assuming that good intentions and relationships are sufficient.

To begin the process of influence, know the outcomes/results you want, identify your resources and the alliances you will need, consider how your perceptions may differ, and plan how you will build rapport.

PROJECT SUPPORT—SUGGESTIONS

Carolyn's answer to Angela's question about why she ran her samples first was, "I know how my work impacts your project and why my analysis is important. You always fill me in and keep me up to date, and I really appreciate that. I feel like I am a part of your team."

Angela's own excitement and interest in sharing her work was simply the way she operated. She'd never considered how this sharing had helped her to build a team member's motivation. In thinking about other project leaders' comments, she also realized that most of them saw Carolyn as providing a required service and didn't really see her as a team member.

Build your relationships—they are likely to help you as much as your technical expertise. As author Ben Sweetland says, "We cannot hold a torch to light another's path without brightening our own" (www.wisdomquotes.com ©1995–2009 Jone Johnson Lewis).

REFERENCES

Acton, G., and Andrews, T. "Impeding Scientist's Productivity." *Research-Technology Management*, Vol. 49, No. 5, September–October, 2006, pp. 59–60.

Demarest, L. *Looking at Type™ in the Workplace*. Center for Applications for Psychological Type, Gainesville, FL, 1997, pp. 40–42.

Domhoff, G. W. *The Scientific Study of Dreams: Neural Networks, Cognitive Development, and Content Analysis*. American Psychological Association (APA), Washington, D.C., 2003.

Gilb, T., and Finzi, S. *Principles of Software Engineering Management*. Addison-Wesley Professional/Pearson Education, Ltd., London, UK, 1988.

Goleman, D. *Emotional Intelligence: Why It Can Matter More Than IQ*. Bantam Books, New York, 1995.

Hallowell, E. *CrazyBusy: Overstretched, Overbooked and About to Snap*. Ballantine Books, New York, 2006.

Harvey, J. B. "The Abilene Paradox: The Mismanagement of Agreement." *Organizational Dynamics*, Summer 1974, pp. 63–80.

Janis, I. *Groupthink: Psychological Studies of Policy Decisions and Fiascoes* (2nd edition). Houghton Mifflin, Boston, 1983.

Klein, G. *Intuition At Work*. Doubleday, New York, 2003.

Lawrence, G. *People Types and Tiger Stripes: A Practical Guide to Learning Styles*, 3rd ed., Center for Applications for Psychological Type, Gainesville, FL, 1993, pp. 161–163.

Locke, E. A., and Latham, G. *Goal Setting: A Motivational Technique That Works*. Prentice Hall, Englewood Cliffs, NJ, 1984.

Sengupta, K., Abdel-Jamid, T. K., and Van Wassenhove, L. N. "The Experience Trap." *Harvard Business Review*, Vol. 86, No. 2, February, 2008, pp. 94–101.

Staw, B. M., and Ross, J. "Understanding Behavior in Escalation Situations." *Science*, Vol. 246, No. 4927, October, 1989, pp. 216–220.

Stone, L. "Living with Continuous Partial Attention." From the article "The Harvard Business Review List of Breakthrough Ideas for 2007." *Harvard Business Review*, Vol. 85, No. 2, February 2007, pp. 28–29.

Treher, E., and Mead, M. *Strategic Partnering, A Five-Stage Process to Improve Strategic Alliances and Outsourcing Relationships.* The Learning Key, Inc., Washington Crossing, PA, 2006.

Treher, E., and Walker, A. C. *Managing Technical Groups.* A program from The Learning Key, Inc., Washington Crossing, PA, 1996.

Wiseman, R. *The Luck Factor: The Four Essential Principles.* Miramax Books/Hyperion, New York, 2003.

BIBLIOGRAPHY

Brousseau, K. R., Driver, M., Hourihan, G., and Larsson, R. "The Seasoned Executive's Decision-Making Style." *Harvard Business Review*, Vol. 84, No. 2, February, 2006, pp. 110–121.

Cohen, A., and Bradford, D. *Influence without Authority.* Wiley, New York, 1991.

Collins, J. *Good to Great: Why Some Companies Make the Leap ... and Others Don't.* Harper Collins, New York, 2001.

Covey, S. R. *Principle-Centered Leadership.* Fireside/Simon & Schuster, New York, 1992.

Crum, T. *The Magic of Conflict—Turning a Life of Work into a Work of Art.* Touchstone/Simon and Schuster, New York, 1988.

Dawson, R. *The Confident Decision Maker.* William Morrow, New York, 1993.

Drucker, P. "What Executives Should Remember." *Harvard Business Review*, Vol. 84, No. 2, February, 2006, pp. 145–153.

Fisher, R., and Ury, W. *Getting to Yes, Negotiating Agreement without Giving in.* Houghton Mifflin, New York, 1981.

Gladwell, M. *Blink: The Power of Thinking without Thinking.* Little, Brown, New York, 2005.

Green, M. *The Project Manager's Partner: A Step-by-Step Guide to Project Management.* HRD Press, Amherst, MA, 2002.

Hurson, T. *Think Better.* McGraw Hill, New York, 2008.

Kash, D. E., and Rycroft, R. W. "To Manage Complex Innovation, Ask the Right Questions." *Research-Technology Management*, Vol. 46, No. 5, September–October, 2003, pp. 29–33.

Klein, G., Orasanu, J., Calderwood, R., and Zsambok, C. E. *Decision Making in Action: Models and Methods.* Ablex, Norwood, NJ, 1993.

Klein, G. *Intuition at Work, Why Developing Your Gut Instincts Will Make You Better at What You Do.* Doubleday, New York, 2003.

Klein, G. *Sources of Power: How People Make Decisions.* MIT Press, Cambridge, MA, 1998.

Lewis, A. *The Seven Minute Difference: Small Steps to Big Changes.* Kaplan, Chicago, 2006.

Luecke, R. *Power, Influence, and Persuasion: Sell Your Ideas and Make Things Happen.* Harvard Business Essentials, Harvard Business School, Boston, 2005.

Miller, J. *The Question Behind the Question: Practicing Personal Accountability in Work and Life.* Denver Press, Denver, CO, 2001.

Patterson, K., Grenny, J., McMillan, R., and Switzler, A. *Crucial Conversations: Tools for Talking When Stakes Are High*. McGraw-Hill, New York, 2002.

Rogers, P., Blenko, M., Pfeffer, J., Sutton, R. I., Mankins, M. C., Steele, R., Bazerman, M. H., Chugh, D., and Davenport, T. H. "Decision Making Better, Faster, Smarter." *Harvard Business Review* Vol. 84, No. 1, January, 2006, pp. 52–126.

Schwartz, P. *The Art of the Long View*. Doubleday, New York, 1991.

Sweetland, B. www.wisdomquotes.com; ©1995–2009 Jone Johnson Lewis and in www.wisdomquotes.com.

Treher, E., and Walker, A. C. *Technical Planning*. A program from The Learning Key, Inc., Washington Crossing, PA, 1996.

Treher, E. *Foundations™—The Project Management Simulation*. The Learning Key, Inc., Washington Crossing, PA, 2008; www.thelearningkey.com.

Ury, W. *Getting Past No, Negotiating Your Way from Confrontation to Cooperation*. Bantam, New York, 1993.

VanGundy, A. B., Jr. *Getting to Innovation: How Asking the Right Questions Generates the Great Ideas Your Company Needs*. American Management Association, New York, 2007.

www.pmi.org for PMP and other professional project management-related certifications.

Zuker, E. *The Seven Secrets of Influence*. McGraw-Hill, New York, 1991.

CHAPTER 11

SUGGESTIONS FOR MANAGING UP

MANAGING UP STORIES

Decision Making

Joe was new to the company, and in a few short weeks he'd become very frustrated with his manager, Art, and his constant redirection. Art seemed to change his mind daily and never thought they had enough data. Joe's university days were behind him, and he wanted to make progress quickly; from his perspective, there wasn't enough time to use all conceivable methods for collecting analytical data after they had enough information to make a decision and move forward. At least data collection shouldn't hold up a decision to move ahead.

Art was the opposite. He liked to run every experiment imaginable. Joe began to see why there had been no new products out of this lab in the last 6 years. Joe turned to Art's manager, the company president, who told him he had to deal with these issues on his own. The question was how?

What should Joe do?

Should Joe have gone to Art's manager?

How would you coach Joe to manage his manager?

See the end of this chapter for what actually happened.

Changing Schedules

LaKeesha had been reporting to her boss for about one year, although she had known her for several years and they had become friends.

A Guide to Success for Technical Managers: Supervising in Research, Development, & Engineering, by Elizabeth Treher, David Piltz and Steven Jacobs Copyright © 2011 John Wiley & Sons, Inc.

Others in the department had worked there longer and had different roles, but they worked together as a team fairly well. The one issue they all faced with their boss was the last-minute meetings she would call—often with no more than a couple of hours notice. Since LaKeesha dealt primarily with contractors and others outside their organization, her schedule was usually booked well in advance. This was also true for a number of others in the department. Yet everyone else dropped whatever they had scheduled and went to the boss's meeting. Some made side comments about LaKeesha's "lack of commitment." Others simply said they wouldn't dare miss a meeting because they were afraid of the consequences.

LaKeesha attended when she could, but infrequently. She knew her boss counted on her to manage these external relationships and keep the projects on track, and she felt she could defend her choices, if asked.

> Would you have attended the staff meetings, if you were LaKeesha?
>
> Were her co-workers correct about her lack of commitment?
>
> Was she managing her boss appropriately?
>
> *See the end of this chapter to learn what happened.*

Screaming Boss

Shortly after joining a new company, Henry began getting not-so-subtle messages from his boss, Andre, that he was not welcome. Andre seemed to go out of his way to shoot down Henry's ideas and to dismiss what he said in front of others. Andre had a reputation for not accepting other's ideas, and Henry quickly saw why he got no participation in meetings. Andre had even screamed at Henry when he was working in the lab with two of his techs. Once he was so loud and belligerent that Henry left the lab, went to his office, picked up his laptop, and drove home in the middle of the afternoon.

> How would you handle this manager?
>
> *See the end of this chapter to learn what happened.*

Your boss may not need to develop the sense of urgency that Art seems to lack, call frequent last-minute meetings, or scream at you, but does your working relationship benefit you both?

Do you understand your boss's goals and concerns and how you can best support him or her? What are they?

Are you able to speak openly and will you get an equally candid response?

Far too often, we don't think about managing our boss at all—unless we have a specific concern. To some, it sounds manipulative. However, impressing your boss and managing to appear in a more favorable, but inaccurate light, is not the goal.

BUILD YOUR RELATIONSHIP

Learning about your manager's goals and priorities can help you each to be more successful. It can certainly provide insight into how to prioritize your own time and help you make a lasting contribution. A better understanding of how your boss prefers to work can improve your efficiency and relationship. Learning how and when to communicate can help establish ways of working together, help develop a trusting relationship, and probably will expand the freedom you have to work. To be effective in your job, you need to build a successful working relationship with your boss.

> ## To be effective in your job, build a successful working relationship with your boss.

Consider the following:

In what ways do your styles support each other?

How do your strengths and weaknesses compare?

If you have both taken the Myers–Briggs Type Indicator, how can you strengthen your "team of two?"

In what ways are you similar? In what ways do you differ?

What is important to your manager?

How does your boss prefer to communicate? How will you keep him/her informed?

MANAGE COMMUNICATION

Managing your boss is similar to managing your staff. The approaches you use with your staff, whether managing performance or working to improve communication, work with your boss as well.

Ask yourself if you clearly understand his/her:

Goals and objectives

How can you best support them?

Priorities

How can you run interference, if necessary, and keep things on track?

Communication preferences

How often do you need to provide updates? What works the best?

Your approach may be different for every manager in your career. For example, Carolyn had three distinctly different managers in her first three jobs. The first felt the need for almost constant contact to get updates on progress. He called her at home, at any time of the day; sometimes at 5 AM and sometimes at midnight. He called when she was across town beginning a 24-hour experiment, he called the lab when she'd returned to process the radioactive target and she had no time to talk. He rarely waited for others to call him. Although she was annoyed, she recognized that he was very interested in the work and that he couldn't wait to hear the latest; a colleague thought he didn't trust her and was trying to check up. Carolyn had the phone removed from the lab to stop the interruptions and have an excuse not to answer it. Certainly, there were better solutions, but the one Carolyn chose solved the immediate problem and gave her the time she needed to do her research. As soon as she was able, she called him to give him updates—and keep him informed.

Her next manager avoided communication with her entirely and went directly to her staff. When she stopped in to talk, he typically picked up the phone to make a call or he left for a meeting. Both she and her employees asked to schedule update meetings, so they could avoid interruptions during experiments. At first he found reasons not to be available and continued to wander in the lab; however, with time, this approach worked. The regular meetings helped them all gain better control of their schedules and improved communication.

Her third manager knew he had the job that Carolyn had applied for, and he expected resistance. She stopped in his office most mornings, and over coffee together, she kept him up to speed on what was going on. He was open to her frequent updates, and their conversations were always enjoyable. They learned from each other. He saw to it that she got one of the largest bonuses in the organization each year she reported to him.

These are real situations encountered by the same person, dealing with three different managers. The examples show that we may face many unexpected challenges in learning to work productively with our managers. To be successful ourselves and with the employees we supervise, we need to develop effective communication channels with our own managers. It isn't optional. In addition, accepting the challenge of working with a difficult boss can be a powerful development experience that will help you in the future in many unforeseen ways.

Your job as a technology manager requires being able to understand others and help them to be more effective. This includes your staff *and* your manager. When we introduced this book, we noted how few of those who have taken our workshops have said they have worked for one or more excellent managers. The odds are you will likely work with a few who don't fall into the "excellent" category.

To be effective, if you happen to have a less-than-skilled boss, you need to find ways to change the situation. This means knowing what is most important to you. If you have a lot of ideas and want to see them implemented, then giving your boss credit for the idea might be required if she or he likes taking credit. In one laboratory, the department head routinely shot down ideas suggested at meetings, unless he had voiced them himself. He, on the other hand, was rarely challenged and many in the group were very frustrated; progress was slow. The group leader realized that making progress on her ideas was more important to her than getting credit for them, so her choice was simple: She gave the ideas away. After a meeting, when her idea was rejected with "we don't have the budget" or "that's too risky" or "it doesn't sound very plausible to me"—she waited a few days. Then, when she passed her boss in the corridor or went to his office, she would comment, "I've been thinking about X," where X is the idea that he had rejected, "I think you were the one who brought it up. It seems like it might be a viable approach, perhaps we should try it." In 4 years, every single time when she used this type of an approach and presented an idea back to her manager as his idea, she got the approval to move ahead. Some of her staff were upset that he was getting the credit, but she explained that getting the ideas implemented was most important to her, and that over time they would all have some degree of credit. On hearing that story, some might call it manipulation, but she felt it was meeting both their needs: hers to get something going, and his to have credit, the essence of managing up. Both were happy.

What benefits do you see in improving your own relationship with your boss? Even if you have a good relationship, if something changed—could it be better?

This doesn't mean kiss up. Many of us in the technical world have kiss-up radar that will immediately activate. Avoid complaining about your employees or colleagues and stick to the issues.

Bring suggested solutions for discussion. Griping about others will lose you points that can be tough to regain. If you can't come up with a solution, approach your boss to discuss your concerns; seek coaching support by asking questions. How do you think I could handle this? Have you faced this before? What did you do? Whenever possible, communicate face-to-face or by phone, even if your boss is half-way around the world and you have to set your alarm for 3 AM; don't rely on email for important conversations.

Keep confidences. If your boss says he or she is going to leave the company or is having problems at home—don't share this information with others.

Go out of your way to support your boss. This doesn't fall into the kiss-up category but into "I'm a team player and she or he is the leader." This can be difficult for some of us to do, especially if we feel our boss is an incompetent moron, so stay silent rather than complain. If you are having issues with your manager, do not share them with your employees or others in your group. Keep it between the two of you, and look for a resolution.

GUIDELINES TO APPROACH YOUR BOSS

If you are uncertain about how to approach your boss and how to discuss a topic, use the following guidelines for a performance management conversation you might have with one of your staff. The principles are the same.

1. *Plan.* How can you describe your concern in an objective way? Avoid interpretations and conclusions and share your observations. Consider how your manager might be viewing the same situation. What is most important to you? What might be most important to him/her?

2. Meet and *describe your concern in an objective way*; follow up with your expectations. For example, "I expected to be able to lead the project independently. You have attended all the project meetings and taken over running them. Have I misunderstood my role? Is there something I need to be doing differently? The team is now looking to you as the project manager."

3. *Ask questions* to explore the causes. This valuable technique is also useful to defuse conflict. Observing an individual in

line to pay a service bill for his car provided a good example of this. The manager behind the counter was yelling—at the customer ahead and at folks in the back no one could see. As each person approached, the manager seemed to get nastier and louder and was a perfect commercial for how not to manage customer service. Most people responded by raising their voices as well. However, when one individual finally got to the front of the line and received another loud shout of "What do you want?" he seemed to look the service manager directly in the eye and said quietly "Have I done something to offend you?" The man stopped instantly and looked shocked, almost as if he hadn't been aware of his behavior. He quickly apologized and his voice and tone dropped to normal. Questions have enormous power. Experience the difference between "What am I doing wrong?" and "How can I do this differently?" by asking yourself these questions. Can you see the advantages of the latter for you, your employees, and your boss?

4. *Generate possible solutions.* Again, use questions. Questions engage each person in a way that suggests information gathering. They do not initially put others on the defensive if you use them to understand each other. To quote Eugene Ionesco: "It is not the answer that enlightens, but the question."

5. *Agree on specific actions.* Record them and follow through. The next time you need to hold a conversation, use the record and the updates as a starting point.

When you prepare to meet with your manager, expect to get some feedback. If you don't, ask for it. Remember the following guidelines on receiving feedback.

GUIDELINES FOR RECEIVING FEEDBACK

☐ The simplest response to feedback is "Thank you." Thank you does not say that you agree with the comments. It simply states you have heard and will take the information into account.

☐ Avoid justification. Do not "explain." If you jump into an explanation, no matter how legitimate it is, you are going to appear defensive. You can always check with others to see if they have a similar impression, but for now, you need to prove that you have heard the feedback and are taking it seriously. Respond only to clarify and to ensure you have understood. "Would you mind repeating that?" or "Let me see if I understand what you are saying. You believe that …"

☐ Ask for an example. This will not only buy you time to think about it, perhaps calm down, and to understand the issue better, but also they can explain the feedback. For example, "Could you give me an example of when you see me cutting people off?"

☐ End by summarizing to check (and to show) that you understood the point that was made. "Let us summarize the feedback. You said …"

The better you can respond calmly and openly to feedback that you perceive as negative, the more you are likely to hear what you need to know. The following story about the walrus makes this point very well (American Management Association, 1961).

The Ill-Informed Walrus

"How's it going down there?" barked the big walrus from his perch on the highest rock near the shore. He waited for the good word.

Down below, the smaller walruses conferred hastily among themselves. Things weren't going well at all, but none of them wanted to break the news to the Old Man. He was the biggest and wisest walrus in the herd, and he knew his business—but he did hate to hear bad news. And he had such a terrible temper that every walrus in the herd was terrified of his ferocious bark.

"What will we tell him?" whispered Basil, the second-ranking walrus. He well remembered how the Old Man had raved and ranted at him the last time the herd caught less than its quota of herring, and he had no desire to go through that experience again. Nevertheless, the walruses had noticed for several weeks that the water level in the nearby Arctic bay had been falling constantly, and it had become necessary to travel much farther to catch the dwindling supply of herring. Someone should tell the Old Man; he would probably know what to do. But who? And how?

Finally, Basil spoke up: "Things are going pretty well, chief" he said. The thought of the receding waterline made his heart feel heavy, but he went on: "As a matter of fact, the beach seems to be getting larger."

The Old Man grunted. "Fine, fine," he said. "That will give us a bit more elbow room." He closed his eyes and continued basking in the sun.

The next day brought more trouble. A new herd of walruses moved in down the beach, and with the supply of herring dwindling this invasion could be dangerous. No one wanted to tell the Old Man, though only he could take the steps necessary to meet this new competition.

Reluctantly, Basil approached the big walrus, who was still sunning himself on the large rock. After some small talk, he said, "Oh by the way, Chief. A new herd of walruses seems to have moved into our territory." The Old Man's eyes snapped open, and he filled his great lungs in preparation for a mighty bellow, but Basil added quickly, "Of course, we don't anticipate any trouble. They don't look like herring-eaters to me—more likely interested in minnows. And as you know, we don't bother with minnows ourselves."

The Old Man let out the air with a long sigh. "Good, good," he said. "No point in our getting excited over nothing, then, is there?"

Things didn't get any better in the weeks that followed. One day, peering down from the large rock, the Old Man noticed that part of his herd seemed to be missing. Summoning Basil, he grunted peevishly, "What's going on, Basil? Where is everybody?" Poor Basil didn't have the courage to tell the Old Man that many of the younger walruses were leaving every day to join the new herd. Clearing his throat nervously, he said, "Well, Chief, we've been tightening things up a bit. You know, getting rid of some of the dead wood. After all, a herd is only as good as the walruses in it."

"Run a tight ship, I always say," the Old Man grunted. "Glad to hear that everything's going so well."

Before long, everyone but Basil had left to join the new herd, and Basil realized that the time had come to tell the Old Man the facts. Terrified but determined, he flopped up to the large rock. "Chief," he said, "I have bad news. The rest of the herd has left you."

The old walrus was so astonished that he could not even work up a good bellow. "Left me?" He cried. "All of them? But why? How could this happen?" Basil didn't have the heart to tell him, so he merely shrugged helplessly.

"I can't understand it," the old walrus said. "And just when everything was going so well!"

MORAL: *What you like to hear isn't always what you need to know.*

At times, especially with some managers, it can be very tough to share what you really need to say. It can be easier to choose not to hold a tough conversation because it feels safer. We may hope it goes away or doesn't become an issue, but the more this happens, the more likely you will someday find yourself in Basil's position. If you find yourself in the habit of backing down or not initiating potentially difficult conversations, step back and assess the short-term and long-term impact on you, your manager, and your organization. If others are involved, perhaps they can help serve as a sounding board by sharing their perspectives and challenging yours. This will build your confidence and perhaps give you insights into better ways to hold the conversation. There may also be a different way of looking at the situation that you hadn't considered. Managing up isn't only for the moment, it's for the future as well. As you build your relationship with your manager, it will become easier to hold difficult conversations.

MANAGING UP STORIES—RESOLVED

Decision Making

Joe decided to take a management skills workshop. He went asking "Can you help me manage my boss?" Although Joe's team was enthusiastic about working with him, and in his short tenure he'd set up productive weekly team and one-on-one meetings for individual discussions and coaching, he felt he needed to find a way to work with his manager, Art.

During the workshop, he learned about the MBTI, and Joe began to realize a number of his issues with Art could be Type related. Joe and the rest of the team liked closure and using experimental results to design the next experiments. Art, on the other hand, seemed to get stressed after making decisions and frequently reversed them.

After the training, Joe asked the department and Art to take the MBTI. He thought it could be a tool to help them talk about their differences. They participated in a facilitated session to discuss the results. When they talked about decision making Art laughed and said, "That's the part of my job that I hate." Joe was thinking, "That is your job," but didn't say it. All laughed and no ones preferences changed, but the group interactions began to improve immediately. Art commented on how his approach differed from the others and the group saw there could be value in not always rushing ahead. Everyone began to relax and laugh as they discussed how past issues linked to their preferences. The meeting was short, but the result was positive and long lasting.

Outcome   When Art changed his mind or asked for additional data, Joe and his staff felt comfortable challenging him and found Art often agreed with them. At other times, Art convinced them to hold off until they had more data. Joe led the group to their first patent-protected new product one year later.

Changing Schedules

Should LaKeesha have attended the staff meetings? No. Based on her understanding of her manager's priorities and the importance of maintaining good relationships with contractors, canceling meetings, especially at the last minute when they were traveling to meet with her, was not a reasonable consideration. LaKeesha could have handled the meetings in several different ways. Assuming she had a conversation with her manager to discuss her reasoning for skipping the meetings, she could meet with anyone who attended to get an update, read the minutes—if any—or try to help her manager understand the consequences of rearranging everyone's schedule. Although last-minute meetings might be needed on occasion, they shouldn't be a way of life.

Actual   LaKeesha and her manager spoke and agreed that when others were involved, she should not change her schedule to attend a department meeting. Others in the department knew this, but remained fearful there might be repercussions. Neither LaKeesha nor her manager viewed her decision to skip the manager's meeting as a lack of commitment on her part. In fact, LaKeesha was highly regarded for her commitment to managing their contractor relationships and projects. Her boss began to give her greater latitude and to solicit her advice on a wider range of issues. However, over time, the spur of the moment meetings continued. LaKeesha sometimes wondered if the meetings were a test that she was the first to pass.

Screaming Boss

The next morning Henry went to his manager's office. "Can we talk calmly now?" was his first question. He then presented what he considered to be guidelines for a professional communication between a boss and a subordinate and they discussed them. They were:

> We speak to each other calmly.
>
> We discuss issues privately.
>
> We do not involve others, either directly or indirectly, unless we need to ask for outside help to resolve the issue.

He asked no questions about "Why did ...?" or "How could ...?", and the focus was looking ahead to a better relationship. The message was simple. "If we are going to work together, this has to change." It did. Andre never again yelled at him and their disagreements were civil. Henry had one advantage many of us don't. He wasn't afraid to quit his job and was confident he would find another, whatever the economic conditions were.

REFERENCES

American Management Association, "Fable for Managers." *Management Review*, October, 1961.

Domhoff, G. W. *The Scientific Study of Dreams: Neural Networks, Cognitive Development, and Content Analysis.* American Psychological Association (APA), Washington, D.C., 2003.

Goleman, D. *Emotional Intelligence: Why It Can Matter More Than IQ.* Bantam Books, New York, 1995.

Hallowell, E. *CrazyBusy: Overstretched, Overbooked and About to Snap.* Ballantine Books, New York, 2006.

Klein, G. *Intuition At Work*. Doubleday, New York, 2003.

Locke, E. A., and Latham, G. *Goal Setting: A Motivational Technique That Works*. Prentice Hall, Englewood Cliffs, NJ, 1984.

Stone, L. "Living with Continuous Partial Attention." From the article "The Harvard Business Review List of Breakthrough Ideas for 2007." *Harvard Business Review*, Vol. 85, No. 2, February 2007, pp. 28–29.

Wiseman, R. *The Luck Factor: The Four Essential Principles*. Miramax Books/ Hyperion, New York, 2003.

BIBLIOGRAPHY

Bossidy, L. "What Your Leader Expects of You." *Harvard Business Review*, Vol. 85, No. 4, April, 2007, pp. 58–65.

Gabarro, J. J., and Kotter, J. P. "Managing Your Boss." *HBR Classic, Harvard Business Review*, Vol. 83, No. 1, January, 2005, pp. 92–99.

Gabarro, J. J. "When a New Manager Takes Charge." *HBR Classic, Harvard Business Review*, Vol. 85, No. 1, January, 2007, pp. 104–117.

CHAPTER 12

LET'S USE IT RIGHT: A SUMMARY OF SUGGESTED APPROACHES

Other chapters covered transitions, motivation, communication, performance management, delegation, team and meeting leadership, managing up, innovation and creativity, and managing projects and decisions. In some cases we suggested steps or provided mnemonics to make it easier to remember. Here we summarize these elements for a quick review reference.

In coaching and delivering training to scientists and technologists over the years, we have worked with two general groups— those who like checklists, templates, and reminders and those who do not. This chapter is for those who do find such summaries helpful in implementing new techniques. Try them yourself or use with your staff and peers.

Our expectation is that you will modify these or create others to fit your own style and experiences. Reviewing the information here will serve as a reminder of steps we often omit in our haste to get to our "real work." Use your creativity and adapt them to your needs.

To introduce this book we said that communication is a theme. Another theme is creativity. Each of the roles you take, the individuals you manage, and the organizations you work in will differ; each will require flexibility, adaptability, and creativity. This means creativity in your science and technology—and creativity in how you manage others. Use your creativity to gain collaboration and build effective working groups. This means knowing your staff and what helps and doesn't. The story of the farmer and his horse, Buddy, illustrates this well (*Reader's Digest*, November, 2009):

A Guide to Success for Technical Managers: Supervising in Research, Development, & Engineering, by Elizabeth Treher, David Piltz and Steven Jacobs
Copyright © 2011 John Wiley & Sons, Inc.

A guy drives into a ditch, but luckily a farmer is there to help. He hitches his horse, Buddy, up to the car and yells, "Pull, Nellie, pull!" Buddy doesn't move.

"Pull, Buster, pull!" Buddy doesn't budge.

"Pull, Coco, pull!" Nothing.

Then the farmer says, "Pull, Buddy, pull!" And the horse drags the car out of the ditch.

Curious, the motorist asks the farmer why he kept calling his horse by the wrong name. "Buddy's blind," said the farmer. "And if he thought he was the only one pulling, he wouldn't even try."

As Peter Drucker (1985) said, "If I put a person into a job and he or she does not perform, I have made a mistake. I have no business blaming that person."

CHAPTER 1   TIPS ON TRANSITIONS FOR TECHNICAL MANAGERS

Four Keys to Making a Successful Managerial Transition
- ☐ Motivation to help others succeed
- ☐ Willingness to give credit to others
- ☐ Openness to other's ideas
- ☐ Interest in taking new roles

CHAPTER 2   ADVICE ON CREATING A MOTIVATING CLIMATE

Benefits to Develop a Motivating Environment
- ☐ Provide focus in spite of distractions
- ☐ Assist in problem solving
- ☐ Increase overall performance

Increasing Motivation Checklist

☐ Learn what motivates others.

☐ Expect success.

☐ Provide opportunities for personal and professional growth.

☐ Recognize accomplishments both formally and informally.

☐ Provide honest feedback and feedforward.

CHAPTER 3   HINTS TO INCREASE INTERPERSONAL EFFECTIVENESS

Modify your communication so that others understand. *In general, communicate with all Type preferences by:*

☐ Starting with a brief overview or conclusion.

☐ Presenting your information.

☐ Providing details only in supporting documents.

☐ Offering conclusions.

To communicate with thinkers:

☐ Plan and organize your presentation.

☐ Divide your comments into sections, "The implementation phase will involve three ..."

☐ Be specific. Rather than "In general, we find ...", try "More than seventy percent of the time, we find ..."

☐ Show you've considered alternatives; give pros and cons.

☐ Provide graphs, charts, or other summaries to support your data.

☐ Use bullets or outlines.

To communicate with feelers:

☐ Be informal.

☐ Use small talk and approach on a personal level.

☐ Show how others will use or benefit from what you are presenting.

To communicate with sensors:

☐ Be brief, focus on your main points, and avoid extraneous/side bar comments.

☐ Emphasize the impact of your approach.

☐ Use visual aids in presentations.

To communicate with intuitives:

☐ Be open to suggestions and new ideas.

☐ Seek their input (and plan extra time for this).

☐ Describe possibilities and the future value.

☐ Use trends.

Planning for a difficult conversation with RACES

Recognize the emotions.

Acknowledge the emotions.

Calm down by taking a few breaths.

Expectations are checked.

Share insights about yourself.

CHAPTER 4   CLUES ABOUT COMMUNICATION PITFALLS AND STRATEGIES

Active Listening Checklist (ADIR)

☐ Pay **Attention** to both verbal and nonverbal gestures.

☐ **Demonstrate** understanding by nonverbal cues and asking clarification questions.

- ☐ Show **Interest** by making eye contact.
- ☐ **Reflect** and share your thoughts.

Writing Effective Emails

- ☐ Start with a comment tied to the interests or prior message of the person you are addressing.
- ☐ Present your own comments.
- ☐ Provide your conclusion.
- ☐ Close.

CHAPTER 5   SECRETS TO MANAGING PERFORMANCE

Setting Goals

- ☐ Be specific.
- ☐ Set time limits.
- ☐ Specify how you will judge performance.
- ☐ Prioritize.
- ☐ Coordinate with other departments if applicable.

Performance Improvement Conversation Process

- ☐ Describe specific observations, not conclusions.
- ☐ Describe your expectations.
- ☐ Check that the employee is clear about expectations.
- ☐ Ask the employee for reasons and causes.
- ☐ Probe and ask questions to understand the employee's perspective.
- ☐ Discuss alternative solutions; ask first for the employee's ideas, without giving yours.
- ☐ Evaluate solutions though questions to help the employee think through advantages and disadvantages of specific approaches.
- ☐ Agree on actions and timeline.
- ☐ Follow up and give the employee supportive feedback on improvement.

CHAPTER 6 INCREASING EFFECTIVENESS THROUGH DELEGATION

Steps for planning to delegate:

Preparing

- [ ] Select a task and individual. Consider the individual, how the task fits into the broad picture, and the need for reliability and dependability or for independent judgment.

- [ ] Decide on how involved you need to be.

- [ ] Define the goal in operational terms so you can track progress and know when the task is complete.

- [ ] Identify what you need to communicate to the employee: critical information, data, constraints, resources, and sources of help or resistance.

- [ ] Identify due dates, checkpoints along the way, and your expectations at each.

Initiating

- [ ] Introduce the topic and get an idea of the employee's interest.

- [ ] Stress your interest and support.

- [ ] Provide an overview of the task. How do you see it? Encourage questions to further define and clarify the assignment. Discuss a second meeting to review the task, especially if the task is complex.

- [ ] Review sources of information. Who may be able to help or needs to be part of the problem-solving process? Describe how you can assist.

- [ ] Indicate special challenges, constraints, or opportunities.

- [ ] Describe what you expect and when. Will it be summarized in a report, written or verbal recommendations, or something else? Don't be vague; make it concrete.

- [ ] Define the level of control (directing, advising, partnering, or conferring) you are proposing. What decisions, activities, and authority, if any, are you retaining?

- [ ] Specify the resources and assistance available. Discuss how to publicize the assignment to those who will need to know about the task.

☐ Define the endpoint and checkpoints, if any, and what you expect at each of them.

☐ Discuss what to do if something does not go as planned.

Implementing

☐ If the task involves the cooperation of others, facilitate the employee's task by publicizing it and requesting cooperation.

☐ Follow the protocol you agree to in the initiation phase. Review progress at each checkpoint.

☐ If problems or misunderstandings occur, provide support and encouragement, but do not take over.

Closing

☐ Review the assignment and how you worked together. Thank your employee and see that the employee gets his/her share of credit.

☐ Solicit feedback about your level of involvement and management style.

☐ Get feedback from the employee on what seemed to work particularly well. Was she or he clear about which actions and decisions to make and which were yours?

☐ Did the employee have a clear picture of the goal and the requirements?

☐ Did you provide information, or did the employee have to ask for it?

☐ Did you share influence? Was there a feeling of mutual trust?

☐ When problems occurred, did you take over or rescue your employee? Did you support and encourage, but leave the challenge with the employee?

☐ Did you treat mistakes, confusion, or errors as part of the learning process?

☐ Would you be happy to delegate another task to this person?

☐ Would she or he be happy to take the assignment?

☐ If you were to repeat this assignment, what would you do differently? Why?

Delegation Styles

☐ *Directing* Use with an inexperienced employee, risky assignments, and/or situations where you know much more than the employee or the employee needs a lot of assistance.

☐ *Advising* Appropriate for working with the employee on some aspects of the assignment to increased performance of a specific task.

☐ *Partnering* Appropriate when minimal help is required and you may need to coach on some elements.

☐ *Conferring* Appropriate when no help is required and you plan to just check in occasionally.

CHAPTER 7 POINTS FOR SUCCEEDING AS A COACH

Coaching Involves

☐ Building connections.

☐ Challenging the status quo.

☐ Looking forward.

Coaching Process—To Begin

☐ Identify topics.

☐ Discuss willingness and readiness to be coached.

☐ Discuss expectations.

☐ Discuss current strengths, weaknesses, challenges, successes, hopes, and aspirations. *Option*: Collect feedback or use a 360-degree survey; review the feedback and look for patterns.

☐ Identify one or two items on which to focus coaching that will result in new skills, knowledge, or behavior.

☐ Draft a schedule for future meetings and close the meeting.

Coaching Process—Follow-up Meetings

☐ Review expectations for the meeting.

☐ Review interim assignments and progress.

☐ Challenge the status quo by asking questions.

☐ Once a goal is reached, begin on the next goal.

CHAPTER 8   TECHNIQUES TO MANAGE GROUPS, TEAMS, AND MEETINGS

Important Team Elements to Clarify

- ☐ Roles
- ☐ Team operating principles or norms
- ☐ Decision making

Whose Decision Is It?

A	Theirs	These are the decisions the leader of the group (or more senior managers) will make independently.
B	Yours	These are the decisions the leader will make with input from the group.
C	Ours	These are the decisions the group will make as a whole. They are the decisions that are important enough to take the time to reach consensus.
D	Mine	These are the decisions that an individual or small subteam can make on its own and communicate back to the entire team.

Effective Meeting Management Steps

- ☐ Identify the meeting purpose.
- ☐ Create an agenda with clear outcomes and expectations of participants.
- ☐ Identify team member meeting roles.

CHAPTER 9   CLUES TO FOSTER CREATIVITY AND INNOVATION

Fostering Creativity and Innovation Reminders

- ☐ Increase self-awareness.
- ☐ Build an environment to support creativity.
- ☐ Use teamwork and collaboration to increase trust.
- ☐ Use creativity tools to get unstuck.

Idea Generation Tools

- ☐ Brainstorming
- ☐ Nominal group technique

☐ Brainwriting and brainsketching

☐ SCAMPER (Substitute, Combine, Adapt, Minify/Magnify, Put to other uses, Eliminate, Reverse/Rearrange)

CHAPTER 10 POINTERS ON MANAGING PROJECTS AND DECISIONS

Reminders

☐ Learn the basics of project management.

☐ Understand and take advantage of different approaches to project planning.

☐ Challenge what does not make sense.

☐ Remember the difference between risk and uncertainty.

☐ Look for ways to improve communication in your project.

☐ Avoid going for the "big bang"—prioritize and proceed incrementally.

☐ Be assertive and work to kill a project that should die.

☐ Make timely decisions and use consensus wisely. *Use the Z-model for decisions.*

☐ Take steps to overcome the "experience trap."

The Learning Key's Modified Z

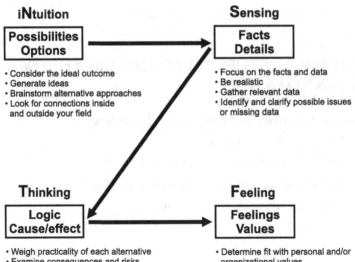

CHAPTER 11   SUGGESTIONS FOR MANAGING UP

Communicating with Your Boss

- ☐ Plan.
- ☐ Describe your concern in an objective way.
- ☐ Ask questions.
- ☐ Generate possible solutions.
- ☐ Agree on specific actions.

REFERENCES

Domhoff, G. W. *The Scientific Study of Dreams: Neural Networks, Cognitive Development, and Content Analysis.* American Psychological Association (APA), Washington, D.C., 2003.

Drucker, P. "How to Make People Decisions." *Harvard Business Review*, Vol. 63, No. 4, July–August, 1985, pp. 22–26.

Goleman, D. *Emotional Intelligence: Why It Can Matter More Than IQ.* Bantam Books, New York, 1995.

Hallowell, E. *CrazyBusy: Overstretched, Overbooked and About to Snap.* Ballantine Books, New York, 2006.

Klein, G. *Intuition At Work.* Doubleday, New York, 2003.

Locke, E. A., and Latham, G. *Goal Setting: A Motivational Technique That Works.* Prentice Hall, Englewood Cliffs, NJ, 1984.

Reader's Digest, "Laugh!" November, 2009, p. 50.

Stone, L. "Living with Continuous Partial Attention." From the article "The Harvard Business Review List of Breakthrough Ideas for 2007." *Harvard Business Review*, Vol. 85, No. 2, February 2007, pp. 28–29.

Wiseman, R. *The Luck Factor: The Four Essential Principles.* Miramax Books/ Hyperion, New York, 2003.

FIFTY-TWO-WEEK LEADERSHIP JOURNAL

To add to our toolbox of skills and knowledge, especially for things that need application and practice, it is easier and more effective to use small segments. This leadership journal covers topics in the book plus a few others. Use it by subject, by week, or occasionally for a day—whatever helps you the most.

Our goal is to provide a vehicle for you to consider, reflect, and perhaps try a few new things. As supervisors, we need to begin with ourselves. Remember Michael Jackson's lyrics for *Man in the Mirror*?

> *I'm starting with the man in the mirror. I'm asking him to change his ways ... If you wanna make the world a better place, take a look at yourself and then make a change.*

TOPICS

Week 1: Using questions

Week 2: Listening

Week 3: Motivation

Week 4: Coaching

Week 5: Leading

Week 6: Empowering

Week 7: Delegating

Week 8: Project management

Week 9: Teamwork

Week 10: Decision making

A Guide to Success for Technical Managers: Supervising in Research, Development, & Engineering, by Elizabeth Treher, David Piltz and Steven Jacobs
Copyright © 2011 John Wiley & Sons, Inc.

Week 11: Managing change

Week 12: Creativity

Week 13: Goal setting

Week 14: Performance reviews

Week 15: Value-based leadership

Week 16: Ethical leadership

Week 17: Professional development

Week 18: Managing

Week 19: Transitions

Week 20: Creating a satisfied workforce

Week 21: Creating an engaged workforce

Week 22: Retaining employees

Week 23: Hiring employees

Week 24: Strategic leadership

Week 25: Inspiring employees

Week 26: Quality management

Week 27: Creating a shared vision

Week 28: Dealing with negativity

Week 29: Exceeding customer's expectations

Week 30: Creating a culture of service

Week 31: Stewardship

Week 32: Lean practices

Week 33: Challenging assumptions

Week 34: Whole brain thinking

Week 35: Using processes to achieve success

Week 36: Leading with emotional intelligence

Week 37: Managing generations

Week 38: Thinking outside the box

Week 39: The attitude of the lucky

Week 40: Using your talents for success

Week 41: Using resources effectively

Week 42: Influencing others

Week 43: Juggling many hats

Week 44: Priorities

Week 45: Time management

Week 46: Leading change

Week 47: Conflict management

Week 48: Self-awareness

Week 49: Training others

Week 50: Networking

Week 51: Creating an inclusive environment

Week 52: Creating a trusting environment

WEEK 1: USING QUESTIONS

Nothing in life is to be feared. It is only to be understood.
—Marie Curie

Questions are one of the most essential and powerful techniques for any technical leader. They do several things. First, they provide the opportunity to learn, explore, understand, and challenge biases, assumptions, and perspectives before responding. Second, they provide an opportunity to clarify and fully grasp another's perspective and situation. Most importantly, they create an environment, when used correctly, of collaboration.

Using questions correctly means recognizing you have a choice—a choice to ask, to listen and learn, or a choice to tell and direct. As a leader, you most likely have had the experience that when you tell and direct the results may be, on the surface, what you want but not have a lasting impact. However, when you choose to use questions you create an environment in which you are giving influence, autonomy, and respect to others.

Asking the right questions means realizing you may not have all the data or answers. Questions help direct, explore options, create solutions, and most importantly, create a lasting impact. They also can build self-confidence in your staff, as they learn they really can solve many of their own problems.

To use questions, first take a deep breath and fight the temptation to jump in and start analyzing, critiquing, telling, or directing. Begin by asking questions such as *What approaches have you tried? How else might you do it? What pros and cons do you see? What do you recommend? How else could we proceed?* By beginning with questions, you will find that those you lead will provide answers based not on fear but on trust. As you practice asking questions, you will find it easier and more automatic to use more of them.

Daily Tips

Monday: Think of a current project where you need a project update or review. Instead of asking for a summary, use questions that begin a conversation such as *What will it take to complete this project? What do you see as the most critical issues to solve?*

Tuesday: Hold a staff meeting to explore the important questions your team needs to answer. Prioritize those questions.

Wednesday: Use brainstorming to solve an issue (no matter how insignificant) where, during the brainstorming, everyone uses only questions. Then answer each question. Do this for approximately 10 minutes and evaluate the results.

Thursday: Think about your goals for the next week. Write a list of five questions you need to answer about these goals.

Friday: Review your company's mission statement and answer *What did I do this week to help meet our mission, and what can I do next week to support the mission?*

WEEK 2: LISTENING

A man should look for what is, and not for what he thinks should be.
—Albert Einstein

We are born with two ears and one mouth, yet it seems that, regardless of our level or role, we tend to speak more than listen. Technical supervisors who master the skill (and art) of listening can accomplish great things. Listening takes self-confidence, self-awareness, trust, and patience. Real listening means you are ready to understand another's perspective and thoughts—and willing to recognize that others have important things to say. This sounds easy, right? But how often as a leader do you truly listen? Do you hear a few things and then begin telling your own thoughts? If so, listening didn't happen.

There are many types of listening—active, reflective, and empathetic. They all have the same CORE skills that are important for a good listener—caring, openness, reflection, and expectations. Caring is noticing that someone else wants to share his or her thoughts and not being critical or judging what is said. Listening with a caring mind-set provides a sense of enthusiasm to learn about someone else. Openness follows since it provides support for listening. Being open means acknowledging that no matter the personality style, this person has something valid to share—even if it seems meaningless to you. It suggests the listener realizes that he or she does not know everything.

Next is reflecting on what is said. Too often, we listen waiting to jump in and share our perspectives. Take a moment and reflect on your latest conversation—how many times did you start talking before the other person was finished? Reflecting suggests that, after hearing, you take time to think before responding. It may take 5 seconds or 20—time to be able to comment on what you have heard to prove you have listened.

Finally, there are our expectations. What expectations do you have when you listen? Do you listen planning to provide an answer or challenge? Do you listen with the expectation of questioning or debating? Your expectations will influence how well you listen. Try to listen without expectations to hear what is really said.

Daily Tips

Monday: Commit to using the CORE method this week. Begin with Caring. Select a conversation and listen through the lens of caring. At the end, take a moment and write down three differences you experienced in listening. How did caring help the conversation?

Tuesday: Identify one conversation and listen through the lens of Openness. At the end, take a moment and write down three differences you experienced in listening that helped the conversation.

Wednesday: Identify one conversation and listen through the lens of Reflecting. At the end, take a moment and write down three differences you experienced in listening that helped the conversation.

Thursday: Identify one conversation and focus on your Expectations as you listen. At the end, take a moment and write down the impact of your expectations. Were you able to set them aside to better listen?

Friday: Observe others conversing. Can you identify those listening? If so, what do you see? If not, what is absent? Take a moment and create a reminder that you can easily access on practices you can implement to be a better listener.

WEEK 3: MOTIVATION

People often say that motivation doesn't last. Well, neither does bathing—that's why we recommend it daily.

—Zig Ziglar

Creating a motivating climate is one of the most rewarding tasks of a leader. The challenge comes from understanding what is important to others and recognizing that your motivators may be very different. A sense of quality, happiness, or duty—all internal drivers—motivate some of us. Money, status, or recognition—external drivers—motivate others. Learning what drives others will help you build motivation to accomplish tasks.

Talent management, placing the right person in the right job or reassigning staff, applies a basic leadership principle—if you know someone's motivation, you can lead them anywhere! What does it take to learn someone's motivation? There are two ways—ask them or watch them. For many supervisors, asking them is problematic so instead of ignoring it, look for it.

Understanding motivating factors and what is important to each of your staff will help improve your delegation and coaching and get the most from your staff.

Daily Tips

Monday: Make a list of those you supervise and think about their typical behaviors. Do you know how they spend their spare time? Write down the things you think help them feel motivated. Test your hypothesis by asking them about the types of jobs they like and why.

Tuesday: Consider how your own motivation may affect those you supervise. Don't assume that what motivates you will work for everyone. Talk with your staff to make sure you aren't imposing your motivators on them.

Wednesday: Reflect on what motivates you. Are these internal or external drivers? Is your job providing the motivators important to you?

Thursday: Call a staff congratulation meeting. Begin by highlighting one item each staff member has contributed to the completion of your goals. Ask others to do the same.

Friday: Ask your staff what makes work fun; keep doing those items. Then ask what could make work more fun and implement what you can.

WEEK 4: COACHING

*What we have to do is to be forever curiously testing new opinions
and courting new impressions.*

—Walter Pater

Coaching can take on many forms but has one goal—helping someone else to develop. Isn't this a goal of supervising? Effective coaches often are self-aware, humble, and have a sense of giving back.

Self-awareness means having the ability to recognize and manage our own insecurities. When leaders do not recognize their own concerns, fears, or insecurities, they may react and make decisions that do not always make sense to their staff. Self-awareness is being able to communicate your needs to others and act accordingly instead of reacting.

Humble coaches share their experiences with others. Effective coaches often coach others as a way to give back. They coach not out of a sense of duty but rather to support an individual and to ensure the organization meets future goals.

Daily Tips

Monday: Take a moment and reflect on a current or future project. List all of your concerns about the project on the left side of the page. On the right side, list individual(s) on the project you might coach to deal with each item.

Tuesday: Show your staff your appreciation and support. Let them know how you rely on their expertise and support.

Wednesday: Take the opportunity to coach someone who may be interested. Explore their interests to see if a short-term coaching relationship would be beneficial. If you are inexperienced, approach someone you respect and think could coach you. Approach that person and ask for coaching. Use that experience to learn more about coaching.

Thursday: Take a moment and reflect on a current or future project where you have provided coaching. Evaluate your approach. What could you have done differently? Ask for feedback to check your perceptions.

Friday: Ask a staff member to show or teach you something. Afterwards, discuss what helped you. What would you change next time?

WEEK 5: LEADING

Make a habit of two things: to help or at least to do no harm.
—Hippocrates

There are many types of leaders in technical organizations. Some focus on their science or technical skills and play a strong leadership role in that way. Those individuals lead primarily through their work. Others inspire and lead through interpersonal skills by helping and guiding individuals and colleagues toward organizational or project goals. In some cases, technical leaders have the ability to focus on interpersonal dynamics of staff and the science or technology and are skilled in leading both.

Of the dozens of theories and models of leading, one of the simplest readily seen in technical organizations is Kurt Lewin's three leadership styles: autocratic, participative or democratic, and laissez-faire. Many managers labeled micromanagers are autocratic leaders. They make the decisions and permit few suggestions. Laissez-faire leaders really don't lead but give free reign to their staff; often this leads to a lack of focus and missed goals. The participative, democratic leader seeks input and builds motivation and collaboration by involving their staff members in operations and decisions.

Daily Tips

Monday: Consider the three types of leaders described. Which style best fits you? One way to evaluate this is to think about what would happen if you weren't at work for a week or two. Would your staff move ahead, almost as if you were there? Would work grind to a halt without you to give direction? Would work pretty much stay the same—perhaps a lot of chaos and not much progress, but a lot of freedom? If one of these fits you, your leadership style is participative, autocratic, and laissez-faire, respectively.

Tuesday: Ask individual staff members to each describe the goal for a project or initiative. Are the answers consistent and accurate? If they are, congratulations, you are an effective leader. If they are not, what can you do to ensure consistency?

Wednesday: Reflect on a recent project. How often did you focus exclusively on what was getting done, instead of helping staff members realize why it needed to get done? What is difficult or easy about doing this? What can you do next time to focus on the why and not just on the what or how?

Thursday: At a staff meeting, ask your staff to share their definitions of leadership. What is similar? Different? Create an open dialogue about leadership with your group.

Friday: Leaders expect different things. What do you expect as a leader? Make a list of your expectations. How well do your staff members understand your expectations? It they don't, share them and hold a conversation about why expectations are important.

WEEK 6: EMPOWERING

Science progresses best when observations force us to alter our preconceptions.

—Vera Rubin

Empowerment is a buzzword that makes some people cringe. For technical leaders, empowering others is challenging since it means giving someone else the power to make decisions you are paid to make or have the expertise to make. Are you a technical supervisor because you are excellent at dealing with people or because you are skilled at your specialty? When it is the latter, you may have to work harder to be comfortable empowering others.

To empower someone else means you need to be okay with the decisions that individual makes. As a specialist, it may be uncomfortable. As a leader, it is essential. So how do you reconcile these seemingly opposite views? The first step is to curb the desire and tendency to tell others how to do something. Instead, set up communication checks and balances at appropriate intervals for updates on progress, just as you would when delegating. Use those meetings to ask questions, and help the individual think through problems, if needed.

Over time, this process not only increases trust and confidence but also builds technical competence.

Daily Tips

Monday: On a scale of 1 to 10, where 1 is little to no empowerment and 10 is complete empowerment, where would you place yourself as a leader? Where would you like to be? What is one thing you can do to increase your ability to empower others?

Tuesday: Ask your staff members how empowered they feel on a scale of 1 to 10. Ask them if they would like the number to change. If so, discuss one thing you each can do to improve.

Wednesday: Create an empowerment schedule for your next project. List all the decisions staff need to make and create a system of updates, so shortly after decisions are made you are engaged. Provide one or two opportunities for you to receive an update prior to the decision point and collaborate on the upcoming decision.

Thursday: Reflect on your previous bosses. With which did you feel empowered? Why? Create a list of characteristics of the relationship. Think of your current boss, how empowered do you feel? Why? If appropriate, talk to your boss about his or her thoughts on empowerment.

Friday: Ask a trusted peer how they empowered their staff. What do they do that you can implement?

WEEK 7: DELEGATING

Anybody who has been seriously engaged in scientific work of any kind realizes that over the entrance to the gates of the temple of science are written the words: "Ye must have faith."

—Max Planck

Delegating helps us accomplish more than we otherwise could. When used correctly it builds skills, can increase motivation, and frees your own time for other activities. Some technical supervisors view delegating as simply a technique to get staff to do things you need to do or don't want to do.

The purpose of delegating is more comprehensive than simply getting things done. Done well, it helps build trust, stronger communication, and increased collaboration with your staff.

Daily Tips

Monday: On a scale of 1 to 10, with 1 being little to no delegation and 10 being complete delegation, where would you place yourself? Where would you like to be? What stops you from delegating? How can you overcome this barrier?

Tuesday: Ask your staff to delegate something to you. Watch how they do it. Afterwards, talk about the process and their perceptions of how you delegate. Decide on one thing you can do differently when delegating.

Wednesday: Think of something you could delegate but have not. Ask yourself these questions: *Am I delegating this to get it off my desk? Who is the best person for this assignment? Am I ready to delegate this?* After answering the questions, reconsider your choice to not delegate.

Thursday: Reflect on your past bosses. Who delegated well? Why? What can you adopt from the best delegators? If appropriate, talk to your boss about his or her thoughts on delegation.

Friday: Ask a colleague about their tips for delegation. What do they do that you can implement?

WEEK 8: PROJECT MANAGEMENT

Aerodynamically, the bumble bee shouldn't be able to fly, but the bumble bee doesn't know it so it goes on flying anyway.

—Mary Kay Ash

For technical supervisors, managing projects is a way of life. It is a skill to practice, to role model, and teach to others. There are many tools and systems available and, whatever your organization uses, there are really only two main components: clarifying and accomplishing a goal. This may seem an oversimplification, and the intent is to not suggest project management isn't complex. However, successful project management has to begin with developing a clear purpose and end with accomplishing goals within applicable constraints such as time, money, and resources.

Projects across the R&D continuum have very different characteristics, and unfortunately, most organizations treat them in a similar way. Development projects have much less uncertainty than do those in basic research. With projects at the development stage, traditional project management approaches, and mapping out a project after careful planning, make sense. For projects with a great deal of uncertainty, you may only be able to plan how to get to a next step where the results at that point will dictate future direction. Not many senior managers are comfortable acknowledging this limitation and, in fact, may not even recognize that it exists. The consequence is detailed project plans that are highly unlikely to be useful for too long.

Daily Tips

Monday: Think of a project you are leading currently. In a sentence or two, clearly describe the project's goal. Without sharing, ask several project members to do the same. Compare. Are they the same? If so, you are doing an incredible job; keep up the good work. If they are not, revisit the project's goal at your next team meeting and clear up any misunderstandings.

Tuesday: How do you hold others accountable for accomplishing goals? Do you wait until the deadline passes before asking? Or do you constantly ask? If you are not already doing this, create a system where, at appropriate intervals before the deadline, you ask for an update. If things are falling behind, get to the bottom of the issue while you still have time to manage it without jeopardizing key milestones.

Wednesday: Talk to your boss about project management. What are the key issues and pointers from his or her perspective?

Thursday: At your next meeting, ask your team to create a list of barriers and risks for your project. Assign each one a barrier or risk and ask them to bring to the next meeting a potential solution or a way to mitigate.

Friday: Assume you have to train a new employee about project management in your organization. In no more than 10 minutes, create an outline of what you would include. Provide that outline to a trusted colleague and ask for input.

WEEK 9: TEAMWORK

None of us is as smart as all of us.

—Ken Blanchard

Effective teamwork is essential in our work and personal environment. The world has grown amazingly complex and information continues to grow exponentially. Highly functioning teams do better than just one individual in developing and delivering products and services. However, teams generally take longer than do individuals who work independently, The skill then is to recognize those times when teamwork makes sense and when it does not.

Great teams have trust, have a common goal or a common purpose, are so in sync they can finish each other's thoughts, and show respect for each other's views. They don't argue; they debate and challenge each other in ways that don't create defensiveness.

Team leaders need to create environments where technical experts see each other as resources with problem-solving skills that can be applied both within and outside their specialty. They need to role model this behavior not by critiquing others but by helping everyone share their thoughts.

Daily Tips

Monday: Spend some time learning something new about each team member. Focus on a personal topic and a technical skill or interest.

Tuesday: Leadership requires knowing when teamwork is appropriate. Are you trying to make everything about teamwork? List the situations where you may be overstressing teamwork. For example, are there decisions you should be making but are leaving them up to the team? Meet with the team to decide where teamwork makes sense and where it does not.

Wednesday: Have members talk about their fears and concerns for the team and their role. Have each person describe a potential concern. Give them time to think about it. As a group, brainstorm ways to minimize the impact of the issues raised.

Thursday: Ask a colleague to observe your staff meeting. Tell your staff the goal is to observe your leadership skills. After the meeting, ask your colleague to share his or her observations. What can you do differently at the next meeting?

Friday: Think of three ways to celebrate with your team— whether your project comes to a successful closure or ends prematurely for any reason.

WEEK 10: DECISION MAKING

Be less curious about people and more curious about ideas.
—Marie Curie

Today, formal decision analysis is taught as the ideal in most business and engineering schools, although research by Gary Klein and others clearly shows that intuitive decisions are more effective and that in most cases when we are faced with a familiar problem, the first solution we identify is going to work. Yes, there might be a better solution, but *better is the enemy of good enough.*

Intuition (the way we translate our experiences) helps us make decisions by using patterns to recognize what is going on and how to react. The more patterns and action scripts (expertise) we have, the easier it is to make decisions.

Like any other skill, making better decisions takes practice and requires feedback for ongoing learning. Often, there isn't time in a typical day to practice making decisions, but tracking the results of your decisions gives feedback. For example, what was the timeline? List key judgments and decisions that you made as the incident unfolded.

Daily Tips

Monday: Think of a difficult decision that you made. Why was this difficult? How did you interpret the situation? Why did you select the actions you did? Looking back, should you have considered another approach?

Tuesday: Sometimes, making the decision isn't the roadblock—it is being clear on whose decision it is. Do you and your team have this issue? Meet to discuss the types of decisions you will make with their input, the decisions you will make by consensus, and those an individual staff member is expected to make.

Wednesday: After working with your staff to make an important decision, do not act on it for 24 hours. Meet again the next day to review it. Often, others will see the situation differently, after taking time to think about it. For all important decisions, this is a good approach. As Benjamin Franklin said,

When those difficult cases occur, they are difficult, chiefly because while we have them under consideration, all the reasons pro and con are not present to the mind at the same time; but sometimes one set present themselves, and at other times another, the first being out of sight. Hence the various purposes or inclinations that alternately prevail, and the uncertainty that perplexes us.

Thursday: Ask each staff member about their individual process for making decisions. Compile their answers and identify similarities and differences. Remove any information that is identifying and share the results with the staff.

Friday: Meet with your staff to list the challenges of making decisions in your group and discuss solutions to the challenges. Solve as many challenges as you can in 15 minutes.

WEEK 11: MANAGING CHANGE

Truth is ever to be found in simplicity and not in the multiplicity and confusion of things.

—Isaac Newton

Being a technical supervisor means dealing with change. Whether it's change in staffing, budgets, strategy, or customer goals, managing change is essential to effective leadership. You may initiate the change or simply be your organization's voice to oversee implementation. Remember that change is personal, change can be scary and exciting at the same time, and change is uncertain. Change is a process, not an event.

Leonardo da Vinci used a painting technique called *sfumato*. It is a painting technique in which you do not see actual paint strokes but rather a softened effect, as through a veil of smoke. It is truly a description of balancing the unknown with the known and the unseen with the seen. It is exactly how technical leaders need to manage change—allowing opposite emotions, opinions, and thoughts to exist simultaneously.

Daily Tips

Monday: List a few changes you have experienced lately. Did you view them as events or processes? What's the difference in your mind? Think of a change you have been through. Which aspects went well? Which didn't? Identify one thing you can do differently.

Tuesday: Ask your boss about how he or she views change management in your organization. How are your views similar or different? If applicable, hold a discussion with your boss on a current change. Identify one thing you can do to support the change process.

Wednesday: Think of a recent change and ask each of your staff how the change personally impacted them. Take notes and compile a list of similarities and differences. Remove all identifying information and share the list with your staff. Discuss what can be improved next time there is a change.

Thursday: Use the Internet and search for an article on managing change in technical organizations. Read it and summarize it for your next staff meeting.

Friday: Ask a trusted colleague how they manage change. What can you learn for the next time you have to manage change?

WEEK 12: CREATIVITY

Give me a lever long enough and a fulcrum on which to place it, and I shall move the world.

—Archimedes

Creativity has many shapes and sizes, processes, and models. They all illustrate the essence—being different. Technology-based organizations generally attract individuals who like to be creative—either to improve or modify or to come up with something new.

Supervising is less about being creative and more about leading creativity by challenging perceptions and assumptions, forcing connections when they seem not to fit, and breaking things down into simpler parts. Helping others to see things that are not obvious is part of leading creativity. It's asking others to go beyond their expertise, experience, and knowledge to find a new solution. This takes time—a commodity in short supply.

Effective technical leaders, however, choose to take time (even if it's a minute or two) to support their staff and projects. Over time, this builds skills and can lead to greater innovation and creativity.

Daily Tips

Monday: Think of a recent project. List all the perceptions and assumptions on the left-hand side of a piece of paper. On the right side, list the opposite of each item. Review both lists. What emerges from the lists? Do you see a new solution you haven't seen before?

Tuesday: Pick five random objects around you. For each object, force a connection to a project or problem. Record the connections. After completing all five connections, review them. What emerges? Do you see a new solution you haven't seen before?

Wednesday: Define creativity. Ask your staff to define it. Collect the definitions and create a list of similarities and differences. Discuss the importance of creativity for your department.

Thursday: Practice creativity on each Thursday for the next month and do something different on your lunch break or while driving to work. If you lunch at your desk, go out or take a break and walk for 15 minutes. If you listen to the news, listen to an audiobook. Vary the routes you use to get to work.

Friday: Ask a friend who doesn't work in your field how they are creative at work. Identify one thing they do that you can implement at work.

WEEK 13: GOAL SETTING

In science, "fact" can only mean "confirmed to such a degree that it would be perverse to withhold provisional assent." I suppose that apples might start to rise tomorrow, but the possibility does not merit equal time in physics classrooms.

—Stephen Jay Gould

Research by Edwin A. Locke and others indicates that goal setting is probably the most important tool a technical manager can use. Goals are a target to provide direction for individual performance road maps. Challenging goals increase effort, stimulate persistence, and can lead to a search for better strategies and tactics.

Goal difficulty, specificity, and acceptance all influence performance. Research has shown that harder goals lead to higher levels of performance. Goals must be difficult enough so they are perceived as challenging, but not so difficult that they seem unattainable. Experience proves that specific goals lead to higher performance levels than goals such as "Do your best." Acceptance or commitment to a goal is correlated with persistence and motivation.

Goal setting is critical and yet often overlooked. Some have the attitude that creating goals just wastes time. Of the many systems to create goals, one isn't necessarily more effective than another. The key is to create goals that are concise, measureable (in the sense that you will know when they are complete) and time bound. Make sure the goals you write wouldn't actually take years to complete. It may take several subgoals to achieve a given task.

Daily Tips

Monday: Analyze your own goals Are they goal clear and concise—do others view them the same way? Vague goals leave too much opportunity for alternative actions.

Tuesday: Write at least one goal or subgoal for each day the rest of this week. Review them to see that they are specific, measurable, and realistic. Are they time bound, or could you spend many days on each?

Wednesday: Review the goals for your staff. Are they well written? For example, how will you measure/evaluate progress and success? Do your employees understand the criteria you will use? Do you consider simply meeting a goal to be average or outstanding performance?

Thursday: Write a list of the challenges to accomplish your own goals. Commit to tackling one at a time until it isn't a challenge.

Friday: Evaluate your progress on the goals you wrote on Tuesday. Did you accomplish them? If you didn't, why not? What do you need to change to write effective goals you can achieve? Summarize what you believe is most important about creating and accomplishing goals. Share and discuss them with your staff.

WEEK 14: PERFORMANCE REVIEWS

Remember the difference between a boss and a leader; a boss says "Go!"—a leader says "Let's go!"

—E. M. Kelly

As a supervisor, one of your tasks is to provide performance feedback to your employees. Almost every organization has a performance review system to follow. You need to document each employee's successes, challenges, growth opportunities, and future goals. This isn't that difficult, especially if you have ongoing communication, give feedback, and coach between formal reviews. What can make it uncomfortable is that performance reviews are often tied to salary increases, bonuses, and promotions, and you may not make those decisions. The process itself can impact motivation if not handled well.

Formal performance reviews should not include surprises and should focus on observable behaviors and outcomes rather than on your interpretation of those events. Many systems today ask that the employee and manager each write a draft review to begin a dialogue. When writing your draft, avoid emotional words, judgments, and assumptions. These are never helpful or constructive. Motivational performance reviews include discussions about additional ways of accomplishing tasks and suggestions to overcome current challenges; they focus on the future and continuous growth. These reviews provide a sense of accomplishment balanced with opportunities for improvement. The goal is to create a review that motivates.

Daily Tips

Monday: Write a one-page mini-review for each of your staff. After writing it, review it and delete any word that is emotional or suggests their way of doing something is wrong. Rewrite it if necessary. What are the differences? Discuss the mini-review with your staff.

Tuesday: Ask several of your staff to write a performance review on you. You may want to choose individuals who have a high level of trust with you. What changes would you make to the performance reviews they wrote for you? How accurate are they and how do they compare with what you would write yourself? What can you do differently the next time you write a performance review?

Wednesday: Meet with human resources; ask them to provide you with additional guidelines on how to write performance reviews. After the meeting, identify one or two things they shared that you will integrate into your next series of reviews.

Thursday: Writing a performance review is only half the story. Holding a performance review is the other half. Using the Internet, research the various ways to prepare, begin, and end performance review meetings. Commit to doing at least one of the ideas at your next review.

Friday: Ask your supervisor for their perspective of the purpose of performance reviews. Is it aligned with your thoughts? Why or why not?

WEEK 15: VALUE-BASED LEADERSHIP

The nineteenth century believed in science but the twentieth century does not.

—Gertrude Stein

Some suggest that value-based leadership is the only way to lead. To others it is so complex it becomes difficult to use. Value-based leadership means leading from a deep sense of self and desiring the best for everyone around you. The self-awareness of value-based leaders helps them understand their triggers, drivers, and motivations, and more importantly, how they can impact others. Value-based leadership uses a set of values (personal and organizational) and associated criteria to make decisions, create goals and visions, build effective teams, empower, delegate, and more. It grounds a leader in a way that provides a foundation that is unmovable and sustainable over time.

When using leadership based on personal values, there can be a disconnect with organizational values or vice versa. This presents a challenge. Values are deeply held beliefs and, if they are not the same as those of the organization, values-based leadership becomes superfluous. For example, if you value teamwork, you will lead from a perspective that creates effective teams and deals constructively with conflict. However, if the organization places value on independence and individual initiative, leading with the value of teamwork is counterproductive. For success, value-based leaders need to lead from a consistent set of values—personally and organizationally.

Daily Tips

Monday: Create a list of your values. Order the list in a way that is meaningful to you, with the first item being the value most important to you. Are any values on your list the same values expressed by your organization? If so, begin leading with these values.

Tuesday: At a staff meeting, ask your staff what values they feel the organization supports. Have each member identify a project and challenge them to incorporate these values into decisions for the project. Continue the discussion as the project progresses.

Wednesday: Find a book or article on values-based leadership. Read it and try to implement one principle from it into your daily work.

Thursday: Before making decisions on a project, select an important value and ask yourself, *does this decision support this value?*

Friday: Talk to your boss and share the results of Monday's activity. Dialogue other ways you both can lead using values.

WEEK 16: ETHICAL LEADERSHIP

There is a single light of science, and to brighten it anywhere is to brighten it everywhere.

—Isaac Asimov

Ethics—doing right instead of wrong—can be complicated. Often, what seems to be the right thing to you is not perceived by others as right. At one point in organizational history, lying on an expense report, or gossiping about something overheard, was being unethical, and embezzlement, making decisions that caused catastrophes, or shredding confidential documents were activities in movies. Unfortunately, some leaders felt it was right to do wrong, so today, considering what is ethical is a common topic of discussion.

We can sum up ethical leadership by—*do no wrong*. It's that simple. When you question your decisions by asking "*is what I am about to do wrong?*", you are practicing the first step of ethical leadership. The second step comes when the answer is yes. If you proceed anyway, then ethical leadership isn't important to you. If you choose not to proceed—in spite of the outcome (fired, demoted, reassigned), then ethical leadership is a core attribute for you.

It's not easy. But instead of ensuring wrong, harmful personal and organizational agendas win, ethical leadership gives insurance that the right decision will be made.

Daily Tips

Monday: Review a current decision you made. Ask yourself, *Is what I am about to do wrong*? If the answer is yes, can you reverse the decision? If not, what can you do next time? If the answer is no, can you think of a time you made a decision that did cause harm? Can you commit to asking the question before making a critical decision?

Tuesday: Talk with your boss about ethical leadership. Do you agree? Why or why not? Can you agree on a definition that can be used daily in your work?

Wednesday: Gather a few key staff members and ask them to rate past decisions on a scale of 1 to 10, where 1 is unethical and 10 is ethical. What differences of opinion surface?

Where is there agreement? Hold a discussion about what it means to be an ethical leader.

Thursday: Using a search engine find three to five current articles or situations about ethical leadership in your field. They can be positive or negative. After reading them, summarize them and decide what you can implement in your work.

Friday: On your company's Intranet, find the ethics or values statement. Make copies and post them in your area. During the day, read them and challenge yourself to uphold those standards.

WEEK 17: PROFESSIONAL DEVELOPMENT

There is one thing even more vital to science than intelligent methods; and that is, the sincere desire to find out the truth, whatever it may be.

—Charles Pierce

Professional development can be technical (learning a new procedure or how to use an instrument) or nontechnical (learning to communicate more effectively with others). It can be formal, such as attending a conference, or informal, such as reading a book. One challenge is viewing professional development as a nonwork activity and not giving time for development during an employee's workday. Thus, development activities may have to be added to an already overbusy work schedule. This creates an environment in which development can be demotivating.

Leaders need to create environments in which employees are motivated for development. As a supervisor, you can support this by understanding the key factors that lead to development and over which you have a great deal of control. These factors include challenging, varied assignments, interacting with a diversity of people, a supportive mentor, and opportunities to participate in training and educational programs.

Guide your staff to explore roles not generally included in job descriptions but known to be useful in development and to the innovation process. These include generating or championing new ideas, taking the lead on small projects, and gatekeeping by collecting and distributing information from internal and external sources. For those who are more comfortable out of the limelight, try a "behind-the-scenes" support or project advocate role and guiding and developing less experienced staff.

Daily Tips

Monday: List the last three things you have done for your professional development. Commit to finding a blog that you can read for the next 5 days on topics specific to your interests. After reading each post, summarize what you learned in one sentence. Share with your staff.

Tuesday: Use a journal or publication your staff knows. Find one article and ask everyone to read it. At your next staff meeting, discuss the article and how it applies to your current projects.

Wednesday: Create a sharing day in which everyone in your group shares one thing from their expertise that would help or interest others.

Thursday: Ask your boss about his or her most impactful professional development experience. Discuss what type of professional development would be impactful for you.

Friday: Learn about something outside your technical skills, like origami. Afterwards create a list of ways that suggest how the skill is similar to your technical expertise. Share your insights with your staff.

WEEK 18: MANAGING

We can lick gravity, but sometimes the paperwork is overwhelming.

—Wernher von Braun

Managing is different from leading. Anyone can lead, regardless of their title or education, if they can influence others around them. Managing, however, is tied to your position. Managing is the role of a technical supervisor. But what does it really mean? For some, it means being involved in daily tasks, and for others, it means hearing about the results. Successful management is somewhere between the two. In many cases, staff needs support and direction, and in those cases, it's appropriate to be involved in task completion. In other cases, staff needs the autonomy and empowerment to use their own skills and knowledge to accomplish the task. The challenge of the technical supervisor/manager is letting go of how you may do it and realize your staff may accomplish the same task differently. Manage by holding staff responsible for the result, not by focusing on how they did it.

Effective technical managers balance being involved and giving autonomy to allow staff to complete a task. The only way to achieve this is through open communication and dialogue with each staff member. Ask them to reiterate the result and available resources to make sure you are on the same page. Discuss with them their preference for updating you and asking for help. Holding discussions like these after the fact doesn't give a positive experience. Agreeing on the process beforehand leads to success.

Daily Tips

Monday: Based on what you know about each of your staff members, decide who likes your involvement and who doesn't. Can you see where conflicts could occur? At a staff meeting, discuss the two approaches and have everyone share their preferences.

Tuesday: Search online for articles on the differences between managing and leading. Print one and share it with your staff. Ask them to read it and identify one or two things to implement from the article.

Wednesday: Find a mentor whom you feel is an exceptional manager. Ask if they are willing to mentor you by sharing their philosophy of managing. It may be a onetime discussion or one that occurs at regular intervals. Implement those elements you learn.

Thursday: Ask a trusted colleague to describe your management style. Share that with your boss. Is there agreement? If not, discuss with your boss what you can do differently.

Friday: Create a personal definition of what managing involves for you. Share with your staff and regularly review your definition. Are you practicing it? Why or why not? Do you need to change the definition or your practices?

WEEK 19: TRANSITIONS

What is a scientist after all? It is a curious man looking through a keyhole, the keyhole of nature, trying to know what's going on.
                                        —Jacques Yves Cousteau

Transitions are everywhere—mergers, promotions, ending projects, or changes in responsibilities. Dealing with transitions can be difficult or easy depending on your perspective and your reaction to change. The challenge for technical supervisors is not only personally dealing with the transition but also dealing with how your staff is reacting to the situation.

Helping others recognize the benefits of a transition is the first step. In some situations, there may be few benefits because the transition is mitigated by environmental factors such as economics, politics, or market share. In those situations, provide a forum for staff to vent while keeping them focused on the future. The challenge is not to lose future focus by dwelling too long in the past.

Providing forums for discussion and exploring how the future will look begins to build a vision and commitment to the future. In creating the vision, be clear about new goals and timelines and where the current staff can fulfill the need.

Daily Tips

Monday: Identify a current transition your staff is facing. Create a list of the benefits of the transition. If there are no known benefits, use your imagination to create one or two. Share the list with your staff and ask them to add to it. As a group, commit to focusing on one or two benefits for the next 30 days. Reevaluate and recommit if necessary.

Tuesday: Call a special meeting to talk openly and honestly with your staff about their perspectives of current or future transitions. Ensure that comments are confidential. Listen and comment as needed.

Wednesday: Call a special meeting where your staff members generate solutions to current or future transition issues. Ensure that comments are confidential. At the end, commit as a group to use one or two ideas for the next 30 days.

Thursday: Meet with your boss and discuss how he or she dealt with work transitions. Discuss the skills used to meet the challenges faced. Commit to one thing you will do the next time you are in a transition.

Friday: Think of a time you went through a transition in your personal life. Record the feelings you had about the transition and what you did to survive it. Now think of a work transition you have dealt with. Were the feelings the same? Will the skills you used in your personal life apply at work? Why or why not?

WEEK 20: CREATING A SATISFIED WORKFORCE

You cannot feed the hungry on statistics.

—Heinrich Heine

Isn't satisfaction the goal for everyone at work—regardless of title? Being a technical supervisor means you have the privilege of creating that satisfaction not only for yourself but also for your staff. Think of what makes you satisfied at work. Is it the people? The work challenges? Your results? The projects themselves? For some, satisfaction can be elusive and nonexistent, while for others, it's everywhere. Satisfaction tends to be connected to happiness, meeting challenges, and looking forward to the future. Creating a satisfied workforce ensures that your staff is happy, meets challenges, and looks forward to each day.

Happiness is different for each person, but it involves feeling needed, appreciated, and recognized at work. Supervisors are in a unique position to help staff feel they are needed, appreciated, and recognized. How often do you provide such feedback to members of your staff? Once a year as part of a performance review isn't enough. Every day is too much, but several times a month creates a positive environment. As staff members feel happy, they are more eager and willing to meet challenges and accomplish tasks. They see work as exciting and fulfilling instead of as a necessity.

Having a satisfied workforce is all about creating interactions with your staff that are positive and sustainable for a long time. The ability to do this is as much a function of your interpersonal skills as your technical expertise.

Daily Tips

Monday: At your next staff meeting, ask everyone to share one thing that makes him or her happy at work. Challenge each person to grow their happiness quotient and discuss what that would do for accomplishing goals and tasks.

Tuesday: Ask a trusted colleague how they define a satisfied workforce. Discuss your thoughts. Identify at least one thing you can do to enhance satisfaction of your staff.

Wednesday: Contact someone in human resources and discuss the programs or initiatives available for staff to increase their satisfaction at work. Commit your support to your staff for a program or initiative. Challenge yourself to participate.

Thursday: Take the first few minutes of a staff meeting to discuss satisfaction at work. Ask people to share one thing that made them happy or satisfied at work since your last meeting. Encourage everyone to participate.

Friday: Find current statistics from the Best Places to Work Survey (search the Web for the results) and share them with your staff. What is one thing you could implement?

WEEK 21: CREATING AN ENGAGED WORKFORCE

Say what you know, do what you must, come what may.
—Sofia Kovalevskaya

Technical supervisors hope that all their staff is engaged at work, but many factors such as assignments, co-workers, or personal issues can cause disengagement. Being engaged means the tasks and work are enjoyable, satisfying, and challenging. Staff feels motivated to perform their best. Creating this type of workforce can be complex as you try and navigate your own reporting and political structure. If you are not fully engaged, how do you motivate others to be engaged?

Providing opportunities for staff to participate in decision making and planning can build engagement. Asking for feedback and opinions allows staff to feel they are part of something. Creating an engaged workforce means involving your staff in multiple ways.

It's easy to fall into the trap of assigning the same tasks to the same person. Create a dialogue with each staff member to explore their interests and the tasks that fully engaged them. Matching tasks with interests increases engagement, which leads to greater productivity and satisfaction.

Daily Tips

Monday: Make a list of the tasks for which you are responsible. Decide if you are fully engaged, somewhat engaged, or not engaged at all. Identify one thing you can do to move a task from the somewhat engaged or not engaged at all category to fully engaged. Challenge your staff to do the same.

Tuesday: At one-on-one meetings with your staff, ask about the tasks that fully engaged them. Are they linked to their interests or motivations? What can you both do to ensure they have more assignments that match their interests or motivations?

Wednesday: Ask your boss to rate your engagement. Does he or she feel you are fully engaged, somewhat engaged, or not engaged at all? Discuss what it would take to become fully engaged in all tasks.

Thursday: Commit to involving your staff more in decision making. Perhaps you will still make the final decision, but providing an open and honest environment where discussions occur will engage your staff more than not providing the opportunity.

Friday: Talk with someone from your human resources department and discover what employment engagement initiatives they have. Commit to participating in at least one.

WEEK 22: RETAINING EMPLOYEES

Ignorance is never better than knowledge.

—Enrico Fermi

One goal of many supervisors is to keep their staff for as long as possible. This may be a great strategy for you, if an employee meets goals and tasks. But what about that staff member who is always negative or misses deadlines? Do you want to retain that person? What about the great employee who has the potential to give far more to the organization if given a chance to broaden his or her experience? Do you want to retain that person?

To respond to either situation, look through two lenses: that of your group and that of the organization and that individual. You may want to keep a great employee with high potential, but instead support their transition to another department because of a greater benefit to the organization.

With the negative employee who misses deadlines, you first need to understand why the employee is negative or late. Why is the employee behaving that way? Some say supervisors get the staff they deserve. What does that mean? If you have a staff member that seems to be negative, ungrateful, or disengaged, are you doing something to foster that behavior? Retaining employees isn't just about numbers, it's about creating an environment where employees are set up for success rather than failure.

If your own behavior hasn't contributed to the problem, use performance management strategies to handle the situation and follow up. Don't let a problem employee remain—creating problems for you—or allow the problem to move to another group in your organization.

Daily Tips

Monday: Make a list that describes the characteristics of your staff. Next to each item, identify what you personally do to promote that characteristic (positive or negative). For those elements that are negative, what can you do to change it to a positive?

Tuesday: At a staff meeting, ask your staff what it would take for them to stay in their exact position for the next 20 years. Listen and take notes. After the meeting, evaluate what you have control over. Share the list with your boss, explore what he or she has control over. Follow up with your staff on any changes made.

Wednesday: Search for articles on how to retain employees. Share one you like with your boss and decide what you can commit to for your staff.

Thursday: Review your organization's mission, vision, and values. Is there anything that suggests why retaining employees is critical to the business? Commit to one thing you can do to support the mission, vision, and values.

Friday: Research the top 10 reasons why employees leave their job. Based on your research, commit to one thing you can do differently with your staff.

WEEK 23: HIRING EMPLOYEES

Any device in science is a window on to nature, and each new window contributes to the breadth of our view.

—Cecil Frank Powell

Filling vacancies due to retirement, promotion, expansion, or replacement can be both exciting and burdensome for technical supervisors. Navigating human resource policies and procedures while reviewing resumés can become overwhelming immediately. During these times, it is easy to forget the key elements in hiring new staff. Beyond technical capability, does this person have the right mix of people skills to collaborate with current staff and work successfully in the organization?

Most interviews tend to focus on the person's technical experience and prowess, while minimizing organizational culture and interpersonal dynamics. Before beginning the hiring process, did you assess your staff and what you need to meet current and future challenges and your goals? If not, begin doing this quarterly. This will better prepare you for when it is time to hire. You will have a picture larger than just the daily tasks to ensure the vision is met. During the interview process, do you provide a copy of the vision, mission, and goals of your group and your company? If so, ask candidates to describe how they can support them. Many wait and don't share that information until after the hiring decision. To ensure the best fit, assess during the interview process how each candidate will support the organizational culture.

Remember, after you hire an employee, your staff will need to spend time getting to know another colleague. Do not expect your team to be exactly the way they were before the hiring. You now have a new staff.

Daily Tips

Monday: Take stock of your employees and where you are. If someone was to leave tomorrow, what could you reorganize? What future initiatives are in the pipeline? What new role would be the best and what skills should that person have to meet your current and future challenges?

Tuesday: Reevaluate your interview questions. Revise them to include questions that give insight into how a potential candidate might operate within your culture.

Wednesday: If you are inexperienced in hiring at your company, meet with your human resources manager and ask them to describe the entire hiring process. You will be ready to manage the process when needed.

Thursday: Talk with your staff about your skills as a group. If you could hire someone, what skills do you need? What tasks would they do? This will prepare you for future challenges.

Friday: Find a blog on the best hiring practices. Commit to the practices the next time you need to hire someone.

WEEK 24: STRATEGIC LEADERSHIP

An idea that is developed and put into action is more important than an idea that exists only as an idea.

—Buddha

Technical supervisors use strategic leadership to chart their direction with a clear end in mind. It focuses daily activities, decisions, and planning on the end result to meet the overall strategy for an area or company. It allows staff to realize they are a part of the whole and each part is needed to achieve the end vision. Strategic leadership focuses staff and supervisors on exceeding the expectations of customers, executives, and stakeholders.

Technical supervisors are often not a part of creating the strategic vision but are expected to implement it. To implement successfully, they need to generate staff buy-in by highlighting the benefits of the vision and how each person's role is critical to achieving that vision. Supervisors need to use creativity to determine the best use of resources. They need to use active listening to ensure they hear everyone's concerns and to manage emotions as changes occur.

Strategic leadership drives focus on time, materials, staff, and the end goal. Productivity, happiness, and engagement increase. They are motivated both extrinsically (benefiting from the company succeeding) and intrinsically (knowing they are part of something bigger than they are). Strategic leadership provides clear direction and purpose with flexibility to achieve the purpose.

Daily Tips

Monday: Read a section of a book on strategic leadership. Identify one thing you can do to move further toward strategic leadership intent.

Tuesday: At a staff meeting, spend 15 minutes writing your group's strategic direction. Ensure everyone agrees with the direction. From this point forward, when decision or planning discussions occur, use the direction to help.

Wednesday: Talk with your boss about what strategic leadership means to him or her. Is there anything from that definition you can implement with your staff?

Thursday: Find a blog or article on strategic leadership and share it with your staff. Identify one thing everyone can do to make decisions and plans more strategic in nature.

Friday: At the start of a new project, create the strategic intent and use it to frame decisions and plans on the project.

WEEK 25: INSPIRING EMPLOYEES

If someday they say of me that in my work I have contributed some-thing to the welfare and happiness of my fellow man, I shall be satisfied.

—George Westinghouse

Technical supervisors have a unique responsibility to inspire their staffs to become the best they can. Technical supervisors can forget that the goal of supervision isn't only to oversee work, or to teach them the skills they lack, but also to inspire them to accomplish things they have never done before.

Inspiring employees is a skill that needs to be honed and practiced. It means acknowledging and appreciating what someone has to offer while believing that he or she can offer more, even when he or she does not. It is providing opportunities to be successful and supportive in times of failure by focusing on what went well and identifying what to do differently next time. When you inspire and believe in employees, they will give 120% and exceed any expectation. The reverse is also true; when employees are berated or told (verbally and nonverbally) they are not good at something, they will disengage and give less than 100%.

Inspiring employees provides a future for accomplishing the seemingly impossible. It ensures employees will do what it takes to get the job done. It creates an environment for staff to want to remain and be engaged at every moment. If there is one skill you can use to ensure your staff works optimally, it is to inspire them to do more than they ever thought possible.

Daily Tips

Monday: Make a list of people who have inspired you. What specifically caused you to be inspired? Can you emulate those qualities with your staff? At your next staff meeting, ask everyone to share something that inspires him or her. Share your thoughts.

Tuesday: For the next 30 days, commit to saying one inspiring thing once a week to each staff member about one of their projects.

Wednesday: Find a blog or article on inspiring others. Share what you find and commit to do one thing you can do that you learned from the article.

Thursday: Discuss strategies for inspiring employees with your boss or another manager. How do they do it? Ask them to share a time they were inspired by someone else.

Friday: Talk to a colleague you trust and ask them to tell you their thoughts on how inspiring you are. Ask them for advice on how to be more inspiring.

WEEK 26: QUALITY MANAGEMENT

Quality is never an accident; it is always the result of high intention, sincere effort, intelligent direction and skillful execution; it represents the wise choice of many alternatives.

—William A. Foster

Quality management is extremely important in any organization. Some in operations refer to the Quality Assurance (QA) Unit as the "dark side" because it can seem that these individuals do all they can to cause delays. However, if you are involved in a service, you are likely to recognize that QA is an essential aspect of customer satisfaction and know just how important quality is.

As a technical supervisor, your role may not be to function like a QA unit, but to lead and instill a quality process in whatever your staff does. Whether it's constantly challenging them to review and revise or to improve or implement cost-saving measures, the concept of quality needs to be at the forefront of every employee's decision.

Daily Tips

Monday: Think of the number of deviations and mistakes that have occurred in your group/department since the beginning of the year. If the number is high, look at your quality procedures and do a root cause analysis of what's going wrong.

Tuesday: Quality needs to be deeply ingrained in the psyches of all of your employees, as quality is whose job? Yes, everyone's. Do you offer quality training? How often? Aim to provide training no less than once a year. If you have a history of quality failures, hold lunch and learn sessions every quarter.

Wednesday: Do you capture lessons learned after each major project? If the answer is no, then put a system in place to do this and ensure everyone's participation. Don't let time constraints and a very fast tempo keep you from doing them. If people don't know the history of quality failures, you are doomed to repeat them.

Thursday: If you hold lessons learned sessions, how do you ensure others learn from them? Are they on a shared drive so everyone is able to view and have access to them? If the answer is no, then work with your information technology group to find a solution.

Friday: Using your lessons learned data, do you do trending analysis on them to identify processes or procedures that may be at fault? Do you do root cause analysis on the trends to eliminate them in the future? Do you do retraining or put on a band-aid? Quality systems that work help keep happy, satisfied customers for very long periods. Look at General Electric and their Six Sigma approach for evidence.

WEEK 27: CREATING A SHARED VISION

The very essence of leadership is [that] you have a vision. It's got to be a vision you articulate clearly and forcefully on every occasion. You can't blow an uncertain trumpet.

—Theodore Hesburgh

A great vision is clear, concise, and short enough for everyone to remember and internalize. Visions should be future oriented and grab people's hearts and minds. John Maxwell captured it best when he said, "[l]eaders must be close enough to relate to others, but far enough ahead to motivate them."

Great visions do just that. They give us a cause to fight for. Something to stand for, something bigger than ourselves that motivates us to come into work every day and make a difference. Great leaders create a shared vision which they live and embody every day and trumpet it to those who will listen, specifically to their staff.

Daily Tips

Monday: Write down your company's vision to the best of your ability without looking at it. Is it too long? Does it motivate and excite you? Your job today is to figure out how you can interpret it for your own group, to motivate you, so you can help motivate others.

Tuesday: Do research on the Internet to look for great vision statements. List three things they have in common. This will help you with the rest of the week's tips.

Wednesday: Based on your activities on Monday and Tuesday, create a vision statement for your division, department, or group that aligns with your company's vision and mission and will motivate your people.

Thursday: Meet with your staff. Discuss your organization's vision and ask each to write a vision statement for your group or for a specific project. Collect them, along with yours, and review them all as a group. Together, create a vision for your group or project.

Friday: What is your personal vision? Write down a 10-word vision that will motivate you in your life.

WEEK 28: DEALING WITH NEGATIVITY

*The difference between **can** and **cannot** are only three letters. Three letters that determine your life's direction.*

—Remez Sasson

Negativity is difficult to deal with. Like the one rotten apple in a barrel, it can turn all around it rotten as well. (A rotten apple releases ethylene which speeds up ripening; as other apples ripen and release ethylene, all can turn rotten.)

Do you have negative individuals on your staff? The negativity may come because some are in the wrong job or perhaps they work hard at a job that a colleague does in one-third the time, so they aren't often praised for their work. Others seem to walk through life with a chip on their shoulder and managers are unlikely to be much of an influence. The wrong job has a solution; a chip on the shoulder may not.

So, what can you do? Remember, a positive attitude brings energy, but positive thoughts are not enough. Don't let the rotting apple influence your attitude. Concentrate on converting your positive attitude into positive actions and initiative. As Henry Ford said, "[w]hether you think you can or you can't, you're right."

Daily Tips

Monday: Consider your own attitude. Where do you fall on the positive–negative continuum? List ways you can improve your attitude at home and at work.

Tuesday: Do you have a negative person on your staff? Talk with them and try to keep them focused on reasons they are unhappy in their work environment. Can you help? Explain the impact of their negative behavior on others. Ask them to consider changes they could make and to plan to meet with you about their thoughts the next day.

Wednesday: Hold a follow-up meeting. If comments indicate this individual is likely to be habitually negative, ask if he or she would be willing to serve officially as the group's "canary"—to warn of potential problems and issues others choose to ignore or may not see. Discuss how you see this role benefitting the team and confirm willingness and commitment.

Thursday: Hold a team meeting and share the new role of this team member—to serve as the team's official canary. Recognize and show appreciation during meetings for the "canary's" comments. Use them as a springboard to explore potential risks and alternative approaches. You may find the canary begins to have suggestions that are more positive as well.

Friday: If you have had no luck with your rotten apple, talk with your manager and human resources in order to get some help for both of you. If you want to first try one more thing, each time you see the individual, ask "what is the best thing that has happened today?" You may get no real answer for some days or weeks, but with time you are likely to have that person come to you (before you even ask) and say "I already know the best thing that has happened today." When that happens you will have turned a corner and begun a new direction.

WEEK 29: EXCEEDING CUSTOMER'S EXPECTATIONS

> *We see our customers as invited guests to a party, and we are the hosts. It's our job every day to make every important aspect of the customer experience a little bit better.*
>
> —Jeff Bezos

This is easily doable, as long as you can learn about your customer's expectations and then exceed their goals on your return on expectations (ROE).

This requires some serious research and customer conversations. Seek out customer-generated expectations for your products or services. Use customer focus groups or customer interviews and don't limit the data by talking only to your satisfied customers. Dissatisfied customers will also give useful feedback. In collecting the data, make your customers feel valued and confident that their feedback is important to you.

After you act on the feedback, let your customers know what you have done and check regularly to make sure their expectations are being met. Then on a regular basis, start the process again to keep up with changing customer expectations. These aren't suggestions directed to a large customer service department. They are appropriate for the many functions in technical organizations that provide a service. You may run an analytical lab and have customers dropping off samples or calling to check on status. Do you know what is most important to each of your customers or how that may change depending on the sample they provide?

Daily Tips

Monday: First things first. Start by listing your customer groups, the assumptions you may be making of each, and what information about them would help you provide a better service. It may help to create a short survey for your customers to fill out. Consider various media, such as electronic or paper surveys and verbal interviews. Different generations are more comfortable with different media and you want as much input as possible.

Tuesday: If you have decided on a survey, meet with your team to get their input and refine your thoughts. Assign tasks such as creating draft survey questions, researching Survey Monkey or other Web resources, and pulling together customer list(s).

Wednesday: Meet to review status and next steps. Identify someone willing to oversee the survey process. Select the approach(es) and target times to connect with your customers to ask for their input.

Thursday: Begin implementation.

Friday: One day is not enough time for the surveys to be completed. Plan who will do what and how you will proceed once you have the survey data. For example, will you share the results with others in your organization or your customers? Others in your division? If so, who will pull the data together and write a summary report?

WEEK 30: CREATING A CULTURE OF SERVICE

The best way to find yourself is to lose yourself in the service of others.

—Mohandas Gandhi

Service to others is really what makes people and businesses stronger. These concepts all link to each other. Customer service is a key focus of lean thinking.

There are a number of steps to creating a culture of service. One important beginning is hiring the right people into the right jobs. Hire into jobs that match talents and skills over specific experience. Job needs and projects change, and those with a basic talent for problem solving will adapt most easily to new requirements. Knowing how to operate a piece of equipment or to run a specific assay can be taught much more easily than teaching those without good problem-solving skills to solve new problems.

Service-oriented companies and cultures are ones where roles and responsibilities are clearly defined and everyone resonates with, and can state, the mission and vision. A classic example of this is Nordstrom Department Stores, which offers an important message for R&D managers. For years, Nordstrom's Employee Handbook was a single 5 × 8-in. (200-mm) gray card with the words:

> *Welcome to Nordstrom—We're glad to have you with our Company. Our number one goal is to provide outstanding customer service. Set both your personal and professional goals high. We have great confidence in your ability to achieve them.*
>
> *Nordstrom Rules: "Rule #1: Use good judgment in all situations. There will be no additional rules. Please feel free to ask your department manager, store manager, or division general manager any question at any time. (Lessons of the Nordstrom Way)*

Nordstrom demonstrated that hiring practices, trust, and training go hand in hand.

Daily Tips

Monday: Does everyone in your group have clearly defined roles and responsibilities? If not, put them in place.

Tuesday: Does everyone in your group know the vision and mission for your company and department? Are they understandable? Meet with your staff to make sure everyone understands the vision and mission. Simplify if needed, so all understand.

Wednesday: Do you hire to put the "right people in the right seats"? If not, list three things you can do to make sure that happens every time.

Thursday: Do a quick assessment. Do your staff meet with external customers? Who are your internal customers? Are your staff friendly and service oriented? If not, list three things you can do to improve. Meet with each person individually to discuss.

Friday: Develop and distribute a short survey to have your customers assess your level of service and give recommendations for service improvements. Review the results with your team and develop a plan for improvement and to follow up with your customers.

WEEK 31: STEWARDSHIP

> *Our commitment should be to leave our environment in better shape than when we found it, our nation's fiscal house in better order, our public infrastructure in better repair, and our people better educated and healthier. To indulge in immediate gratification and exploitation is an insult to previous generations, who sacrificed for us, and thievery from the next generation, who depend on our virtue.*
>
> —Eric Liu and Nick Hanauer

The definition of stewardship is the careful and responsible management of something entrusted to one's care such as natural resources, the environment, or our people.

In today's business environment, there is a slow, steady, and inexorable move toward going green or decreasing the waste and destruction of our natural resources. Our global population keeps growing and our natural resources are finite. This is a concern for many people—concern not only about us but also about our children and their children's children.

There are growing efforts to figure out ways to lessen the wastefulness of our departments, our businesses, and ourselves. Many emails now say "Please don't print this and waste valuable resources" at the bottom. It's a start.

Daily Tips

Monday: Write out the definition you have for stewardship in your business and ask some colleagues about theirs.

Tuesday: Look at your programs. Can they be greener and less resource wasteful?

Wednesday: What are the resources you see wasted around you every day? Talk with your staff and come up with two or three ways you can reduce waste in your group.

Thursday: Do the same exercise as yesterday, but now figure out how to influence others around you to stop wasting resources.

Friday: Make a list of the things around you that might be considered resources. How about your people's natural talents and motivation? Take some time to talk with those you manage to see what you can do to support and help develop them. Gandhi said, "[t]he fragrance always remains on the hand that gives the rose." How many roses have you given recently?

WEEK 32: LEAN PRACTICES

The most dangerous kind of waste is the waste we do not recognize.

—Shigeo Shingo

Lean is an important concept for any of the processes you have in your organization. The high level goal of lean thinking is to eliminate waste. This is a lofty, valuable ideal with two challenges. The first is to recognize how to identify the waste; the second is how to eliminate the waste. It takes time, effort, and change management on the part of an organization implementing the lean practices. Identifying the waste requires you to map your processes and look for the redundancies, as well as continuing to ask the question, "Why do we do this and is it value added for our business?"

There are two types of added value. The most important is "customer value add" and the second, and less important, is "business value add." Strive for the largest percentage of your processes toward customer value add (90% is a good goal).

We once did a project on the waste (or nonvalue add) versus the value add of the warehouses for distribution. After our assessment, what do you think the customer value add, versus the business value add, versus the nonvalue add was? It should have been 85%, 10%, and 5% if we were good. It turned out to be 7%, 15%, and 78%. This was a great exercise, as we were able to change those percentages very quickly, with some lean practice changes, to benefit our company and our bottom line.

Daily Tips

Monday: In your department, are your processes mapped? If not, how can you figure out what is redundant and wasteful? Start mapping your processes.

Tuesday: Once you've mapped your processes, put them on the walls for all those doing that process to check to make sure the map truly reflects the process. Write on the map, if it's not correct.

Wednesday: Work with those individuals who are doing the processes and keep asking the questions, "Why do we do this?" and "Is this of any value to our customer?"

Thursday: Once you map your processes, put them in the categories "customer value added", "business value added" and "nonvalue added." What are your percentages?

Friday: As you improve your processes, make sure you involve those using the processes. Get buy in from them as to why it's important to do this. Until they reason for themselves why it's a good idea to change, they are not likely to do so. Good change management programs get those impacted to accept the change before the change is implemented.

WEEK 33: CHALLENGING ASSUMPTIONS

Euclid taught me that without assumptions there is no proof. There-
fore, in any argument, examine the assumptions.

—E. T. Bell

Assumptions allow us to believe something where there is an absence of facts, something to avoid in many situations. They can also be valuable when you don't have facts and need to understand better a concept, person, or system. Scientific theories are based on assumption(s) that need to be tested and proven.

Good experimental design is a combination of confirming and disconfirming assumptions. A simple quiz we often give in workshops is to have individuals list "experiments" to discover a simple mathematical "rule." The "experiments" are in the form of three numbers to test their hypothesis. For example, "Do 8, 10, 12 fit the rule?" They learn if their numbers do or do not fit the rule. Frequently, a large percent of these highly trained technologists and scientists ask many confirming "experiments" in a row and can even need prompting to challenge their assumptions and do "experiments" to disprove their working hypotheses. By repeating similar "experiments," they learn no new information and seem unaware of their approach. How much wasted laboratory time on the job does this indicate?

Daily Tips

Monday: How many times have you heard "That's the way it's always been done?" How can you communicate that it is an unacceptable answer for you?

Tuesday: Think of the assumptions you've made recently, about processes, systems, or people. What data do you have to support the assumptions? Figure out how you can turn an assumption into a fact.

Wednesday: Consider your own work or that of someone you manage. To what extent do you waste time confirming what you already know or suspect rather than challenging your assumptions or conclusions to see if they will stand?

Thursday: Meet with your team. List two or three times making an assumption has gotten you in trouble. Discuss ways to avoid this in the future.

Friday: What assumptions are you making about individual staff members? How can you check your assumption or challenge it to prove yourself wrong? Follow through.

WEEK 34: WHOLE BRAIN THINKING

Whole Brain Thinking: Ignore It At Your Peril.
—Ann Herrmann-Nehdi

Knowing about whole brain thinking and brain styles can help lead to success in your organization. The brain, according to work done by Ned Herrmann, has four quadrants the front cerebral cortex, the back brain stem and limbic system, and the left and right sides. Front thinkers think in ways that merge concepts, while back thinkers are driven more by pain and pleasure and basic instincts. Left brain thinkers are more analytical, while right brain thinkers link multiple points of data together. Even with these different ways of thinking, the brain is designed to function as a whole. Yet, each brain develops dominant quadrants so that ways of learning and thinking differ from person to person. The quadrants break into the four Fs. People are oriented toward Fact, Form and Function, Feelings, or the Future. Opposite styles of thinking are Facts versus Feelings and Form and Function versus the Future.

If your boss is a Fact thinker and you are more right brained and think Future and Feelings, you may see a trend your boss does not. However, if you have a feeling, and don't know or communicate the facts to support your conclusion, your boss may not listen to your warnings. Learn what and how you need to communicate with the individuals with whom you work. We have to learn to communicate with other's brain styles. We can't expect others to change to ours.

Daily Tips

Monday: Do some research on whole brain dominance. Which brain style do you think fits you? Ask your staff if they agree with you.

Tuesday: What brain style do you think fits your boss? How might you need to change your approaches to better work with that individual? Make a list of three things you need to do.

Wednesday: Now that you have a feel for the concept, which brain style do you think fits your company/corporation? Often employment at a company with a different thinking style than yours can feel oppressive or nerve racking.

Thursday: Think of your dream team. What brain styles would you want to get the greatest outcomes and success? Make a list of the people that would be on that team. You never know when you might have the freedom to create your own team.

Friday: Now that you know about the different brain styles, how might you remember those with whom you work so you know the way they think when you walk in their office?

WEEK 35: USING PROCESSES TO ACHIEVE SUCCESS

We should work on our process, not the outcome of our processes.
—W. Edwards Deming

Do you have documented processes or standard operating procedures (SOPs) in your department? How do you build in quality? How can you improve?

For routine work, we all need a road map in order to follow a process. It ensures we stick to the ways proven to work and with quality built in.

You can always tell a great place to work and departments that produce consistently excellent products and services. They're the ones with processes built over time and created with input from those doing the processes. When processes and procedures are not created by the folks who do them, they become senior management concepts that are not easily accepted, internalized or executed by those doing the work.

Processes and procedures go hand in hand with roles and responsibilities. People want to do a good job. By letting them know what they are expected to do for their job and for the processes they use, you help them to build quality into everything they do.

Daily Tips

Monday: Review your processes and procedures. Were they developed with feedback from the people doing them? If not, ask how they can be improved.

Tuesday: Look at the mistakes and deviations from your department. Is there an issue with your procedures? Are they being followed? Talk with your staff to find ways you can avoid repeating mistakes in the future.

Wednesday: Talk to the individuals following your processes. Were they trained on all the processes and procedures they use? Do you have a training matrix for them?

Thursday: Are your processes efficient and reasonable? Are your SOPs clear? Many process descriptions and SOPs are too long, short, or confusing. They should be clear, concise and provide operators with flexibility.

Friday: Do you have a clear approach for identifying needed processes or SOPs? Put one in place if the answer is no.

WEEK 36: LEADING WITH EMOTIONAL INTELLIGENCE

> *If your emotional abilities aren't in hand, if you don't have self-awareness, if you are not able to manage your distressing emotions, if you can't have empathy and have effective relationships, then no matter how smart you are, you are not going to get very far.*
>
> —Daniel Goleman

Emotional intelligence (EQ) became a popular concept beginning in the late 1990s. The key tenets of EQ, according to Daniel Goleman, are self-awareness, self-regulation, empathy, motivation, and social skills. Leaders exhibit these traits, especially in times of crisis. Being a good leader can seem easy when all is going well. Great leaders rise to the occasion when things go wrong. Intelligence and technical skills are important for success, while emotional intelligence is more important to achieve excellent performance for jobs at all levels of an organization.

Many technical supervisors fail to recognize the importance of the ability to manage relationships or build networks (social skill). Competence to listen, to influence and persuade, to manage conflict effectively, and to guide others are social skills.

Daily Tips

Monday: Think about the words you use throughout the day to influence and persuade others or manage conflict. Make a list of them and consider the positive and negative impact those words could have. This helps you to see how powerful words are to motivate or turn off people.

Tuesday: Every time you have a negative emotion take a moment afterward and ask yourself the question, *Why did I just experience that?* The answer to this question builds self-awareness and insight into what holds you back from exhibiting high emotional intelligence.

Wednesday: Look back on your attitude throughout the last few days. Has it been good or bad? How did others react to you? Did you maintain control? Self-regulation is essential for establishing trust and leading.

Thursday: Play a game called "How much do I know about my people and how they're doing?" If the answer is a lot, congratulations, you rank high on empathy and social skills. If you don't know much about these individuals, take steps to learn more.

Friday: Find a person you trust to be honest with you and ask him or her if you have a reputation for being trustworthy. How much do those around you trust you? Everyone needs a "canary," the person who sings and tells you the truth just before you walk into danger.

WEEK 37: MANAGING GENERATIONS

The true test of character is not how much we know how to do, but how we behave when we don't know what to do.

—John W. Holt

In today's world of work, employees come from multiple generations. We see each generation in the roles of staff, supervisors, managers, directors, and executives. Younger managers may supervise older employees. Research on different generations shows that people grow up with cultural events and icons that influence their worldview and outlook on life. That research shows that respect is key. When staff respect each other, generational differences become strengths.

Values in dress, meeting times, technology, problem solving, and decision making may differ. For some generations, deference to authority is appropriate, while others need to challenge authority. Balancing the dichotomous views creates an environment where respect grows. Create open dialogues among your staff about their views based on their generational perspectives.

Daily Tips

Monday: Do some research on generations and try to identify how many generations you have at work. Share your research with your staff and discuss how the various generations can work together.

Tuesday: Think about your boss. What generational influences does he or she bring to work? Are they similar or different from yours? Meet to discuss your perceptions and how you may strengthen your working relationship.

Wednesday: List three ways you'll have to modify your behavior to accommodate and respect your boss or a staff member.

Thursday: Find an article that has statistics of generational influences in your field. Share with your staff and discuss the results. What is one thing you can to do capitalize on your unique generational staff makeup?

Friday: Talk to a trusted peer about how they handle generational differences. Identify one thing you can implement based on what they shared.

WEEK 38: THINKING OUTSIDE THE BOX

I'll be more enthusiastic about encouraging thinking outside the box when there's evidence of any thinking going on inside it.
—Terry Prachett

A great deal has been written about thinking outside the box or shifting paradigms. The ability to think in different ways is a skill you can develop, once you exercise your brain and concentrate on doing things in new ways. This may be difficult and some suggest practicing by taking a new route to work or starting with breaking other small routines. The concept of paradigm shifting has to do with breaking out of preconceived notions and expectations.

Technical supervisors must not only be able to shift their own paradigms to accomplish tasks but also be able to help their staff do the same. Helping others see what they don't see takes time and patience, characteristics that are not valued in a fast-paced work environment.

Daily Tips

Monday: Go to the library or purchase magazines from completely different industries and read them. How does learning about another industry help you become more creative in your own? Consider a specific challenge you are facing—look for parallels you can apply to your challenge.

Tuesday: If people on your team are from other countries and cultures, ask them about their views on a problem you face. Listen to their responses and consider how their perceptions differ from yours. Practice seeking and listening to the perspectives of those from different cultures; they are likely to see things differently.

Wednesday: Take a problem you are trying to solve and look at it in a different way. Start with the end in mind and then work backward.

Thursday: One reason it is so difficult to think outside the box has to do with how easy it is to fall into context traps. For example, agendas are a form of planned context to reduce the likelihood of being trapped by side discussions that can take over a meeting. List three other things you can do with your staff to minimize context traps from forming.

Friday: Try to increase your creative thinking by focusing your mind and then do something relaxing. Go for a run, drive in the country, take a shower, or stare at the color blue. Letting your mind relax and then sleeping on a problem overnight allows the subconscious to take over. Many individuals claim they solved a particularly vexing technical challenge during a dream, although Domhoff (2003) claims that there is no evidence to support this common assertion.

WEEK 39: THE ATTITUDE OF THE LUCKY

I've always worked very, very hard, and the harder I worked, the luckier I got.

—Alan Bond

Many people feel that luck is ephemeral and some people have it and some don't. There is research that shows luck is not happenstance and lucky people have a different attitude and outlook on life than unlucky people. What goes along with this attitude is a willingness to take risks and learn from failure to create one's own luck, and to exploit opportunities when they occur and not try to analyze things until the opportunity passes.

Research shows that people with this attitude bounce back faster from adversity and failure and they have an interesting mindset of turning lemons into lemonade. Also, they have a high level of self-esteem and confidence. In Richard Wiseman's book, *The Luck Factor*, he talks about the fact that hard work is not part of being lucky. When you work too hard, you may focus so much that you miss opportunities that are right in front of your eyes.

As a technical supervisor, you set the tone for your staff. Is your attitude positive and resilient, able to face and conquer any challenge, or is it negative and pessimistic? An outlook of optimism creates an environment that can feel lucky and in some cases becomes lucky.

Daily Tips

Monday: Do you believe you're lucky? The power of positive thinking is impressive. Allow yourself to believe you are lucky. Don't be swayed throughout the week, just firmly believe it and see what happens at the end of the week.

Tuesday: How many times have you had a gut feeling or an intuition, about something, ignored it, and then something bad happened? Take some time to listen to your gut and go with it. Lucky people do this more than unlucky people.

Wednesday: Talk with your colleagues about what good fortune would look like for you all. Today, and for the rest of the week, expect this good fortune and work to believe in it when you make decisions.

Thursday: When bad things happen, avoid self-pity. Think of the solution and how you can reverse the outcome to be what you want. Lucky people can do this on the fly.

Friday: Look back over the week and write down each of the times it seemed you got lucky. See if there's a trend or if you surprised yourself. Keep doing what you've been doing and see how things change for the future.

WEEK 40: USING YOUR TALENTS FOR SUCCESS

Great things are accomplished by talented people who believe they will accomplish them.

—Warren G. Bennis

Everyone has talents and skills; sometimes they are in the same area and sometimes they are not. Talents are those things that are natural to us where skills are the things we learned along the way. For example, I may have a talent for mathematical games but learned the skill of calculus and differential equations. For many, matching one's talents with skills is the ultimate goal. However, there are many situations where that is not the case.

As a technical supervisor you have the talent and skill of your specialty and perhaps the talent for supervising others but maybe not the skill. When discrepancies exist for anyone between talents, skills, and job tasks, the workplace can become a frustrating environment. The challenge you have is to ensure the talents and skills of your staff are aligned.

Daily Tips

Monday: Take some time today and list at least one talent you have. How can you further develop your skills in this area?

Tuesday: Are you in a job that utilizes at least one of your talents? If the answer is no, now is the time to start looking around for a job that will utilize your talents. If the answer is yes, then what are you doing to keep your talents sharp?

Wednesday: Is there anyone in your group or on your team who clearly doesn't know what his or her talents are? Take some time today to think about these talents. Plan to talk to them.

Thursday: What skills would you like to develop or learn? You may want to be a better typist or better with spreadsheets. You may want to learn a new lab technique. Take time today to identify some classes or mentors you can use to sharpen your skills.

Friday: Consider those you work with. Do some have skills that could be taught to others? How can you build greater depth in this group?

WEEK 41: USING RESOURCES EFFECTIVELY

Anthropology demands the open-mindedness with which one must look and listen, record in astonishment and wonder that which one would not have been able to guess.

—Margaret Mead

Technical supervisors are the liaison between upper management and their staff. You may feel caught in the middle. Upper management may say there is no money and you already have plenty of resources, or your staff is adamant that equipment is outdated and useless. Managing these dichotomous perspectives becomes your job.

To negotiate for resources and work with upper management, you'll need to provide data and details about your current resources, utilization, and gaps. In addition to providing the costs to fill the gaps, know the short- and long-term benefits of filling the gaps. For example, if a machine is purchased for $Y today and will be used over the next 5 years on projects in your pipeline, the cost per year per project for the resource may be negligible, especially if your efficiency will also improve. Convince your management of the benefits not just the need.

In working with your staff, challenge them to think differently and creatively to achieve their goals with current resources. Your task becomes helping individuals break down their paradigms and become part of the solution in using current resources to the fullest.

Daily Tips

Monday: At your next staff meeting, challenge your staff with this question: *If today we lose half of our current resources, what would it take to continue our work without adding anything?* Conduct a brainstorming session to answer the question. Have fun. At the end of the discussion, review the answers and identify one thing you can implement immediately.

Tuesday: Find a blog or article on creatively using resources in a technical environment to the fullest. Share the article with your staff and discuss one thing everyone can do to use resources more effectively.

Wednesday: Take an inventory of all the resources you have available. Share the list with a trusted peer and discuss if there are any resources you could share. Identify those resources and create a plan to share them.

Thursday: Discuss with your bosses their perspective of using resources effectively. Do they feel that you and your staff already do? If not, what is one thing you can do differently based on your bosses' thoughts?

Friday: Find mentors or peers who use resources effectively. Meet with them to learn their secrets. Identify one thing you can do to improve how resources are utilized.

WEEK 42: INFLUENCING OTHERS

Science and technology revolutionize our lives, but memory, tradition, and myth frame our response.

—Arthur M. Schlesinger

Technical supervisors are in key positions to influence those above them, those who report to them, and their peers. Certainly, for those who lead projects with staff from other functions, influence skills are essential. There is no one way to influence. Influencing takes many directions and forms—seeking support, persuading and inspiring others, and partnering to achieve a goal. It builds connections between people and across organizations, departments, and units.

Many well-known authors write about how organizations silo themselves and create competition between units rather than partnerships in which everyone is vested in the outcome. Successful influencers are able to focus outside their own group and recognize that collaboration with others creates the momentum to accomplish more than could be done alone.

The skills of effective influencers include listening, communicating and presenting, collaborating, and partnering, presenting, and assertiveness techniques.

Daily Tips

Monday: Identify a unit with which you have difficulty working. Make a list of your reasons for why it is difficult to work which them and make a commitment to influence them to collaborate on one thing in the next 30 days.

Tuesday: Attend a program or read a book on influencing skills. Identify one thing you can do differently to influence and collaborate with the unit you identified above.

Wednesday: Find an article on influencing and share it with your staff. Discuss what your staff is good at and where everyone could grow. Ask everyone to commit to one thing to do differently in influencing others.

Thursday: Ask about your manager's perspective of your ability to influence others. Identify one thing you can do differently based on the conversation.

Friday: Find a mentor who you feel influences and collaborates effectively. Ask them to share with you their secrets. Identify one thing you can practice to improve your influence skills.

WEEK 43: JUGGLING MANY HATS

The world cannot be governed without juggling.

—John Selden

As life gets more complex, and we have more things to do in less time, it becomes extremely important to learn the fine art of juggling. Today, many of us try to solve this dilemma with multitasking until it seems to be second nature. Technology appears to make multitasking easier—although recently, studies have shown that such activities can be fatal (as in using electronic devices while driving).

New terms have been coined, such as "continuous partial attention" (*The Harvard Business Review List of Breakthrough Ideas*, 2007). Edward Hallowell (*CrazyBusy*, 2006) calls multitasking a "mythical activity in which people believe they can perform two or more tasks simultaneously." This is especially counterproductive in technical environments that require coherent periods for thinking, planning, and working. Research from J. B. Spria at Basex estimates that extreme multitasking costs the U.S. economy $650 billion each year in lost productivity (*NY Times*, 2007).

As a technical supervisor, you probably multitask at meetings or while checking email and talking on the phone. The disadvantage is instead of giving 100% to tasks, you give 50% or less. When your staff only gives 50% of their energy to something, is that acceptable? Probably not! The key to multitasking is to recognize it as a skill that can be useful but should never become the norm for workplace behavior.

Daily Tips

Monday: Make a list of the times you fall into multitasking. Do you continue working on your computer when a staff member stops to speak with you? Do you write or review email when you speak on the phone? Practice focusing on one task (listening?) for the rest of the day. What did you experience? How was your meeting or phone call different when you weren't doing other things?

Tuesday: What can you do to protect your staff from "crazy-busy" feelings and interruptions, so they have longer blocks of time for work? Discuss interruptions and solutions with your staff to get their suggestions.

Wednesday: Think about your work day. Identify what is out of balance. How might you manage things differently to be more effective?

Thursday: Try this when you find yourself stressed or unfocused. When you are stressed, stare at a picture with a lot of blue coloring in it or look out the window at the sky, thinking of the all the good things that happened to you recently. If you feel unfocused, look at the color red. It allows the mind to sharpen.

Friday: Do a Web search and read more about multitasking and current research on its impact. How can you improve your own skills or those of your staff so that you can pay greater attention?

WEEK 44: PRIORITIES

I learned that we can do anything, but we can't do everything ... at least not at the same time. So think of your priorities not in terms of what activities you do, but when you do them. Timing is everything.

—Dan Millman

The first step to prioritizing is to organize yourself and what you need to accomplish each day and every week. This is tough to do, given the lean organizations most of us work in. According to Peter Drucker, effectiveness comes from doing what is needed. This means prioritizing. He said knowledge, intelligence, and imagination do not bring effectiveness by themselves. His habits necessary for effectiveness include the following:

- Know where your time is spent.
- Focus on results not activities.
- Concentrate on the areas likely to give outstanding results from superior performance.

One approach is to list the things you want to do that day. Check your list throughout the day. Evaluate the things that pop up and whether you should change your priorities. Don't fall into the trap where the urgent drives out the important. Change your priorities for things that are both urgent *and* important. This is tough to do; in most of our work and personal lives, we find ourselves with too many things to do and they all can feel important. Weigh each against your list of priorities for that day.

Another approach to handle prioritization is to follow the principles for risk management. Make a matrix with impact (high to low) on one axis and probability it will happen on the other axis. Shade the low areas close to the origin in medium gray, the middle areas light gray, and the high areas dark gray, like this:

		Probability		
Impact	High			
	Medium			
	Low			
		Low	Medium	High

If you do this quick assessment with each of the tasks you need to do, you'll find that the dark gray ones need to go to the top of the list, followed by the light gray ones and then the medium gray ones. Move the medium gray ones to the next day if you are short on time. Quick and easy, but you still need to understand how things change to influence the impact and the probability.

Daily Tips

Monday: Write down tonight all the things you want to accomplish tomorrow.

Tuesday: Set a timer to ring every 2 hours to remind you to look at your list and see how you are doing. At the end of the day, analyze how well you stuck to your plan.

Wednesday: Make a list of all the things that came up at the last minute on Tuesday. Which items delayed your accomplishing the list? See if there's a trend to them and if there is a way to mitigate them.

Thursday: Meet with your staff to discuss prioritization. Let individuals share their own approaches. Discuss the ways you typically prioritize and those described here. Decide on next steps to improve prioritization.

Friday: Do a process check on your prioritization. How did it work this week? How can you improve it?

WEEK 45: TIME MANAGEMENT

The automobile engine will come, and then I will consider my life's work complete.

—Rudolf Diesel

Managing time is an essential for success. Technical supervisors need to manage their own time as well as protect the time of their staff. Thousands of books and articles exist on the topic. Many time management systems are available. However, the truth of good time management is balancing structure with flexibility and planning with change. Some people prefer structure to flexibility and vice versa. The same is true with planning and change. Whatever your preference, a successful time management system includes all four elements.

As a technical supervisor, you have another issue, however, which stems from the type of work you manage. The activity patterns of managers tend to be highly fragmented, with many relatively short interruptions. Trying to do research and development in that environment provides no coherent thinking time—or sometimes even enough time to run an experiment.

Perhaps your most important role as a technical supervisor is to ensure interruption-free work intervals for your staff.

Daily Tips

> *Monday:* Using the Web, find a free online time management assessment that would provide insight into your style. Learn about your strengths and growth opportunities. If you find the assessment valuable, share it with your staff and discuss the results as a group.

> *Tuesday:* Create a time management system that someone else could use. Find a trusted colleague and ask them to try it and provide you with feedback as to its strengths and weaknesses. Based on the feedback, identify one thing you can do to improve your time management system.

> *Wednesday:* Find a mentor who manages time very well. Ask about his or her secrets of time management. Identify one thing you can do to improve your time management.

Thursday: Monitor how frequently you experience interruptions. What is the average length of time you can work without an interruption? Ask your employees to do the same. Also, look at how often you interrupt someone else working in your group. How can you reduce those interruptions? Discuss with your group how you can work toward longer periods without interruption.

Friday: Find a blog or article on time management appropriate to your type of work. Share with your staff and discuss what can be applied to your initiatives.

WEEK 46: LEADING CHANGE

There is nothing wrong with change, if it is in the right direction.
—Winston Churchill

Leading change is probably one of the most difficult things that we do as leaders. There are many models for change. Whatever the model, almost 70% of change initiative programs fail (http://blogs. hbr.org/cs/2010/06/four_ways_to_know_whether_you.html).

Many of us forget it's not systems, organizations, or specific programs that need to change, it's the people. A lot has been written about the fear and resistance people have to change. For many, the resistance comes from not seeing value to the change. The fear comes from a possible threat, such as "Will I lose my job when this is done?"

Good leaders realize there are key tenets to leading change. They engage their people in the change from the beginning and communicate whatever they know—even if it's "I know nothing yet." It's useful to find individual champions for change since many of us are more influenced by our peers than by management. Communicate the reasons for the change, foster dialogue, and welcome questions. Do this and your chances of launching successful change escalate dramatically.

Daily Tips

Monday: Think of the last change initiative you experienced. Make a list of what went right and wrong. How can you avoid the things that went wrong in the future?

Tuesday: What is your own reaction to change? How comfortable are you with change? Are you a change agent or do you prefer things to stay with the status quo? As a leader, if you don't believe in the change, how will that impact your staff? If you are responsible for leading a change effort, what can you do to find a way to believe in the change or to challenge and influence senior management about the change?

Wednesday: What percentage of your staff are change agents who quickly grab hold and accept change? What percentage of your staff resist change with a passion, and what percentage of your staff are typically on the fence? What can you do to surface and address the fears and issues of the resisters and convert those individuals on the fence?

Thursday: Think of Wednesday's tip. Meet with your group to discuss a current or prior change initiative. Lead a discussion on how the change was presented, and what happened (or should happen) next. Find ways to manage resisters and those on the fence.

Friday: List ways to communicate during a change initiative and decide about how often to use them without overdoing it.

WEEK 47: CONFLICT MANAGEMENT

The resolution of revolutions is selection by conflict within the scientific community of the fittest way to practice future science. The net result of a sequence of such revolutionary selections, separated by periods of normal research, is the wonderfully adapted set of instruments we call modern scientific knowledge.

—Thomas S. Kuhn

Conflict and disagreement, competing theories, and conflicting views on best approaches are at the heart of an effective R&D&E community. Arguing is something that comes naturally to (and even enjoyed by) many with technical backgrounds. That said, personal disagreements are another matter and often the source of great discomfort. Many of those in our workshops are even conflict avoiders.

There are several available instruments to help assess individual preferences when it comes to dealing with conflict. Simple ones are the Myers–Briggs Type Inventory® and the Thomas–Kilmann Conflict Mode Instrument (TKI). The TKI uses two axes called assertiveness and cooperativeness and identifies five styles of conflict. They are Competing (assertive, uncooperative), Avoiding (unassertive, uncooperative), Accommodating (unassertive, cooperative), Collaborating (assertive, cooperative), and Compromising (intermediate assertiveness and cooperativeness). Each of these styles is appropriate in certain circumstances. The key is to use them as circumstances dictate and not overuse, underuse, or rely on just one or two.

When conflict is handled with tact that results in understanding and collaboration, conflict is healthy. When issues are avoided and neglected, conflict can be detrimental.

Daily Tips

Monday: Look up the TKI online and read more about it. Learn enough to be able to describe the instrument and its purpose to those you manage.

Tuesday: Consider the conflicts you have faced and managed. In thinking about the TKI conflict styles, which one seem(s) to fit you the best? Is there a style you almost never use or one you rely on most of the time? How might you broaden your reactions to interpersonal conflict?

Wednesday: How does your group at work manage conflict? Do you have healthy disagreements and reasoned arguments, or do disagreements become heated and angry? What can you do to help the group better manage conflicts?

Thursday: Think of the last time you got into an argument with your manager. Why did it happen? What was the root cause? Would you handle the situation differently if you had it to do over? If so, approach your manager and discuss the conflict and get his or her feedback.

Friday: Figure out ways you can build cooperation in your team. Play the "What's in it for us?" game and meet together to discuss how the team handles conflict and ways to improve conflict management.

WEEK 48: SELF-AWARENESS

Everything that irritates us about others can lead us to an understanding of ourselves.

—Carl Jung

Self-awareness is a first key tenet of emotional intelligence (Goleman, 1995). If you don't know yourself, how can you identify things about you that you need to change or to foster? Self-awareness leads to happiness and success. Your ability to know your strengths and weaknesses helps you stay away from jobs or organizations that make you work to your weaknesses. Without knowing your hot buttons, others will be able to push them again and again and you'll fall into the same traps. Self-awareness leads to self-regulation, so you don't lose your temper or self-control.

Self-awareness is essential to growth and development. Great leaders with self-awareness surround themselves with those who compliment their weaknesses and whose weaknesses they compliment. Leaders know they do not know everything, nor should they. They know the importance of others to a successful initiative or project.

As technical supervisors are promoted, they typically work with others who have greater (or different) technical competence and expertise than their own. Self-awareness and self-confidence lead to accepting and valuing what others offer.

Daily Tips

Monday: Identify a character from a movie, book, or a cartoon that personifies you. Identify the characteristics that are similar to you. Now go ask a friend if they agree with your assessment. They can help guide you on a journey of self-awareness.

Tuesday: Find a rock garden (a garden filled with rocks with patterns raked into them), a stream, or a lake, and sit and look at it. Then focus not on what you see but reflect on your strengths and weaknesses. You might want to run this by your good friends too.

Wednesday: Make a list of what makes you happy and play the game, "How can I do that more?" Once you have your list of things that make you happy, figure out the jobs where you could do those things most of the time.

Thursday: Meet with your team to write your team's eulogy. Discuss the things you've done you want others to know about. Consider the things you would like to do. Now figure out a way you can do those things.

Friday: Today is question day. Ask yourself the question, *Who am I when no one else is around?* The answer might surprise you.

WEEK 49: TRAINING OTHERS

On the mountains of truth you can never climb in vain: either you will reach a point higher up today, or you will be training your powers so that you will be able to climb higher tomorrow.

—Friedrich Nietzsche

There are two ways to look at training. The first is, it is the best way to stay sharp and to keep up in your field, to keep growing, to continue to learn new things that may help you now or later. When you continue learning new things, you keep yourself flexible and increase your value. Estimates are that a week's worth of information in the *New York Times* contains more information than a person would come across in a lifetime in the 18th century. The amount of new technical information doubles every 2 years. Training will keep you competitive in today's and tomorrow's business world.

The second aspect of training is the joy of teaching. It is a great joy to share something and see the "aha" moment when a person really gets a concept that had been out of his grasp. Even if you're not teaching for selfless reasons, the secondary benefit of teaching or training is you become an expert when you teach. The Latin proverb states it best, "By learning you will teach; by teaching you will understand."

Daily Tips

Monday: Take some time today to research a topic you have wanted to learn more about.

Tuesday: Set up a lunch and learn this week on a subject about which you are an expert, and share it with others in your department.

Wednesday: Arrange for a vendor to meet with your team to present changing technology, new equipment, or other relevant topics.

Thursday: Ask an expert in your company to come in and share their knowledge on a subject that will be of value to your team.

Friday: Bring in a customer to meet and discuss their needs. Follow up with your group on ways you can better support, or educate, your customers.

WEEK 50: NETWORKING

It's not what you know but who you know that makes the difference.

—Anonymous

No one knows everything. It's an advantage to work with colleagues who know more than we do. If you are a "two" and surround yourself with enough "tens," you look like an "eight." As funny as this may sound, it works.

The growth and maintenance of a network is not easy. Like a garden, it requires you plant the seeds (akin to meeting new people, especially those who are honest, fun, and compliment your skills and talents). You need to fertilize and water (this is where you get to know the folks in your network and give them something back in return for allowing you to be part of their network). You enjoy and nurture them so they continue to grow strong (you have to keep in touch with those in your network to keep it vibrant and active; they need to know you're out there for them and ready to help).

Studies show that the most effective scientists and technologists use their networks differently from those rated less effective. The most highly rated know that the more you give to networking, the more you get. That's why it is analogous to a garden. Taking care of your network, sharing information, and maintaining contact, even when you don't need something, will provide great returns when you do. An effective network looks out for you, provides help when you need it, gives recommendations, tells you about jobs and learning opportunities, and keeps you informed. Your net worth is your network.

Daily Tips

Monday: Today is your day to become a member of LinkedIn (http://www.linkedin.com). Set up your profile and connect to the friends you have in the industry that are members. If you are already a member, think of others you could invite to join you.

Tuesday: Bring your team together and discuss how networking could improve the functioning of the team. Make specific plans to expand or refresh your team's network.

Wednesday: At your next conference, play the game "How many business cards can I bring home?" Introduce yourself to as many as you can. Who seems interesting or friendly? Who asked good questions? They are likely to be good additions to have in your network.

Thursday: Register on social networks that include many of your friends. This can be Facebook, Blogster, Hotlist, PartnerUp, MySpace, or another.

Friday: Go through the business cards you have collected. Contact those you remember but with whom you haven't stayed in touch. Try to offer something of interest; if you have nothing specific to say, ask how they've been and what they have been doing. Remember, ask questions and listen.

WEEK 51: CREATING AN INCLUSIVE ENVIRONMENT

We need to give each other the space to grow, to be ourselves, to exercise our diversity. We need to give each other space so that we may both give and receive such beautiful things as ideas, openness, dignity, joy, healing, and inclusion.

—Max de Pree

There is no better feeling than when you are included in decisions and information is transparent at every level of your team.

Why is sharing information not automatic for some of us? Some say "There wasn't enough time" or "I forgot" and "I didn't think it was that important." It is clear teams make better team decisions when everyone knows all the pertinent facts, expectations, outcomes, and influencers.

Inclusion isn't just demonstrated by transparency with information. Inclusion is also about making sure everyone is involved in key decisions that could impact the whole team. This doesn't mean they have the final decision, but they have the opportunity to influence that decision. Inclusion empowers the team and gives the team ownership in all that is done. Inclusion builds openness, camaraderie, and trust.

Daily Tips

Monday: Ask your group if they feel they know how decisions are made in the team. Then ask if they feel they are part of those decisions. If the answer is yes, you have passed the inclusion test. Ask them to describe the types of decisions that are theirs to make. If they know those as well, you are doing far better than many of your counterparts in other organizations.

Tuesday: During a meeting today, play a game called "Wait for it." Ask for suggestions for a solution, or ideas, or ways to improve your department or your processes. Then sit back and wait for it. Don't say a word. Count to 20 if you have to. Eventually, the silence will be filled with comments, and feelings of inclusion will escalate.

Wednesday: Pick the quietest person in your group and ask for their ideas on how you can improve. If they can't think of anything, say you will come back to it. (If you can, tell him or her ahead of time you will be asking for input so that he or she will have time to think.) Their feeling of inclusion in your circle will be motivating.

Thursday: Go out for a drink after work, or set up a lunch for your whole department at a local, reasonably priced place. (Pay as you go if you don't have the budget.) Keep it informal and let everyone get to know each other.

Friday: Today is your day to listen and ask open-ended questions. Talk to those in your group or other colleagues in the company. Actively listen to what they say, ask pertinent questions, and give feedback. You will be including them in your circle. Watch for smiles at the end of your conversation.

WEEK 52: CREATING A TRUSTING ENVIRONMENT

To be trusted is a greater compliment than being loved.
—George MacDonald

Every leader needs to create an environment of trust. Without trust there is no team, there are only survivors. When teams don't trust their leaders, their leaders are no longer leading the team. What's worse is without trust a lack of communication and collaboration quickly follows.

Trusted leaders usually demonstrate specific qualities that engender trust in their teams. Four easy components are necessary to build trust—the four Cs. They are Consistency, Competence, Commitment, and Character.

How many of us have walked into our boss' office afraid we might step on a mine and get blown up by someone who loses his or her temper? This shows a lack of consistency, and without consistency, trust diminishes. Competent bosses engender trust quickly. Bosses who are honest and admit when they don't know something create trust more quickly; nothing engenders trust faster than vulnerability. Commitment is indeed another key element of trust. Leaders who are not committed lack the drive and determination to win; teammates notice and stop following. If the leader shows no energy about a goal, why should anyone else?

Finally, character is essential to build trust. In many corporations in the news today, character seems to be missing at senior levels. It is nonnegotiable and never to be compromised. To waver with your character leads to a slippery slope from which it is hard to recover. People demonstrate character when they do the right thing, even when no one is looking.

Daily Tips

> *Monday:* Keep a daily journal this week and record the number of times you lose control or send an inconsistent message to your colleagues. This allows you to assess whether you are consistent.

> *Tuesday:* Talk to a close friend who will be honest with you. Ask them if you have any opportunities for improvement in the four Cs.

Wednesday: Bring your team together to talk about the four Cs. How do you as a team demonstrate each of them? What could you do to improve?

Thursday: Have a lunch and learn with your staff today to focus on a specific topic or issue related to your work. This engenders a sense of learning, sharing, and a drive to keep developing competence.

Friday: Ask yourself, if you found a $20 bill on the ground would you ask around to see if someone lost it? If you got a good idea from a colleague, would you take credit? Make up your own litmus test for character and see if you pass it.

REFERENCES

Domhoff, G. W. *The Scientific Study of Dreams: Neural Networks, Cognitive Development, and Content Analysis.* American Psychological Association (APA), Washington, D.C., 2003.

Goleman, D. *Emotional Intelligence: Why It Can Matter More Than IQ.* Bantam Books, New York, 1995.

Hallowell, E. *CrazyBusy: Overstretched, Overbooked and About to Snap.* Ballantine Books, New York, 2006.

Klein, G. *Intuition At Work.* Doubleday, New York, 2003.

Locke, E. A., and Latham, G. *Goal Setting: A Motivational Technique That Works.* Prentice Hall, Englewood Cliffs, NJ, 1984.

Stone, L. "Living with Continuous Partial Attention." From the article "The Harvard Business Review List of Breakthrough Ideas for 2007." *Harvard Business Review,* Vol. 85, No. 2, February 2007, pp. 28–29.

Wiseman, R. *The Luck Factor: The Four Essential Principles.* Miramax Books/ Hyperion, New York, 2003.

INDEX

Printed in the United States
By Bookmasters